THE *abundant table*
Recipes from The Bishop's Ranch Kitchen

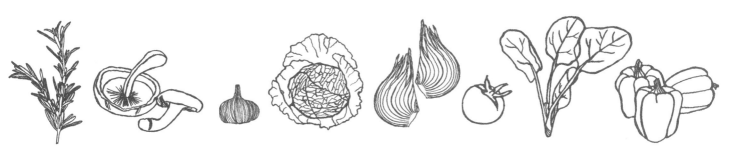

THE *abundant table*
Recipes from The Bishop's Ranch Kitchen

Elizabeth Schmidt & Ariel Ross
Illustrations by Meg Mateo Ilasco

Text copyright © 2007 by Elizabeth Schmidt and Ariel Ross

All rights reserved. No part of this book may be reproduced in any form without written permission from the publisher.

ISBN 978-0-9802464-0-7

Printed in China.

Designed by Laura C. Deleot, Crookston Design

10 9 8 7 6 5 4 3 2 1

The Bishop's Ranch
5297 Westside Road
Healdsburg, CA 95448
www.bishopsranch.org

To Marion Schmidt,

our mother and grandmother, who taught us that margarine is bad, butter is good, and always to prepare food with love in your heart.

contents

- 5 **Dedication**
- 13 **Foreword**
- 15 **Introduction**
- 20 **Our Kitchen and the Cookbook**
- 23 **Acknowledgments**

25 Breakfast
- 27 Bishop's Ranch Granola
- 28 Oven-Baked Home Fries
- 29 Bishop's Ranch Pancakes with Honey Butter
- 30 Buttermilk Oatmeal Pancakes
- 31 Scrambled Tofu with Vegetables
- 32 Zucchini Frittata
- 33 Spring Vegetable Frittata
- 34 Apple Strudel
- 35 Blueberry Buckle
- 36 Pumpkin Date Muffins
- 37 Coffee-Spiked Poppy Seed Muffins
- 38 Oatmeal Muffins
- 39 Banana Coconut Muffins
- 40 Cranberry Muffins
- 41 Blueberry Muffins
- 42 Dried Fruit Scones
- 43 Orange Currant Scones
- 44 Herbed Biscuits

45 Bread

- 49 Whole Wheat Bread
- 50 Walnut Rosemary Beer Bread
- 51 Seeded Dinner Rolls
- 52 Sourdough Bread
- 54 Italian Herb Bread
- 55 Struan Bread
- 56 Onion Rye Caraway Bread
- 57 Cheese Onion Poppy Seed Bread
- 58 Ariel's Focaccia
- 60 Fruit Bread
- 61 Breadsticks
- 62 Cornbread with Chiles and Cheese

63 Soups

- 65 Vegetable Stock
- 66 Chicken Stock
- 67 Fresh Corn Stock
- 68 Fish Stock
- 69 Curried Butternut Squash Soup
- 70 Corn, Bean, and Squash Stew
- 71 Potato Corn Chowder
- 72 Potato Leek Soup
- 73 Vegetarian French Onion Soup
- 74 White Bean Soup with Rosemary Toast
- 75 Hot and Sour Soup
- 76 Tomato Soup
- 77 Black Bean Chili
- 78 "Mo-Rockin" Lentil Soup
- 79 Watermelon Gazpacho
- 80 Spicy Carrot Soup

81 Salads and Dressings

- 83 Sesame-Ginger Vinaigrette
- 84 Balsamic Vinaigrette
- 85 Gorgonzola Dressing
- 86 Buttermilk-Herb Dressing

87   Citrus Vinaigrette
88   Fresh Tomato Dressing
89   Champagne Vinaigrette
90   Ariel's Vinaigrette
91   Bishop's Ranch Vinaigrette
92   Black Bean Salad with Cumin Vinaigrette
93   Romaine with Ruby Grapefruit, Jicama, and Avocado
94   Caesar Salad
96   Lemon-Chicken Pasta Salad with Greens
97   Chinese Noodle Salad with Roasted Eggplant and Ginger-Soy Dressing
98   Roasted Vegetable Salad with Lime-Honey Dressing
99   Roasted Potato Salad with Bacon and Spicy Pecans
100 Middle Eastern Platter with Pita Triangles
101 Hillary's Salad
102 Jicama with Lime and Chili

103 Poultry and Meat

105 Orange Chicken with Olives and Thyme
106 Korean-Style Chicken with Black Sesame Seeds
107 Chicken Breast with Lemon-Caper Sauce
108 Roasted Chicken with Rosemary and Garlic
109 Grilled Chicken Breast with Adobo Sauce, Citrus Butter, and Tropical Fruit Salsa
110 Braised Chicken with Thyme and Apple Cider
111 Enchilada Mole con Pollo
112 Focaccia Sandwich with Chicken, Roasted Eggplant, Red Bell Pepper, and Basil Aioli
114 Cornish Game Hens with Butternut Squash and Sage
115 Bishop's Ranch Turkey Meatloaf
116 Turkey Mole
118 Grilled Pork Tenderloin
119 Slow-Roasted Pork with Sage and Garlic
120 Moroccan Lamb Kabobs with Yogurt Mint Sauce
122 Grilled Hanger Steak
123 Beef Short Ribs Braised in Barbeque Sauce
124 Beef Stew with Cabernet and Hoisin Sauce

125 Fish and Shellfish
- 127 Rock Shrimp and Sweet Corn Fritters
- 128 Fettuccine with Rock Shrimp, Sun-Dried Tomatoes, Basil, and Cream
- 129 Pescado con Jugo de Naranja
- 130 Baked Cod with Basil and Parmesan
- 131 Grilled Salmon with Italian Salsa Verde
- 132 Fish Stew with Garlic Rouille
- 134 Fish Kabobs with Citrus Marinade

135 Vegetarian Main Dishes
- 137 Cheese and Nut Loaf
- 138 Winter Curry
- 140 Spanakopita
- 141 Chilaquile Casserole
- 142 Pizza Dough
- 144 Roasted Eggplant, Red Bell Pepper, Red Onion, Fontina, and Rosemary Pizza
- 145 Greek-Style Pizza with Spinach, Feta, and Oregano
- 146 Pizza with Caramelized Onion, Smoked Chicken, and Gorgonzola
- 147 Shiitake Mushroom Ragoût
- 148 Baked Polenta Layered with Spinach, Mushrooms, Fontina, and Gorgonzola
- 149 Vegetable Egg Foo Yong
- 150 Summer Pesto and Tomato Lasagna
- 152 Tart and Galette Dough
- 154 Butternut Squash Galette
- 155 Cheese and Tomato Galette
- 156 Chard Tart

157 Side Dishes and Vegetables
- 159 Roasted Brussels Sprouts with Sage and Squash
- 160 Roasted Summer-Vegetable Ragoût
- 162 Maple-Glazed Carrots
- 163 Herb-Baked Tomatoes Provençal
- 164 Chinese-Style Broccoli with Oyster Sauce
- 165 Roasted Green Beans with Shallots and Hazelnuts
- 166 Marinated Vegetables with Fresh Herbs
- 167 Wilted Greens
- 168 Creamed Swiss Chard

169 Braised Sweet and Sour Red Cabbage
170 Roasted Winter Vegetables
171 Potato Pancakes
172 Soft Polenta
173 Soft Polenta with Red Pepper and Orange
174 Homemade Pinto Beans
175 Fragrant Rice
176 Fiesta Rice

177 Condiments and Sauces

179 Cilantro Pesto
180 Basil Aioli
181 Pickled Red Onions
182 Red Tomato Chutney
183 Tamari Sunflower Seeds
184 Caramelized Nuts
185 Gorgonzola Butter
186 Barbeque Sauce
187 Tomato Sauce
188 Chipotle Red Chile Cream
189 Salsa Verde
190 Salmoriglio
191 Hummus
192 Salsa Fresca
193 Tropical Fruit Salsa
194 Crème Fraîche

195 Desserts

197 Blueberry Sauce
198 Raspberry Sauce
199 Caramel Sauce
200 Crème Anglaise
201 Pastry Cream
202 Caramel Frosting
203 Quick Orange Icing
204 Chocolate Ganache
205 Candied Citrus Peel

- 206 Fruity Oatmeal Cookies
- 207 Persimmon Cookies
- 208 Cowboy Cookies
- 209 Orange Crispies
- 210 Gingersnaps
- 211 Black-Footed Macaroons
- 212 Chocolate Mint Cookies
- 213 Corn-Lime Cookies
- 214 Almond Biscotti
- 215 Chocolate and Candied Orange Peel Biscotti
- 216 Italian Sesame Cookies
- 217 Vanilla Nut Wafers
- 218 Butter Tart Bars
- 219 Meyer Lemon Bars
- 220 Fudge Brownies
- 221 Dream Bars
- 222 Citrus-Olive Oil Cake
- 223 Lemon Pudding Cake
- 224 Black Magic Cake
- 225 Chocolate Torte
- 226 Almond Tart
- 227 Banana Cake Filled with Rum Pastry Cream
- 228 Orange Chiffon Cake
- 229 Pumpkin-Ginger Cake with Praline Pecans
- 230 Fresh Pear Cake
- 231 Summer Fruit Tart
- 232 Buttermilk-Lemon Pound Cake
- 233 Ginger-Peach Upside-Down Cake
- 234 Apple-Cranberry Crisp
- 235 All-Butter Pie Crust
- 236 Mom's Best Ever Pumpkin Pie
- 237 Cherry-Peach Pie

239 Suggested Reading
240 Index

foreword

Sunday morning, about an hour after daybreak, she pushes open the glass door that leads onto a wide porch on the edge of the valley. Sunlight from the east overlaps the contoured bands of hills, silver belts of fog, and the geometry of vineyards and orchards. Taking a thick cotton rope in both hands, she gives a strong pull and sends the peals of an old brass bell past a white-plastered chapel, beyond a gracious house under moss-mottled tiles, and through the gardens and oak trees to call the hungry.

Welcome to The Bishop's Ranch: a place where the simple hunger of our bodies is sated with delicious, nourishing food, and the subtler hunger of our minds and souls finds respite in nature's hospitality and beauty.

Situated on a knoll at the edge of the Russian River Valley, in the Sonoma County wine region near Healdsburg, California, the land that would become The Bishop's Ranch was purchased from the White family by Bishop Karl Morgan Block in 1947. Set aside by the Episcopal Church as a place of renewal for individuals and communities, the Ranch has developed its facilities and mission, serving the church and non-profit groups of many kinds, as well as individuals and families. The mission of the Ranch is to serve God by providing for people of all walks of life a place where lives are changed, a place where renewal of spirit, mind, and body can occur in a natural setting that fosters individual growth and strengthens community. To that end, the Ranch provides comfortable lodging, inspiring programs, delightful food, restful gardens, and a 300-acre land preserve.

The savory meals, which the Ranch kitchen excels at creating, are a fundamental part of our hospitality. When the bell rings, the dedicated women and men of the Ranch kitchen see that guests are fed amiably in body, so that they are renewed in soul and spirit as well. As you open this book in your own kitchen, please find it an extension of Ranch hospitality.

Sean Swift
Executive Director, The Bishop's Ranch

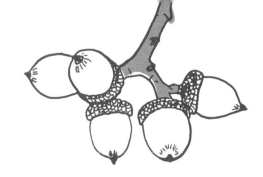

introduction

I still remember my first visit to The Bishop's Ranch. It was August of 1987 and Mark Farmer had offered me the job of kitchen manager. Mark himself had just been hired as executive director with the mandate of expanding the facilities and increasing the number of guests.

I had met Mark at a family gathering and he had liked the food I'd brought: a pot of chili. We had talked and enjoyed each other's company and he had learned that I loved to cook.

And I did. I grew up spending winters a few miles down the road from The Bishop's Ranch and summers in Canada's Yukon Territory, where my father had a gold mining company. During those summers in the 1950s on the Sixty Mile River, we ate dinner at the cookhouse with about 30 other people who worked for the company. The food was cooked on two huge, black woodstoves and was served family-style at long tables. We bused our dishes to a table that was between the dining hall and the kitchen, where the dishes were washed by hand in a big wooden sink. There was no refrigeration. It was a long drive into Dawson on a dirt road.

The cook, Ada, was a tall red-haired woman and a magnificent person of awe-inspiring ability to me. She had muscled arms and strong hands. She always wore a white apron and kept her hair hidden in a cleverly knotted scarf. As a young girl, I treasured the afternoons I was allowed to help make lunches for the men. I spread Miracle Whip on 120 slices of bread (all baked in that kitchen in the giant woodstoves). I wrapped cookies in waxed paper, filled thermoses, and packed each lunch in a battered, black box. The sounds, the smells, the huge pieces of equipment, and the sheer quantity of it all filled me with excitement. Out in the world of placer mining, the men were always talking about "moving

the yardage." Ada sure knew how to "move the yardage," or get things done, in that kitchen.

Back home in Healdsburg, as the oldest of five children, I had no trouble convincing my mother to let me experiment in the kitchen. She was happy to have an extra batch of cookies or some banana bread on hand. Before long, I was making dinners.

We moved when I was twelve to a smaller operation on Dominion Creek, and I soon had the opportunity (work was always termed an "opportunity") to be the cook for a crew of 8 to 12. Through my high school years, I had lots of "opportunities" to hone my skills cooking for my dad's crews.

I went on to university, motherhood, and teaching and I started Live Oak Preschool in Healdsburg, where I directed and taught for nine years. My cooking, while still an important part of my life, was relegated to family and friends. Enter Mark Farmer and The Bishop's Ranch.

I walked past the thriving vegetable garden that August day and there it was, the closest approximation I had ever seen to my childhood cookhouse—the huge pots, the long tables, and stoves that would make anyone named Hansel or Gretel tremble. I was especially drawn to the walk-in refrigerator with the wooden door and to the butcher block table. I wandered through the kitchen knowing with such certainty that this was for me. And so I said "yes" and was glad that I knew my multiplication tables.

Soon The Bishop's Ranch began to grow from an occasional weekday group, with an average of 30 or 40 people on the weekends, to 39,636 meals served in the year 2005.

Over the years, many of my former preschool students ended up working in the kitchen and both of my daughters did too. Hillary worked for us in between college semesters and then went on to other careers, but Ariel soon became a full-time employee. She had been interested in cooking from an early age and was always fearless in creating new recipes. The most memorable was "Watermelon Soup" at age ten. It was delicious.

Ariel spent a summer in Europe and returned with an even higher standard for her culinary arts. She soon became a cook I looked to for guidance and advice. She worked at The Bishop's Ranch for 10 years, and managed the kitchen when I took summer leaves to cook once again in my beloved North, this time for Alaska Wildland Adventures at their backcountry lodges. When I needed to take an extended leave to care for my mother, Ariel took over as manager.

Looking back over these 20 years, I have deep gratitude for the opportunity to have participated in both my own growth and that of the kitchen. To have done this surrounded by the beauty of the Ranch and the kindness and good humor of many people is a blessing indeed.

Elizabeth Schmidt

I grew up in the garden and the kitchen. I was lucky to be raised by a father and mother who loved to work the land. They taught my sister and me how to grow flowers and vegetables, and we helped with weeding in the garden. We harvested our own carrots and potatoes and made applesauce and jam. There were eggs to collect from the hens and the annual feather plucking of the homegrown chickens headed for the freezer. For years, our family had a cow and we learned to milk. In my childhood, I despised those chores. But now I am so thankful for that experience because I realize how much this life contributed to my love of fresh, vibrant food.

My mother, Liz, increased my fascination with food by cooking meals that were made from "scratch." Even the peanut butter was freshly ground. As a young girl, I learned how to make bread, butter, yogurt, cookies, and pesto as I helped her in the kitchen. At the time, I longed for the Skippy and white bread that my friends were eating, but know now that those were the experiences that conditioned and educated my palate.

My sister, Hillary, and I spent our free time playing "restaurant," creating menus and then surprising our parents with dinners that we made from the cupboard, the fridge, and the garden. As I ended my teenage years, my passion for cooking increased. I reveled in the challenge of duplicating meals that we had at Chinese or Thai restaurants. I would spend endless time "getting the flavors right." My experimentation grew and blossomed. I had a compelling need to take things to the next level and pursued this by taking culinary classes at the local junior college.

When I was 16, I took a job at Madrona Manor. Working at this high-end restaurant was a great experience: I learned the front of the house and soaked up the fast pace, the aesthetics, and the new food styles of the time. The sophistication of that restaurant set my standards for food higher again.

In 1988, my mother suggested I check out her new place of work, The Bishop's Ranch. Soon, I was cooking there a few times a week. I enjoyed the peaceful environment and the warm and caring atmosphere created by Mark Farmer and his parents, Beva and Peter Farmer. I appreciated the trust and respect I was given in the kitchen.

The following year, I boarded a plane on a sojourn to Europe for three months. My companion and I traveled to Italy, France, England, and Spain and finally ended our trip in Portugal. Those Europeans knew how to live! This was where my taste buds came alive and I truly began to understand food as an expression of culture. I felt like I was home. The land and the people were rich with history and food told the story. We had cappuccinos and porchetta at the farmers' markets in Rome, pastries in Florence, pizzas in Napoli, cheese and wine in Paris, flan and paella in Spain, and blood sausages and caldo verde in Portugal.

Returning home to the United States was difficult. I was disheartened by the mass-produced food and vegetables. Inspired by the bakers in Europe, I started a little artisan business and sold my baked goods weekly to a local restaurant and to private homes in the area. At the same time, I continued working at the Ranch where we prepared beautiful, wholesome meals based on local, fresh ingredients. This was as close to my European experience as I could get.

I continued working and managing at The Bishop's Ranch for over 10 years. During this time, I spent a good chunk of time rewriting the recipes for this cookbook. I became a mother, and moved on to work with other chefs in local restaurant and winery kitchens, did catering and then moved into the wine business.

Every once in a while, I know it's time for a visit to the Ranch. When I come back, I have the sense that things just keep getting better. Under Sean Swift's direction, the warm and friendly atmosphere continues. After working in other environments, I feel it is a true accomplishment that the Ranch and its kitchen have been able to grow in size, while maintaining high professional standards and the warmth and care that makes it such a special place.

When I visit, it brings back some very powerful and comforting feelings. I feel lucky to have had the chance to explore and perfect my passion for food in such a loving and nurturing environment in the early years of my life.

I appreciate the opportunity to have helped in the creation of this cookbook and I hope you will find a recipe or two that sparks your interest and ignites your creativity.

Cheers to The Bishop's Ranch and its creators, its vision, its purpose and spirit!

Ariel Ross

our kitchen and the cookbook

The Bishop's Ranch can be found sitting on a beautiful knoll, overlooking the serene and expansive Russian River Valley, five miles outside of Healdsburg, California. The Ranch is home to rolling hills, gorgeous gardens, and an extremely efficient, productive, and talented kitchen crew.

Visiting the Ranch, you may see our kitchen staff picking tomatoes, fresh herbs, zucchini, or flowers from our organic gardens. You may smell bread, cookies, and granola baking, stocks simmering, and the wonderful aroma of garlic and onions wafting up from the sauté pans. You will hear sounds of whirling kitchen equipment, conversation, and lots of laughter.

Our goal in The Bishop's Ranch kitchen has always been to nourish, both nutritionally and spiritually. We are an inspired and passionate group of people, and we create each meal with love, thought, and care.

In our kitchen, we believe that the food we present on the table really begins in the field. It is our wish to honor the earth that nourishes us by supporting agricultural practices that are renewing and sustaining rather than depleting of the soil. Because good food begins with good ingredients, as much as possible we use local organic produce. All our flours and grains are grown organically. To avoid excess chemicals and preservatives, we make our desserts, muffins, and salad dressings from scratch. Not only are such foods better for both us and the environment, but there is a huge improvement in flavor using ingredients that are not artificially pumped up with chemicals. Just think of the succulent sweetness of organic, fully ripe strawberries and tomatoes in contrast to their hard, flavorless, mass-produced counterparts.

To us, food is creative artistry. We consider how the ingredients will work together and if they fit the season and weather of the day. We imagine the visual appearance of the meal and work both toward compatibility and contrast of flavors. We ask if the meal has balance in color, taste, and texture. All of these components are integral to a fantastic meal—one that will be thoroughly enjoyed and not soon forgotten.

There are significant benefits to taking a quiet moment in one's day to both prepare and eat a meal. Sharing even a simple meal is an opportunity for nourishment beyond the physical. And don't forget what a difference to your mood a few lit candles can make, even if the meal is just you, alone, with a bowl of soup.

Over the years, there would always be the guest who would thank us for the meal and then say, "You should write a cookbook." Sigh, right. Like we have time for that? But the request kept recurring, and eventually we realized that we did

in fact have a great collection of recipes in those binders on the shelf.

Putting the cookbook together has been a long process because most of it was done when we were busy managing and working in the kitchen. Ariel began the cookbook, during her last year as manager, with the initial rewrite of the recipes. Often this involved turning a recipe that fed 30 or 100 into one that worked for 6 or 8. She established a format for the existing recipes and developed some new ones. Then we sent them out to family and friends for testing in home kitchens. Next Liz began inputting the corrections, retesting recipes where needed, and writing additional text and editing. It was quite a moment of celebration when we printed out the first rough draft of the book in December 2005—the culmination of many years of experience filled with memories.

And so, here it is. The recipes we have included represent some of our favorites, some basics, and some of those most requested by guests. Many have personal history and some have been adapted from vintage classics, regional travels, gathered from friends, or are simply a stroke of creative brilliance. We hope this book inspires you to cook and that you use it as a starting place for your own improvisation, invention, and creativity. Bon appétit.

acknowledgments

First and foremost, we are so grateful to every person who has ever worked in The Bishop's Ranch kitchen. It has always been a team effort. Our wonderful cooks brought in ideas, recipes, and always enthusiasm. Their talents and dedication have helped develop the quality of our food.

Thank you to the guests who encouraged us to begin and continue this book. All those queries of "Have you ever thought of writing a cookbook?" have come to fruition!

Over the years, guests have generously donated money to improve the kitchen. We were able to do a major remodel in 1998 and have been helped with the occasional purchase of new equipment. We are grateful for this financial help that improved our working conditions and assisted us to a new level of sophistication.

This book would not have been published without the enthusiasm and skilled assistance of Ann Wilson Spradin, our managing editor. Ann was a pleasure to work with and cheerfully steered us in the right direction.

A big thank you to all who helped test recipes in their home kitchens. Each person's effort was appreciated. A few people tested many and always returned them with helpful suggestions. So special thanks to Hillary Ross Hoessle, Pete and Marla Strebel-Young, and Mark and Jean Farmer.

We have been blessed to live in a wonderful community of farmers and grocers who have provided us with tasty and healthy produce. How could we fail with such excellence as our base?

Thank you to Joe and Phoebe Pummill, to Mark, Beva and Peter Farmer, who were at the Ranch in those first years, and left us a legacy of love and service.

Thank you to Jack Dowling, computer wizard extraordinaire, who rescued Liz from many technological catastrophes and always with patience.

And to Sean Swift, current director of The Bishop's Ranch, thank you for always saying, "Oh, yes, we're going ahead with it" with a smile.

breakfast

breakfast

Breakfast at the Ranch is abundant and filled with choices: fruit in season, homemade granola with yogurt, pancakes and sausage, eggs and toast, a fresh muffin or scone, hot cereal, and maybe even a sticky bun. Breakfast is the chance for our guests to enjoy the views over the valley, linger over tea or coffee, and watch the sun rise.

Back in the kitchen, we keep to a tight schedule. Many of the foods have been prepped the day before. Some fruit has been cut up, the bacon is precooked and only needs reheating. We have just enough time to make pancakes or muffins, scramble eggs, and put out the food. At home, you can use prepping the night before to help make your own busy mornings go more smoothly. We have noted any opportunities for prepping ahead in the recipes.

Preparing food should be a wonderfully satisfying activity. Here are a few suggestions to help keep your experiences in the kitchen positive.

- Read through the recipe to make sure you have all of the ingredients on hand before getting started.

- Once you get going, think ahead so that you can re-use measuring cups and bowls.

- Keep a sink filled with warm, soapy water and wash as you go, or at least rinse off bowls, knives, and utensils to simplify your cleanup.

The muffins and scones in the following recipes will all benefit from a light touch in the mixing. We have found that they bake better if you heat the oven 25 to 50 degrees hotter than called for in the recipe, put the muffins or scones in the oven, and then turn the oven down to the proper temperature immediately or after a few minutes. A lot of heat can be lost while you are arranging the trays in the oven and having preheated it to a higher temperature helps keep it where you want it. We have put the muffins and scones in the breakfast section, but they are also popular as an afternoon snack or a light dessert.

BISHOP'S RANCH *granola*

This is a staple at all our breakfasts—we make large amounts every week. It is easy to make and nothing is more satisfying than eating your own homemade cereal in the morning. The variations are endless, and we substitute ingredients with the changing seasons. In the fall, we dry lots of persimmons from the Ranch and use them instead of apricots. Pumpkin seeds or any nuts can be added. Dried apples, blueberries, peaches, and pineapple are also delicious.

- 1½ quarts rolled oats
- 1 cup wheat germ
- ¼ cup whole wheat flour
- ½ cup sesame seeds
- ½ cup shredded, unsweetened coconut
- ½ cup hulled sunflower seeds
- 1 cup whole almonds, coarsely chopped
- ¾ cup honey
- ¾ cup vegetable oil
- ¼ teaspoon vanilla or almond extract
- ⅓ cup raisins or sultanas (golden raisins)
- ½ cup dried apricots, chopped
- ½ cup dried cranberries or dried cherries

Preheat the oven to 350°F. Place the oats, wheat germ, flour, sesame seeds, coconut, sunflower seeds, and chopped almonds in a very large mixing bowl. Stir to combine. Meanwhile, heat the honey, oil, and extract in a medium saucepan over low heat until warm. Pour the honey and oil mixture over the dry ingredients and stir until evenly coated.

Pour the oat mixture onto a large cookie sheet. Level the granola with a spoon until even and place in oven. Check and stir granola every 10 to 15 minutes. The whole baking process will take approximately 45 minutes to 1 hour. Toward the end of the baking, you will need to check and stir the granola more frequently as it can burn rather quickly. When it is golden brown, remove the granola from the oven and add the dried fruit. Stir once or twice as it cools to keep the granola loose. Wait until it is completely cooled before placing in an airtight container. Store in the refrigerator if keeping more than a few days.

MAKES APPROXIMATELY 6 CUPS

OVEN-BAKED HOME *fries*

No muss, no fuss with the frying pan or the griddle. These are easy to prepare for a weekend breakfast. We offer the recipe more as a process, with variations, and you can adjust to your taste and the number of people to be served. Allow 1 potato per person.

1 pound Yukon gold or red potatoes, cut into ¾ to 1-inch chunks
Olive oil
Salt and freshly ground black pepper
Cajun spice, paprika, dried thyme, or dried oregano

Scrub the potatoes and remove any bad spots. Cut into cubes and place in a saucepan. Cover with cold water and bring to a boil. Boil gently until a cube is just tender when pierced with a fork. Sample to make sure there is no "raw" taste left. Drain the potatoes and refrigerate if done the night before.

Preheat the oven to 450°F. Place the potatoes in a bowl and add oil, salt, and pepper as well as any spices you might wish to add. Toss all to coat and spread onto an oiled baking sheet. Bake for about 25 minutes, turning occasionally with a spatula. When done, the potatoes should be starting to brown and become crispy on the outside.

Variation: Try adding diced onions and/or bell peppers with the spices. Toss, coat, and bake as directed in the original recipe.

MAKES APPROXIMATELY 4 SERVINGS

BISHOP'S RANCH *pancakes*
WITH HONEY BUTTER

These 100 percent whole wheat pancakes are amazingly light, especially when the flour is freshly milled from wheat berries. Serve the pancakes with our Blueberry Sauce (page 197), Honey Butter, or maple syrup. They are also delicious served with sliced fruit and yogurt.

- 2 cups whole wheat flour
- 1½ teaspoons baking powder
- ¾ teaspoon baking soda
- 1 teaspoon salt
- 1 tablespoon brown sugar (optional)
- 3 eggs, separated
- 2¼ cups buttermilk
- ¼ cup vegetable oil
- plus additional oil for greasing the griddle

Sift the flour, baking powder, soda, salt, and brown sugar (if using) into a large mixing bowl. In a separate mixing bowl, beat the egg whites until soft, medium-stiff peaks form. Set aside.

In a third mixing bowl, combine the egg yolks, buttermilk, and vegetable oil. Whisk until well blended. Mix the wet ingredients into the dry, stirring until just moistened. Gently fold the egg whites into the batter. Do not overmix. The egg whites should still be visible, and the batter will be somewhat lumpy. It should be thick but pourable. If too stiff, add a bit more buttermilk.

Meanwhile, heat a heavy-bottomed skillet or griddle over medium heat. When it's hot, add a thin layer of oil or butter. The classic test for frying pancakes is that a few drops of water sprinkled on the griddle will sizzle and dance. Spoon or pour the batter onto the pan with a large spoon or quarter-cup measure. The pancakes should be about ¼-inch thick. Cook until bubbles break on top, 2 to 3 minutes. Turn and cook until lightly brown.

MAKES APPROXIMATELY 18 (4-INCH) PANCAKES

HONEY BUTTER

This is delicious on French toast or pancakes. Refrigerated, it will keep for weeks.

- ½ cup unsalted butter
- ½ cup honey

In a small saucepan, melt the butter and honey together over medium heat. Whisk until smooth and creamy. Serve warm.

MAKES APPROXIMATELY 1 CUP

BUTTERMILK OATMEAL *pancakes*

These are hearty breakfast treats—a good choice before a long weekend bike ride or a day of chopping wood. They are delicious with homemade applesauce and maple syrup. The rolled oats are soaked overnight in buttermilk, so a bit of planning is involved.

- 2 cups rolled oats
- 2 cups buttermilk
- 2 eggs, lightly beaten
- ¼ cup unsalted butter, melted
- ½ cup raisins or dried cranberries (optional)
- 2 tablespoons honey
- ½ cup unbleached flour
- 1 teaspoon baking powder
- 1 teaspoon baking soda
- ½ teaspoon ground cinnamon
- ¼ teaspoon salt

Combine oats and buttermilk and stir well. Cover and refrigerate overnight. In the morning, add eggs, butter, raisins or cranberries, and honey and stir. In another bowl, sift together the flour, baking powder and soda, cinnamon, and salt. Add these dry ingredients to the oat mixture and stir until just moistened. This is a very thick batter and does not pour like regular pancake batter. However, oats can really soak up the buttermilk so, if it seems overly thick, add a bit more buttermilk.

Heat a lightly oiled griddle or skillet over medium heat until a drop of water sizzles and dances when flicked onto the surface. Using ¼ cup of batter for each pancake, cook until brown on bottom, then flip and cook the other side. Serve warm.

MAKES APPROXIMATELY 16 PANCAKES

SCRAMBLED *tofu* WITH VEGETABLES

We make this occasionally to accommodate special diets and always receive requests for the recipe. Molly Katzen in The Sunlight Cafe *suggested the technique of boiling silken tofu prior to sautéing it. This keeps the tofu from disintegrating into crumbs, and fluffs it up into a close approximation of scrambled eggs. Add a pinch of ground turmeric if you need the yellow color and, of course, you can scramble the tofu without the vegetables. Silken tofu comes in vacuum-packed boxes and is found shelved with other Asian products or in the refrigerated section.*

- 6 ounces silken tofu
- Olive oil, to coat pan
- 2 tablespoons finely diced red or yellow onion
- ¼ cup finely diced carrot
- 2 tablespoons finely diced celery
- 2 tablespoons finely diced red or yellow bell pepper
- 2 tablespoons finely diced zucchini or summer squash
- 2 tablespoons coarsely chopped Italian parsley leaves
- Pinch of salt or dash of Bragg's Liquid Aminos Seasoning
- Freshly ground black pepper

Slide the tofu into a small saucepan. Add water to cover and bring to a boil. Simmer for 10 minutes, then drain in a fine-meshed sieve. Transfer to a plate and cut the tofu into ¼-inch cubes.

Heat a small skillet and add the olive oil. Sauté the onion, carrot, and celery for 2 minutes, stirring occasionally. Then add the tofu and sauté another few minutes; add the bell pepper, squash, and parsley and continue sautéing until the vegetables are tender and the tofu is light golden brown, about 5 to 8 minutes. Season to taste and serve.

MAKES 1 TO 2 SERVINGS

zucchini *frittata*

Well, this won't use up all that zucchini in your garden, but it is a great light dinner dish or perfect for a slow weekend morning. The zucchini can be grated the night before and left to drain in the refrigerator overnight. The original recipe called for ricotta and Parmesan, but we prefer it with a mixture of ricotta, feta, and Parmesan. If you are using ricotta, check to see if it is very wet and, if it is, put what you will use in cheesecloth and let it drain overnight.

- 1½ pounds zucchini (approximately 6 cups grated or 6 small zucchini)
- 1 teaspoon sea salt
- Freshly ground black pepper
- 1 tablespoon olive oil
- 1 garlic clove, minced
- 6 large eggs
- 1 tablespoon chopped fresh marjoram
- ⅓ cup grated Parmesan cheese
- ½ cup crumbled feta cheese or drained ricotta or a mix of the two

Coarsely grate the zucchini, toss with salt, and set aside in a colander or sieve to drain for at least 30 minutes. Rinse briefly to remove excess salt and, using your hands, squeeze dry.

Preheat the oven to 350°F. Heat the oil in a skillet over medium high heat. Add the zucchini and cook, stirring frequently, until it is dry, about 6 minutes. Just before the zucchini is done, stir in the garlic to let it cook briefly. This will take away a bit of its sharpness. Remove the pan from the heat and set aside.

Break the eggs into a large bowl and beat until well mixed. Add a grinding of pepper. Stir in the zucchini and garlic mixture, and add the marjoram and cheeses.

Grease an 11 by 7-inch Pyrex pan and pour the mixture into it. Bake for 45 minutes or until the frittata is set and slightly browned on top. Cut into squares and serve.

MAKES 6 SERVINGS

SPRING VEGETABLE *frittata*

This works well as a brunch dish or a light dinner entrée. The potatoes, onion, and asparagus may be prepared the day before to save time.

½ pound Yukon gold potatoes, skin on, diced into ½-inch cubes
1 medium yellow onion, thinly sliced
½ pound asparagus, trimmed and cut in ½-inch diagonal slices
Mild tasting olive oil to coat vegetables and sauté the garlic, about ½ cup
Salt
2 medium garlic cloves, minced
10 eggs
2 cups grated sharp Cheddar cheese
¼ cup freshly grated Parmesan cheese
2 tablespoons chopped Italian parsley
Pinch of cayenne pepper
Salt and pepper

Preheat the oven to 450°F. Each vegetable will roast in a different amount of time, so keep them separate as you work with them. Toss the potatoes, onion, and asparagus with oil and sprinkle with salt. Roast the vegetables in the oven, turning with a spatula to ensure even roasting. Leave them in until they are starting to brown, about 15 minutes for the potatoes and onions and 10 minutes for the asparagus. If preparing ahead, let cool and store in refrigerator overnight or until needed.

Preheat the oven to 300°F. Briefly sauté the garlic in a small amount of olive oil. (If the potatoes, onion, and asparagus have been refrigerated, heat them up in this same pan before proceeding.) In a large bowl, crack the eggs and whisk them together. Add the garlic, potatoes, onion, asparagus, cheeses, and parsley. Stir together and season with salt, pepper, and cayenne.

Pour into an oiled 9 by 13-inch glass Pyrex pan or equivalent ovenproof casserole dish. Bake until the top is puffed and starting to brown. This will take approximately 1 hour.

MAKES 8 TO 10 SERVINGS

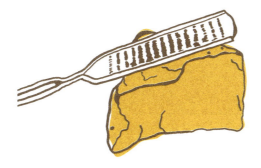

APPLE *strudel*

This beautiful, moist strudel comes to us from Liz's grandmother. The layered apples blend with the butter and sugar and bake to form a delectable caramel-flavored apple pastry, delicious for breakfast or dessert.

4 large apples
1 cup unbleached flour
2 teaspoons baking powder
½ teaspoon sea salt
⅔ cup sugar
1 egg
½ cup milk

Topping:
3 tablespoons unsalted butter
⅓ cup firmly packed brown sugar
¼ teaspoon ground cinnamon

Preheat the oven to 350°F. Grease a 9 by 13-inch Pyrex pan with butter. Peel and slice the apples ¼-inch thick. Set aside. Sift the flour, baking powder, salt, and sugar into a medium-sized bowl. In a separate bowl, whisk together the egg and milk and add it to the flour mixture, stirring until just combined. Do not overmix. Pour the batter into the greased pan. Arrange the apple slices on the batter, overlapping in 3 lengthwise rows with the curved outer side almost straight up, but slightly diagonal.

Mix together the butter, brown sugar, and cinnamon. Sprinkle over the top of the apples. Bake for 30 to 35 minutes, or until the dough has set and the strudel is beginning to brown and pull away from the edges of the pan. Remove from the oven and let cool slightly. Cut and serve.

MAKES 8 TO 12 SERVINGS

blueberry BUCKLE

We normally use frozen blueberries for this breakfast treat. Fresh blueberries or huckleberries are even better when in season and shorten the baking time a little. If using frozen blueberries, do not thaw them.

½ cup unsalted butter
¾ cup sugar
1 egg
2 cups unbleached flour
2½ teaspoons baking powder
¼ teaspoon salt
½ cup milk
1½ to 2 cups frozen blueberries

Cinnamon Topping:
½ cup sugar
½ cup unbleached flour
½ teaspoon ground cinnamon
¼ cup unsalted butter

Preheat the oven to 375°F. Cream the butter and sugar. Add the egg and beat well. Sift the flour, baking powder, and salt together and add to the butter mixture alternating with the milk. Spread this thick mixture in a greased 11 by 7 by 1½-inch Pyrex pan. Scatter the blueberries over the top.

To make the cinnamon topping, mix the sugar, flour, and cinnamon together. Cut in the butter until the mixture is the size of peas. Sprinkle this evenly over the buckle.

Bake for about 1 hour, until the top springs back when lightly touched and a toothpick inserted comes out clean. It may take up to 1½ hours depending on your oven and if the berries were frozen. Cut into squares and serve warm.

MAKES 8 TO 10 SERVINGS

PUMPKIN DATE *muffins*

Perfect for the fall, these muffins are moist and not too sweet. You can make them with canned pumpkin, baked fresh pumpkin, or butternut squash. We make this recipe for groups that request "no dairy" as part of a special diet.

- 4 ounces dates, pitted, approximately ¾ cup
- 1¾ cups unbleached flour
- 1 teaspoon baking soda
- 1 teaspoon ground cinnamon
- ¾ teaspoon salt
- ½ cup vegetable oil
- 2 eggs, room temperature, lightly beaten
- 1 cup fresh or canned pumpkin purée
- ¾ cup honey or 1 cup sugar
- ¾ cup toasted walnuts or pecans, chopped (optional)

Preheat the oven to 350°F and grease muffin tins. Chop the dates and set aside. In a mixing bowl, sift together the flour, soda, cinnamon, and salt. Add the chopped dates and stir to coat. In another bowl, combine the oil, eggs, pumpkin, and honey or sugar; stir until well blended. Add the wet ingredients to the dry ingredients and stir until just blended. Fold in the nuts, if you're using them.

Using a 2-ounce ice cream scoop or spoon, fill the greased muffin tins about two-thirds full. Bake for 30 minutes, rotating pans halfway through, until muffins are lightly browned and spring back when lightly touched. Let cool about 10 minutes before removing from pans. Serve warm.

MAKES 14 MUFFINS

COFFEE-SPIKED POPPY SEED *muffins*

These muffins are packed with flavor. Spiked with fresh coffee, moistened with buttermilk, crunchy with poppy seeds and streusel topping, they are a morning treat. Due to the moisture content, they keep well and can be reheated successfully. This recipe was adapted from the wonderful bakery-café, Los Bagels, in Arcata, California.

Topping:
¾ cup firmly packed brown sugar
1½ tablespoons unbleached flour
2 teaspoons ground cinnamon
1½ tablespoons unsalted butter, softened
¾ cup walnuts, chopped

Batter:
1 cup firmly packed brown sugar
¾ cup sugar
3 eggs, room temperature, lightly beaten
1½ cups buttermilk
2 teaspoons vanilla extract
⅓ cup strongly brewed coffee
1 cup unsalted butter, melted, cooled
3 cups unbleached flour
¾ teaspoon baking powder
¾ teaspoon baking soda
¾ teaspoon salt
⅓ cup poppy seeds

Preheat the oven to 400°F. Grease 18 muffin tins.

To make the topping: Add all of the ingredients together in a small bowl and mix until combined. Set aside.

To make the batter: Combine the sugars and eggs in a medium bowl and beat until light and fluffy. Add the buttermilk, vanilla, coffee, and melted butter and beat until blended. Sift together the flour, baking powder, soda, and salt and add it to the butter mixture. Add the poppy seeds and stir together until blended. Do not overmix.

Fill the muffin tins two-thirds full with batter and sprinkle topping over each one. Bake for 20 to 25 minutes or until light, golden brown, and the muffins spring back when lightly touched on top. Let cool in tins for 5 minutes before removing.

MAKES 18 MUFFINS

oatmeal MUFFINS

Butter and oats combine to produce a muffin rich in flavor, light and fluffy inside, yet crispy on the outside. The cranberries add a tart contrast to the buttery sweetness. The trick here is to not overmix the batter; folding the butter in gently will ensure a beautiful light texture.

- 1 cup rolled oats
- 1 cup buttermilk
- 1 egg, room temperature, lightly beaten
- ½ cup firmly packed brown sugar
- 1 cup unbleached flour
- 1 teaspoon baking powder
- ½ teaspoon salt
- ½ teaspoon baking soda
- ¼ teaspoon nutmeg, freshly ground (optional)
- ⅓ cup salted butter, melted and cooled, plus a small amount extra for greasing the tins
- ½ to 1 cup dried cranberries or dried cherries (optional)

Preheat the oven to 400°F. Soak the oats in the buttermilk for 20 minutes to an hour. While they are soaking, melt the butter, grease the muffin tins and sift the dry ingredients together. Add the egg and brown sugar to the oats and buttermilk. Add the dry ingredients to the wet and mix until just moistened. Gently fold in the ⅓ cup cooled melted butter and the dried cranberries, if you are using them. Do not overmix.

Using a 2-ounce ice cream scoop or spoon, fill the tins two-thirds full. Bake for 20 minutes or until golden brown. Let the muffins cool in the tin for a couple of minutes before removing. Cool on a rack. Serve while still warm. They are also delicious cold and keep well.

MAKES 12 MUFFINS

banana coconut MUFFINS

This recipe is simple to make. The coconut is rich but subtle and adds a nice texture to these moist muffins, which are so good they can also be used as dessert.

- 1½ cups unbleached flour
- ½ teaspoon salt
- 1 teaspoon baking soda
- 10 tablespoons unsalted butter, softened
- ½ cup sugar
- ½ cup firmly packed brown sugar
- 2 eggs, beaten
- 3 or 4 ripe bananas, puréed or mashed, approximately 1½ cups
- 1 cup shredded unsweetened coconut

Preheat the oven to 350°F. Grease the muffin tins. Sift the flour, salt, and soda together. Cream the butter and sugars together until light and fluffy. Add the eggs to the butter mixture and blend until well incorporated. Add the bananas, dry ingredients, and coconut to this mixture and stir until just blended.

Using a 2-ounce ice cream scoop or a spoon, fill the greased muffin tins two-thirds full. Bake for 25 to 30 minutes or until a toothpick, inserted in the center, comes out clean and the muffins are golden brown. Let the muffins rest a few minutes before removing from tins.

Note: This recipe makes excellent banana bread. Grease a large loaf pan and spread the batter evenly, filling to two-thirds full. Bake for about 1 hour, or until a toothpick comes out clean and the top springs back when lightly touched.

MAKES 8 TO 10 MUFFINS

cranberry MUFFINS

This recipe was originally from Liz's family in the Yukon where wild cranberries are plentiful in the late summer. Frozen or fresh cranberries work just fine in this recipe and make a moist muffin that keeps well for days. We often pulse the large, domestic berries briefly in the food processor to make them a little smaller so they distribute more evenly throughout the batter. Small, wild berries may be left whole.

¾ cup orange juice
1 tablespoon orange zest
2 cups unbleached flour
1 cup sugar
1½ teaspoons baking powder
½ teaspoon baking soda
1 teaspoon salt
¼ cup unsalted butter, cut into very small pieces
1 egg
½ cup chopped pecans or walnuts
1¼ cups cranberries

Preheat the oven to 350°F. Grease muffin tins. Zest the orange and then squeeze it for juice. Set aside the zest and juice. Sift the dry ingredients together in a bowl. Add the butter to the dry ingredients and cut in with a pastry blender or two knives until the mixture resembles coarse crumbs. Beat the egg and combine with the orange juice and zest. Pour all at once into the dry ingredients and mix just to moisten. Carefully fold in the nuts and cranberries. Using a 2-ounce ice cream scoop or spoon, divide the batter into the greased muffin tins. Bake for 25 minutes.

MAKES 12 MUFFINS

blueberry MUFFINS

These muffins have a rich, creamy, vanilla flavor highlighted with juicy blueberries and tops that sparkle with turbinado sugar. Be careful when folding in the blueberries. If you overmix, they will turn into tough, bright purple, smurf muffins. Don't thaw frozen berries; they will hold up better if still frozen when stirred into the batter. In this recipe, you might consider using paper liners to assure easy removal of the muffins from the tins.

- 1 cup unsalted butter, softened, room temperature
- 1½ cups sugar
- 4 eggs, lightly beaten, room temperature
- 4 teaspoons vanilla extract
- 1½ cups sour cream
- 4½ cups unbleached flour
- ½ teaspoon baking soda
- 1½ teaspoons salt
- 2 cups fresh or frozen blueberries
- ½ cup turbinado sugar

Preheat the oven to 400°F. Grease muffin tins or line with paper liners. In a medium bowl, combine the butter and the sugar. Cream until light and fluffy. Add the eggs and beat until incorporated. Mix in the vanilla and the sour cream. Sift together the flour, soda, and salt. Add the flour mixture to the wet batter and stir until the dry ingredients are just moistened. Gently fold in the blueberries until evenly incorporated, being careful not to overmix. The dough will be very thick.

Using a 2-ounce ice cream scoop or spoon, scoop the batter into the tins. Make them full and slightly mounded. Normally we wouldn't fill them so high, but since this dough is thick and has very little leavening agent, they expand only slightly. Sprinkle the tops with the turbinado sugar.

Bake for 10 minutes, then turn the oven down to 350°F if the tops seem to be browning too fast. Bake until muffins are golden brown and spring back when lightly touched, about another 10 or 15 minutes. Let muffins sit a minute or two before turning out of the tins.

MAKES 20 MUFFINS

DRIED FRUIT *scones*

The cream in this recipe produces a delicate scone with a lighter texture than those made with butter. Tangy dried apricot and candied ginger keep the palate intrigued. Serve with fresh fruit and frittata for brunch.

- 2 cups unbleached flour
- 1 tablespoon baking powder
- ½ teaspoon salt
- ¼ cup sugar
- ½ cup dried fruit (an equal mix of currants, apricots, and candied ginger), chopped
- ¼ cup golden raisins
- 1 teaspoon lemon or orange zest (optional)
- 1¼ cups heavy cream
- 2 tablespoons unsalted butter, melted
- 2 tablespoons turbinado sugar

Preheat the oven to 400°F. Sift together the first 4 dry ingredients into a large mixing bowl. Add the chopped dried fruits, raisins, and the zest and stir until the fruit is separated and evenly distributed. Stir in the cream until just moistened.

Lightly flour a dry surface and pat the dough into an 8 to 9-inch round and cut into 8 or 10 wedges. Lay them gently 1 inch apart on a baking sheet lined with parchment paper and brush with the melted butter. Sprinkle the tops with the turbinado sugar and bake until the tops and bottoms are browned, approximately 15 to 20 minutes. If they seem to be getting too dark, turn the oven down to 350°F after the first 10 minutes. Let cool slightly before handling as they are delicate.

MAKES 8 TO 10 SCONES

ORANGE CURRANT *scones*

This classic scone with its flaky, crunchy texture is reliant upon cold, tiny pieces of butter, a gentle but fast handling of the dough, and a hot oven. The egg wash gives a nice sheen and holds the turbinado sugar. You can use cream in place of the egg wash for a similar effect.

- 1 orange (zest and 4 tablespoons juice)
- ½ cup dried currants
- 3 cups unbleached flour
- 5 tablespoons sugar
- 1 tablespoon baking powder
- ½ teaspoon salt
- ¼ pound cold unsalted butter
- ⅔ cup buttermilk
- 1 egg yolk
- 2 tablespoons milk
- ¼ cup turbinado sugar (optional)

Preheat the oven to 400°F. Zest the orange and then squeeze the juice. Place the currants in the orange juice to plump a bit. Sift the dry ingredients together into a bowl. Cut the butter into small, pea-sized pieces and then, using a pastry blender or whisk, add it to the dry ingredients and mix until it resembles coarse meal. Combine the currants, orange zest and juice with the buttermilk and add these wet ingredients to the dry ingredients, stirring until the mixture is just moistened. You may need to add a little more buttermilk. Do not overmix.

Turn the dough out onto a floured surface and, with a few light pats, gather the dough together. Then gently press into a round about 1 inch high. Cut the round into 8 wedges and place 1 inch apart on a baking sheet lined with parchment paper. Whisk the egg yolk and milk together and lightly brush the scones with the mixture. Sprinkle the tops with turbinado sugar if using. Bake until the scones are lightly browned, about 20 minutes.

MAKES 8 SCONES

HERBED *biscuits*

We serve these delicious biscuits regularly for breakfast with scrambled eggs, fresh salsa, and pinto beans. Of course, they are equally good at dinner with a bowl of stew. If you want the tops darker, you can brush the biscuits with heavy cream or melted butter before baking.

- 2 cups unbleached flour
- 2 teaspoons baking powder
- ¾ teaspoon salt
- ½ teaspoon baking soda
- 2 tablespoons chopped fresh Italian parsley
- 2 tablespoons chopped green onions or chives
- 5 tablespoons unsalted butter, cold and cut into ¼-inch pieces
- ¾ cup plus 2 tablespoons buttermilk

Preheat the oven to 400°F. Sift the flour, baking powder, salt, and soda into a large bowl. Mix in the parsley and green onions. Add the butter to the dry ingredients and mix with a pastry blender until the mixture resembles coarse meal. Make a well in the center and pour in the buttermilk. With your hand or a wooden spoon, blend the dough just until combined. It will be sticky.

Turn the dough out onto a floured work surface. Wash and dry your hands and flour them. Gently knead or fold the dough back on itself just until the dough feels smooth, about 6 times. Pat out the dough to ½ to ¾-inch thickness. Dip a 2½-inch biscuit cutter into flour and cut out the biscuits, lightly patting the scraps together and then cutting again. Place the biscuits at least 1 inch apart on a baking sheet lined with parchment paper. Bake until golden brown, rotating if necessary, for about 10 minutes.

MAKES 10 BISCUITS

bread

bread

There is nothing more wonderful than the aroma of baking bread. Once you master some simple techniques and understand a few facts, breadmaking really is an easy process. Allow yourself to experiment as you develop a feel for the dough and learn how dough reacts in your own oven. Don't give up if you have a batch that rises too much or comes out oddly shaped. The bread will still taste good. Remember, you want your bread to look homemade, right? Just plunge in and know that bread dough is very forgiving.

To make bread requires a commitment of a few hours for the whole process, but not in actual work. The actual work time is more like 30 minutes to do the initial mixing and kneading, and another 10 minutes to punch down and form the loaves. Pop them in the oven and you just have a few minutes of work left to do: checking the loaves, pulling them from the oven, and cooling them down. When you understand the way dough works, you can devise ways to make the process fit your own schedule by, for example, leaving your dough overnight in the refrigerator or even freezing it.

You must use high-quality ingredients to obtain good bread. Your flour should be unbleached all-purpose flour or bread flour specially designed to give your dough the necessary gluten. King Arthur, El Molino, and Giusto's are brands that produce such flour.

These recipes have been written and tested with active dry yeast. Fresh cakes of yeast will also work, if that is what you prefer to use. One cake of compressed yeast equals 1 tablespoon of active dry yeast. One envelope of dry yeast is 2½ teaspoons. If you have a good local health food store, you might consider buying yeast in bulk because it is better quality than that in the packets.

So, a few facts. Yeast is alive. As the yeast multiplies, it feeds on sugars in the dough and makes carbon dioxide gas. These gas bubbles are held in place by the gluten in the flour, which has the ability to become stretchy. You can slow the yeast way down by chilling it or you can kill it with too much heat. Yeast is killed if the water or conditions are hotter than 115 degrees. It is safer to work with things on the cool side. If the day is really warm, say more than 80 degrees, you might want to start with water cooler than "warm to the touch," which is around 90 to 100 degrees.

Do NOT forget the salt. If you have a tendency to forget things, put your salt container right next to your cookbook or work area. Salt is extremely important, not just for the taste it imparts, but also because it controls the speed at which the yeast works. If you omit the salt, your bread will rise spectacularly and then collapse. You will most likely find the dough less alive when you go to mold it and end up with a tasteless, flat, dense loaf.

And now, on to technique. Kneading is a rhythmic, physical activity that can be done in a machine, but why give up the joy of feeling the shaggy mass of dough transform into a shiny, springy, smooth ball? Add flour gradually to the bowl of yeast, salt, oil, and liquids, stirring in as much as you can. It will be a rough mass, and you probably will not be able to get all the flour into the dough. Sprinkle flour over your kneading surface and keep a cup filled with extra flour nearby. Using a rubber spatula or dough scraper, scrape the dough out of the bowl onto the kneading surface. Flour your hands and pull the outer edge of the dough up and then fold and push it down into the middle of the dough with the palms of both hands. Rotate the dough a quarter turn and repeat. Lift and fold the outer edge in, push down, then rotate or turn. Keep repeating this process of fold, push, turn. Put your whole body into the movement and chant the words "fold, push, turn" out loud if it helps you. Establish a rhythm. If the dough starts sticking, sprinkle more flour under the dough and on your hands.

If you have small hands, knead using both together. If you have large hands or are working with a small batch of dough, then use one hand for lifting and pushing and the other for turning. After kneading for 5 to 10 minutes, you will feel the texture of the dough change. It will become more elastic, smoother in appearance, and should begin to be springy and bounce back a bit as you push. Admire what you have created. It is now ready to rise.

To let your dough rise, lightly oil a bowl that is large enough to accommodate the dough as it swells to twice its bulk. Recipes often advise you to put the dough in a "warm place to rise," but please make sure it isn't too warm. If the room is over 65 degrees, you don't need to seek out a special warm place. Your dough will rise perfectly at that temperature. Put your dough in the bowl, with the bottom-side down, swirl it around to get oil over all the dough, then flip it over so the oiled, smooth bottom is now on top. Cover the dough with plastic wrap or a damp towel and let it rise for an hour, or until it has doubled in size.

To punch down the dough, slightly oil your hand and stick it right in the middle of the dough to the bottom of the bowl. The whole mass will sink down around your hand. It is rather dramatic. Turn all the edges into this hole and knead the dough a few times. You will now either turn the dough bottom-side to the top, if the recipe asks for a second rise in the bowl, or proceed to forming your loaves.

To form or shape the loaves, divide the dough into the number of pieces indicated in the recipe. There are a variety of techniques to obtain the shape of the loaf and, basically, they all work. If forming a loaf to fit into a pan, we begin with the smooth side of the dough down and stretch or push the dough to form an oblong loaf. We pinch together a seam of the two sides, lengthwise, then flip the loaf over, turning the ends under. At this point, cradle the loaf between your palms and jiggle it back and forth on the seam to settle it together. Then into the greased pan it goes, seam-side down, smooth-side up.

Now it is time to preheat your oven. We like to preheat the oven 25 to 50 degrees higher than the recipe suggests to counteract the heat that is lost when the oven door is opened to insert the loaves. Leave the loaves at this higher temperature for a few minutes and then turn it down to the temperature requested in the recipe for the remainder of the baking.

While the oven is preheating, your bread will be rising in the pans. A common error is to allow this rising to go too far. Unfortunately, many recipes call for the bread to rise until doubled in the pans. But "oven spring," which is the sudden rise when the bread first encounters the heat of a hot oven, can be as much as 15 percent. If you have allowed your loaves to fully double in size, they will be too airy. Often just 20 minutes is enough for this final rise. This is especially true with light roll dough or dough that has eggs in it. Heavier, denser bread can use more rising time.

Recipes frequently ask you to slash the bread either after you have put the loaves in the pan or just before you put them in the oven. This is done to help the bread expand evenly and avoid an uneven crack in the loaf. Use a razor or a sharp knife and do it quickly.

To bake the bread, put the loaves into the preheated oven and, if you have heated it at a higher temperature, don't forget to turn the oven down. About halfway through the estimated baking time, check your loaves and rotate the pans as necessary. If you are baking a bread with honey or molasses in it or with an egg glaze, you should check to see if it is browning too fast and cover it with aluminum foil if it is burning. When the loaves are evenly browned and you think they are done, remove them from the oven and take them out of the pans. The bottom should be brown and it should sound "hollow" when tapped with the knuckles of your hand. It is almost a sensation as much as a sound. Somehow you will just know. We promise. If it is not done, put the loaf back in the pan and put it back in the oven, but check it frequently now, every 5 minutes or so.

When the loaves are done, turn them out of the pans onto a rack and let them cool. They should be on a rack so they don't collect moisture on the bottom and become soggy. It is best to allow your bread to cool thoroughly before slicing. You will be able to slice it more evenly and the texture changes for the better as it cools. Then, get out the butter and enjoy, enjoy.

whole wheat BREAD

Liz brought this bread recipe to the Ranch in 1988 and we've been making it ever since. The milk, honey, and oil make this a moist and flavorful bread.

1 cup lukewarm water
1 tablespoon active dry yeast
2 cups warm milk
¼ cup honey
4 cups unbleached flour, approximately
3½ cups whole wheat flour, approximately
1 tablespoon sea salt
¼ cup vegetable oil

Egg Wash:
1 egg
½ cup cold water
Sesame seeds or poppy seeds (optional)

In a large mixing bowl, combine the warm water and yeast and let sit for about 10 minutes or until the yeast is active. Meanwhile, heat the milk over low heat until lukewarm. Add the milk to the yeast, and then stir in the honey. Add 1 cup of white flour and 2 cups of whole wheat flour. Stir vigorously (about 100 strokes by hand) to develop the gluten. The resulting sponge should be the consistency of mud. At this point, you can let the sponge rest, covered, for up to an hour or you can proceed with the rest of the recipe immediately. Add the oil and salt to the sponge, and then add the remaining whole wheat and unbleached flour, one cup at a time, until the dough is pulling away from the sides and is difficult to stir with a wooden spoon.

Turn the dough out onto a lightly floured work surface and knead for about 10 minutes, adding small amounts of flour as needed to keep from sticking, until the dough has formed into a smooth elastic ball that springs back when pushed with your hand. Place the dough in a lightly greased bowl, cover with plastic wrap or a damp dishtowel, and place in a warm spot to rise. Let the dough rise for 1 hour or until it has doubled in bulk.

While the dough is rising, preheat the oven to 400°F. Grease 2 large bread pans, 9 by 5 inches. Punch down the dough, divide into two pieces and form into loaves. Place the loaves, seam-side down into the pans. Cover with plastic wrap or a damp towel and let rise for approximately 30 minutes or until the dough is cresting the pan. Make an egg wash by whisking together the egg and the cold water. Brush this over the loaves with a pastry brush. This is the time to sprinkle the loaves with the seeds if you are choosing to use them. With a sharp knife, quickly slash the tops of the loaves. We usually make three diagonal cuts that run ¼ to ½-inch deep. This will allow the bread to expand in the first 10 minutes of baking.

Place the loaves in the oven and then turn it down to 350°F. Bake the loaves 45 to 50 minutes until golden brown. Remove from pans. Loaves should sound hollow when tapped on the bottom with your hand. Let cool on racks before slicing.

MAKES 2 LARGE LOAVES

WALNUT ROSEMARY BEER *bread*

This is a stunningly beautiful bread. It pairs well with goat cheese. The bread can be served as an unsliced braid to be broken apart "family style," or the dough can be made into individual rolls. The beer helps to activate the yeast and gives the bread a malty flavor. However, it can be made using water in place of the beer.

½ cup walnuts
1½ cups beer, slightly warmed
2 tablespoons active dry yeast
½ cup olive oil
4½ cups unbleached flour, divided
½ cup rye flour
2 tablespoons sugar
1 tablespoon salt

1 cup yellow onion, chopped
1 tablespoon fresh rosemary leaves, chopped

Egg Wash:
1 egg
2 teaspoons water

Preheat the oven to 350°F and toast the walnuts for about 10 minutes. Remove and rub with a towel to remove some of the skins, then chop them. In a medium bowl combine the beer with the yeast and let sit for 10 minutes or until the mixture dissolves and is active. Add the olive oil. Set aside ½ cup of the unbleached flour to use when kneading. In a large bowl, combine the remaining unbleached flour, the rye flour, sugar, salt, onion, walnuts, and rosemary. Add the yeast mixture and, with a sturdy spoon, stir until all ingredients have been incorporated and the dough has formed a shaggy ball and is pulling away from the sides of the bowl.

Dump the dough onto a lightly floured work surface and knead for about 10 minutes, sprinkling little bits of flour when needed, until the dough forms into a smooth, elastic ball that springs back when pushed with your hand. Place the dough in a lightly greased bowl, cover with plastic wrap or a damp towel, and let rise in a warm place for about 1 hour or until doubled in bulk.

Punch down the dough. Cut it into 2 pieces. Divide each piece into thirds. Using your hands, roll each piece into an 8 to 10-inch rope. Braid the 3 pieces together to form a loaf. Pinch the pieces together at each end and tuck under. Repeat with the remaining three pieces and place them on a greased baking sheet or sheet lined with parchment paper. Cover and let rise for about 30 minutes or until doubled in bulk.

While the loaves are rising, preheat the oven to 350°F. Beat the egg and water together in a small bowl. Brush the tops of the loaves with the egg wash. Bake for 45 minutes, rotating pans halfway through for even baking, or until bread is dark brown and sounds hollow when tapped on the bottom with your hand. Let bread cool on the pan for 10 minutes before moving to racks to cool completely.

Note: For individual rolls, form the dough into 3-ounce balls (about the size of a lime). Let balls rise until doubled in size and then bake for about 20 minutes or until rolls are dark brown on top and bottom and sound hollow when tapped with your hand.

MAKES 2 LOAVES OR APPROXIMATELY 20 TO 24 ROLLS

seeded DINNER ROLLS

These rolls are tender, lightly sweetened with honey, and sprinkled with flavorful seeds. They are perfect for an informal soup and bread meal, and also as a beautiful contribution to a holiday feast. We like to bake them as pull apart rounds, although they may be baked individually too. Many variations are possible with this recipe. You can vary the amount of whole wheat flour or bake the rolls with only one seed or none at all. If using just one variety of seed, poppy or sesame are both fine, but the fennel is too strong to use alone.

1¼ cups lukewarm water
1 tablespoon active dry yeast
¼ cup honey
1 egg, beaten
1 teaspoon salt
1 cup whole wheat flour, approximately
3¼ cups unbleached flour, approximately

Egg Wash:
1 egg
2 tablespoons water
1 tablespoon each of
   poppy, sesame, and fennel seeds
Kosher salt, for dusting

In a large mixing bowl, combine the warm water and the yeast. Let sit for 10 minutes or until the yeast is active. Add the honey, the beaten egg, and salt and mix well. Stir in the whole wheat flour and some of the white flour (one cup at a time) until the batter resembles thick mud. Beat well to develop the gluten in the flour. Continue adding the white flour (now ½ cup at a time, stirring after each addition) until the batter turns into a mass of dough that is too difficult to stir with a spoon.

Turn the dough out onto a lightly floured work surface and knead for approximately 10 minutes, adding small amounts of flour only when needed to prevent sticking. Knead until a smooth, elastic ball has formed that springs back when pushed with your hand. Place the dough in a lightly oiled bowl. Cover with plastic wrap or a damp towel and set in a warm, draft-free area to rise for 1 hour or until doubled in bulk.

Grease one 9-inch round cake pan. When the dough has doubled, punch it down. Grease your hands with oil and pull off a 3-ounce piece of dough (about the size of a small lime). Form it into a ball by cupping your hand around the dough and then rapidly rolling it in a circular motion on the table. It will form into a tight round ball after about 30 seconds of rolling. Place 12 rolls in each pan, 3 in the middle and the rest around the side. Leave about ½ inch between each roll. Repeat with the remaining dough. Cover with plastic wrap or a damp towel and let rise in a warm place for about 30 minutes or until rolls are cresting the pan.

While the rolls are rising, preheat the oven to 400°F. If you plan to sprinkle them with seeds, make an egg wash by whisking together the remaining egg and water in a small bowl. Brush the tops of the rolls with the wash and then sprinkle on the seeds and a light dusting of kosher salt. Place in the oven and bake for about 20 to 25 minutes, or until the tops and bottoms of the rolls are a deep golden brown and they sound hollow when tapped with your hand on their tops. Let cool in pans for a minute before moving to racks for further cooling.

MAKES 12 TO 15 ROLLS

sourdough BREAD

For many years, this sourdough bread has been a mainstay of our lunch and dinner menus at the Ranch. Once you have your starter, the bread can be made in the space of a day or spread out over a few days. Either way, it is easy to make and the result is a shiny, crunchy exterior with a chewy interior and good flavor. The starter is also used as a base for our Fruit Bread (page 60).

>Sourdough Starter:
>¼ teaspoon active dry yeast
>2 cups lukewarm water
>2¼ cups unbleached flour
>
>Bread:
>2 cups lukewarm water
>1 teaspoon active dry yeast
>2 cups sourdough starter
>2 teaspoons salt
>1 cup whole wheat flour
>7½ cups unbleached high-gluten bread flour, approximately
>Kosher salt

To make the starter: Dissolve ¼ teaspoon yeast in 2 cups warm water in a glass or stainless bowl. Add the flour and beat well until the mixture is smooth. Cover with plastic wrap and let sit at room temperature for 24 to 32 hours. After this period, refrigerate if not using immediately. Once you have made your starter, it needs to be used or "fed." To feed the starter, add equal amounts of flour and water and stir well. Let sit out overnight and then refrigerate. Store in a glass or plastic jar, using and feeding the starter at least once a week. It will gain in flavor with time. Or simply make the starter the day before you want to bake this bread, use it up, and make anew for the next batch.

To make the bread: Combine the warm water and the yeast in a large bowl. Let sit for 10 minutes or until the yeast is active. Add the sourdough starter and stir well until the mixture is smooth. Then add the salt and the whole wheat flour. Add about 2 cups of the unbleached flour or enough to get the mixture to the consistency of mud. Beat vigorously to develop the gluten, then continue adding flour, one cup at a time, and stirring until it becomes difficult to stir in more flour. The dough will pull away from the sides of the bowl and form into a loose, shaggy, round shape.

Sprinkle about ½ cup of the flour on your board or table and turn the dough out to knead. Knead for about 10 to 12 minutes, sprinkling on more flour as necessary to prevent sticking. The dough should form into a ball that is taut and elastic, shiny and springy to the touch but still moist. Return the dough to a clean bowl that is lightly greased with oil. Cover with plastic wrap or a damp towel.* Let rise 2 hours in a warm spot. Punch down and remove the dough from the bowl. Cut the dough into the desired number of pieces and form into rounds, loaves, or baguettes. Place the breads seam-side down on baking sheets lined with parchment paper with at least 6 inches between loaves. Cover with plastic wrap or a damp towel and let rise for about 45 minutes or until doubled in bulk.

After 15 minutes of rising time, begin preheating the oven to 425°F. When the loaves have risen, spray them liberally with cold water and sprinkle with kosher salt. Slash the tops of the loaves. Put in the oven, turn it down to 400°F, and bake for about 30 minutes for baguettes, 40 to 45 minutes for the rounds and loaves, rotating the pan and loaves half way through for even baking, until the loaves are a medium golden brown, sound hollow when tapped with your hand, and have a nice shiny hard crust. Remove from the oven and let cool on racks for about 30 minutes before slicing.

MAKES 2 LARGE 14-INCH LOAVES, 2 ROUNDS, OR 6 BAGUETTES

*At this point, you can put the dough in the refrigerator and leave it overnight. The sourdough flavor will be stronger if you do. Pull it out 2 hours before molding, to allow it to come to room temperature, and continue with the remaining steps.

italian herb BREAD

Ariel worked up this recipe for a chewy, sourdough-style bread that makes great toast and sandwiches. It is best if you give the starter a good twelve hours to get going, but if necessary, a shorter amount of time will work.

Starter:
1 cup warm water
1 tablespoon active dry yeast
1 tablespoon honey
1 cup unbleached flour
½ cup whole wheat flour

Bread:
2 cups warm water
1 tablespoon salt
1 tablespoon chopped fresh oregano or 2 teaspoons dried
⅓ cup chopped fresh Italian parsley
3 tablespoons chopped fresh basil
7 cups unbleached flour, approximately
olive oil to grease the bowl

To make the starter: Dissolve the yeast and honey in the water in a glass or stainless bowl. Add the flour and stir well. It will form a sticky ball. Cover with plastic wrap and let sit at room temperature for a minimum of 4, but preferably 12 to 24 hours.

To make the bread: In a large bowl, combine the starter with the water and salt. Stir vigorously to combine. Sprinkle the herbs in and begin to add the flour, one cup at a time. When it becomes difficult to add more flour and the dough is starting to pull away from the sides of the bowl, turn the dough out onto a surface dusted with flour. Knead, adding ¼ cup flour at a time, until the dough forms a springy, elastic ball, about 10 to 15 minutes.

Return the dough to a clean bowl that is lightly greased with oil. Cover with plastic wrap. Let rise 2 hours or until doubled in size. Punch down and remove the dough from the bowl. Cut the dough into 2 pieces and form into 2 round or long loaves. Place each on a baking sheet lined with parchment paper or a sheet oiled and sprinkled with polenta. Cover loosely with plastic wrap and let rise for 45 minutes.

Preheat the oven to 450°F. Slash the tops of the loaves, spray with water and place in the oven. After 10 minutes, spray the loaves again with water and then turn the oven down to 350°F. Continue to bake until loaves are brown on top and sound hollow when tapped on the bottom, approximately another 40 minutes. Let cool before slicing.

MAKES 2 ROUND OR OBLONG LOAVES

struan BREAD

We found this wonderful bread in Brother Juniper's Bread Book. *Peter Reinhart, the author and renowned baker of Brother Juniper's, describes it as an ancient Scottish bread that celebrates the harvest. It was baked each fall on the eve of the feast of St. Michael the Archangel, the guardian of the harvest, and so included the various grains that had been grown during the year. The bread is beautiful in appearance with a rich, golden color and delicious as a side for soup, as a sandwich bread, or as croutons or toast.*

3 tablespoons active dry yeast
¼ cup lukewarm water
7 cups unbleached high-gluten bread flour, approximately
½ cup uncooked polenta
½ cup rolled oats
½ cup firmly packed brown sugar
⅓ cup wheat bran
½ cup cooked brown rice

4 teaspoons sea salt
¼ cup honey
¾ cup buttermilk
1½ cups water, divided

Egg Wash:
1 egg
½ cup water
3 tablespoons poppy seeds

In a large bowl, dissolve the yeast in ¼ cup of warm water for 10 minutes or until the yeast is active. In another large bowl, mix together the flour, polenta, oats, brown sugar, bran, cooked rice, and salt. Add to the proofed yeast the honey, buttermilk, and 1¼ cups of the water, reserving about ¼ cup for adjustments during kneading. Stir to combine, add the wet ingredients to the dry ingredients, and stir with a wooden spoon until the dough pulls away from the sides of the bowl. Gather up the dough and press together to form a ball. If the dough is dry and crumbly, add a bit of the reserved water.

Sprinkle your work surface lightly with flour and knead the dough for 12 to 15 minutes. This dough requires a longer kneading than others because of the whole grains. The finished dough should form into a taut, shiny ball. It will be tacky but not sticky, lightly golden, stretchy, and elastic. When you push the heels of your hand into the dough, it should give way but not tear. Place the dough in a lightly oiled bowl. Cover with plastic wrap or a damp towel and allow to rise in a warm place for about 1 hour, or until it has doubled in size.

Preheat the oven to 350°F. Grease 2 bread pans measuring 9 by 5-inches with butter. Punch the dough down and cut into 2 pieces and form into loaves. Place in the greased bread pans. Cover with plastic wrap or a damp towel and allow the dough to rise until cresting the tops of the pans or until it has risen about 80 percent.

Whisk together the egg and the water and brush this egg wash over the tops of the loaves. Sprinkle with the poppy seeds and quickly but carefully slash the tops with a sharp knife. Bake the bread in the oven for about 45 to 50 minutes, rotating the pans halfway through for even baking, until the loaves are dark gold and sound hollow when tapped with your hand. Allow the bread to cool thoroughly for at least 40 minutes before slicing.

MAKES 2 LOAVES

onion rye caraway BREAD

This is a very moist bread, lightly accented with onion and caraway seed, and makes delicious ham sandwiches with Gruyère cheese. The rye flour makes the dough a bit sticky and trickier to knead than others. Don't get discouraged when kneading, just keep sprinkling small amounts of flour on your hands and board as you work.

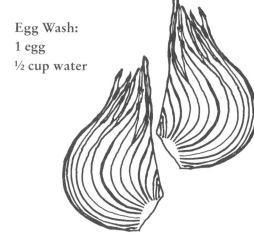

- 1 cup lukewarm water
- 1 tablespoon active dry yeast
- 2 cups milk, warmed
- ¼ cup molasses
- ¼ cup vegetable oil
- 2½ cups rye flour
- 3 cups whole wheat flour
- 4 teaspoons sea salt
- 1 yellow onion, chopped (approximately 1½ cups)
- 2 tablespoons caraway seeds
- 3 cups unbleached flour, plus more as needed

Egg Wash:
- 1 egg
- ½ cup water

Place warm water in a large bowl and sprinkle with the yeast. Let dissolve for 10 minutes or until the yeast is active. Add the milk, molasses, and oil and stir together. Add the rye flour and the whole wheat flour, stirring with a spoon, until the batter resembles thick mud. Beat for about 1 minute to develop the gluten. Add the salt, onion, caraway seeds, and the unbleached flour (one cup at a time) until the dough is pulling away from the sides of the bowl and has formed into a shaggy ball. When it is difficult to stir with a spoon, turn the dough out onto a lightly floured work surface and knead, adding more white flour as needed. Continue kneading and adding flour ¼ cup at a time, for about 10 minutes, until the dough has become a smooth, shiny, elastic ball that springs back when pushed with your hand. It will still be a bit tacky from the rye flour.

Place the dough in a lightly greased bowl, cover with plastic wrap or a damp towel, and let rise in a warm place for about 1½ hours or until doubled in bulk. Grease the bread pans. Punch down the dough with your fists and shape into 2 loaves. Place the loaves in the pans, cover with plastic wrap or a damp towel, and let rise for 25 minutes or until the dough is cresting the top of the pan.

While the loaves are rising, preheat the oven to 350°F. In a small bowl, whisk together the egg and water. Brush the egg wash over the tops of the loaves. Quickly make 3 diagonal slashes on the tops of the bread with a sharp knife and place in the hot oven. Bake for about 45 to 50 minutes, rotating pans halfway through for even baking, until the bread is dark brown. The loaves should sound hollow when tapped on the bottom with your hand. Let cool before slicing.

MAKES 2 LOAVES

cheese ONION POPPY SEED BREAD

This bread recipe was developed by Liz and can be made into beautiful large braids or into delicious hamburger buns. It can also be made in regular loaf pans and makes a good sandwich loaf, especially for ham and cheese.

1 tablespoon yeast	2 cups whole wheat flour
½ cup lukewarm water	4½ to 5 cups unbleached flour
1½ cups milk	1 cup chopped onion
¼ cup honey or sugar	1½ cups grated sharp Cheddar cheese
1 tablespoon salt	
¼ cup vegetable oil	Egg Wash:
1 egg, beaten	1 egg yolk
2 tablespoons poppy seeds	2 tablespoons water

Dissolve the yeast in the warm water and let it sit until the yeast is active. Heat the milk to lukewarm and add to the yeast along with the honey, salt, oil, egg, and poppy seeds. Add the whole wheat flour and enough unbleached flour (approximately 3 cups) to make a sponge the consistency of thick mud. Beat well by hand or in a mixer with a dough hook for about 3 minutes. Add the onions and the cheese. Then continue adding unbleached flour until a firm dough is formed. Turn out onto a floured board and knead until the dough is smooth (or knead in mixer with the dough hook). Cover with plastic wrap and let rise in greased bowl until doubled, about 1 hour.

Preheat the oven to 350°F. Punch down the dough and make into braids or buns.

To make braids: Divide the dough into 6 pieces and roll them back and forth with your hands until they form 24-inch-long ropes. Braid 3 at a time to form the loaves. Tuck the ends under to finish. They will each be about 12 inches long. Place on a baking sheet lined with parchment paper or greased with oil. Beat the egg yolk and water together and then brush braids with this egg wash. Let the loaves rise for 20 minutes. Bake at 350°F for 30 minutes, then turn oven down to 325°F and continue baking for another 20 to 30 minutes, or until the loaves are browned and sound hollow when tapped with your hand.

To make hamburger buns: Divide the dough into 12 pieces. Roll into balls and flatten with the palm of your hand till about 3½ inches across. Place on a baking sheet lined with parchment paper or greased with oil. Let the rolls rise for 10 minutes, then push down again to stretch them out more. Brush with egg wash and let rise an additional 10 minutes. Bake buns at 350°F for 20 or 30 minutes or until done.

MAKES 2 LARGE BRAIDS OR 12 TO 15 HAMBURGER BUNS

ARIEL'S *focaccia*

This excellent dough was developed by Ariel and won a gold medal at the Sonoma County 1998 Harvest Fair. It can be made into flatbread for a focaccia sandwich, into delicious dinner rolls, or into flat rounds with savory toppings to be used as an appetizer. To make the dough into flatbread or rounds, use as little flour as possible and keep the dough soft. For rolls, use the larger amount of flour and make your dough a little stiffer.

2½ cups lukewarm water
3 teaspoons active dry yeast
5½ to 6½ cups unbleached flour
3 teaspoons sea salt
¼ cup olive oil plus extra for coating and brushing
2 tablespoons fresh rosemary or sage, chopped
Polenta, for sprinkling on baking sheet
Kosher salt, for sprinkling

Pour warm water into large mixing bowl, add yeast, and let sit for 10 minutes or until the yeast is active. Begin adding flour, 1 cup at a time, incorporating with a whisk at first, until a soft "mud" forms. Whisk vigorously for about 1 minute. Add the salt, oil, and rosemary and switch to mixing with a wooden spoon. Stir, adding smaller amounts of flour now, until the dough balls up in the bowl and you can no longer stir with a wooden spoon.

Turn the dough out onto a counter, using flour to keep it from sticking. Keep sprinkling handfuls of flour, only as needed. The idea is to keep the dough very moist without adding too much flour. Knead for about 10 minutes. The dough will slowly take the form of a ball and will look slightly shiny and smooth and will spring back to the touch when it is ready. Brush the dough with olive oil, cover with plastic wrap, and let sit for 1½ hours in a warm room away from cold drafts. If you are making it ahead, you can coat it with oil, cover with plastic wrap, and refrigerate overnight.

After 1 hour, or when the dough has doubled in bulk, punch down the dough and let it rest for about 5 minutes. If it has been in the refrigerator, pull it out and bring to room temperature before punching down and proceeding with the following steps.

To make flatbread: Lightly coat a 13 by 18-inch baking sheet with oil. Sprinkle with polenta. Alternatively, line a pan with parchment paper and coat that with oil. With a rolling pin, or with your hands, roll or push out the dough to a rectangle. Place it on the pan. Dough should be about 1-inch thick. It might not stretch out to the full size of the pan at first, but if you let it rest a few minutes, you will slowly be able to coerce it to the sides of the pan with your fingertips. Sprinkle the dough with flour and cover with plastic wrap. Let the dough sit, in a warm place, for 35 to 45 minutes to rise.

Preheat the oven to 450°F. Make indentations in the dough with your fingers, brush liberally with oil and sprinkle lightly with salt. Bake in the oven for 20 to 30 minutes, checking and turning pans halfway through to ensure even baking, or until crust is lightly browned on bottom and top. Remove and let cool on wire racks. When cool, cut into 8 to 12 equal pieces.

To make rounds: Divide the dough into 5 to 7 equal pieces and roll out into circles. Once again, it is important to roll out the dough, let it rest for about 20 minutes, and then reroll after it has relaxed. Put on toppings (see suggestions below). Moist toppings may be put on before baking but it is best to add dried tomatoes or grated hard cheeses such as Parmesan or Asiago when the focaccia is almost baked and has just a few more minutes to go in the oven. Preheat the oven to 450°F and proceed to bake following the previous instructions for flatbread.

Suggested Toppings:
Caramelized onions
Roasted vegetables such as eggplant or bell peppers
Roasted garlic
Bits of moist cheese, such as Gorgonzola, mozzarella, or feta
Oven roasted tomatoes or sliced fresh Roma tomatoes

To make rolls: Add a little more flour for a stiffer dough. Divide into 3-ounce balls (about the size of a lime). Form each ball by cupping your hand around the dough and rapidly rolling in a circular motion on the table. The dough will form into a tight round ball after about 30 seconds of rolling. Place the rolls on a baking sheet lined with parchment paper and allow to rise for about 20 minutes. Meanwhile, preheat the oven to 400°F. Lightly brush the rolls with oil and sprinkle with salt. If desired, the rolls can be snipped with scissors or slashed with a razor to make an "X" on top. When the rolls have risen to almost double in size, place in the oven and bake about 20 minutes or until golden brown and done.

MAKES ONE 13 BY 18-INCH FLATBREAD OR 5 TO 7 FLAT ROUNDS OR 24 TO 30 ROLLS

fruit BREAD

This bread is delicious fresh or toasted. It uses our sourdough starter as its base, so if you don't have that on hand, plan to start a day ahead to have it ready. This bread can be made into breakfast buns too. The dough is quite heavy, so you might want to consider mixing it by hand.

1½ cups lukewarm water
5 teaspoons active dry yeast
2½ cups sourdough starter (page 52)
1 cup rolled oats
3 tablespoons honey
5 tablespoons packed brown sugar
½ cup rye flour
1½ cups whole wheat flour
Pinch of ground cinnamon, nutmeg, allspice, or cardamom (optional)
2 tablespoons salt
4 cups unbleached flour

1 cup dried chopped apricots or chopped candied citrus peel (orange or lemon)
1 cup raisins or currants
½ cup dried cranberries or dried cherries
1 cup toasted pecans, coarsely chopped

Glaze:
2 tablespoons unsalted butter
2 tablespoons honey
2 teaspoons lemon juice

In a large bowl, dissolve the yeast in the warm water. After about 10 minutes or once the yeast is active, add the sourdough starter. Stir to mix. Add the oats, honey, sugar, rye flour, whole wheat flour, and spices if you are using them. Stir vigorously with a spoon for about 2 minutes or beat with paddle attachment for 2 minutes in stand mixer. Add the salt, and begin adding the flour, stirring or using the dough hook on a mixer. After 3 cups of flour have been added, you will have a very stiff dough. If your mixer is strong enough, you can continue with the dough hook, or turn the dough out onto a floured board and finish by hand. Knead at least 5 minutes by hand, slowly adding the final cup of flour and trying not to use much more than that. Now you can add the fruits and nuts, ½ cup at a time, kneading well after each addition. Use just enough flour to keep the dough from sticking too much.

Place the dough in a well-oiled bowl, cover with plastic wrap, and let rise at room temperature for 1½ hours, until doubled. Punch down. Let the dough rest for 15 minutes. Form into 2 free-form, 12-inch-long loaves. Grease a baking sheet or line it with parchment paper and place the loaves on it. Let the loaves rise 1 hour. Preheat the oven to 425°F. Place bread in the oven and turn down heat to 350°F. Bake for 40 to 45 minutes, rotating the pan once during the baking. The loaves should be browned and crusty on top. Remove from the oven and cool on racks for at least 1 hour before cutting.

While the bread is cooling, mix the butter, honey, and lemon juice in a small saucepan and heat just to blend. Brush on the still-warm loaves, letting as much as possible be absorbed.

MAKES 2 LARGE LOAVES

breadsticks

Breadsticks, or grissini, *are convenient to have on hand for appetizers or to serve with soup. These are fast and easy to make, and they freeze and reheat well. Lots of variations are possible: cracked black pepper, flakes of red pepper, fennel seed, dried red tomato, or dried herbs such as thyme and rosemary. The grissini can also be brushed with oil and sprinkled with poppy or sesame seeds prior to baking. We always sprinkle the breadsticks with kosher or flaked salt.*

- 2 teaspoons active dry yeast
- Pinch of sugar
- 1¼ cups lukewarm water
- 3 to 3½ cups unbleached flour, approximately
- 1½ teaspoons salt
- 1 tablespoon olive oil plus more for brushing
- 1 cup grated aged hard cheese such as Parmesan, Asiago, or pecorino
- Kosher or flaked salt for sprinkling

Stir the yeast and sugar into the warm water. Let it sit for about ten minutes or until the yeast is active. Add half the flour, the salt, and the oil. Stir until incorporated.

Stir in the cheese and any other flavoring you might choose, and mix well. Add the remaining flour, ¼ cup at a time, or as much as you can until you have a dough that you can knead. You might not need the full 3½ cups.

Turn the dough out onto a well-floured surface and knead for 7 to 10 minutes. If the dough is sticky, add more flour in small amounts until you have a fairly stiff dough. Cover the dough and let it rest for 10 minutes. This allows the dough to relax and it will be easier to roll out.

Place the dough on a well-oiled surface that can be used to roll and cut the dough. Using your hands and/or a rolling pin, roll the dough into a 20 by 6-inch rectangle. Brush with oil, cover with plastic wrap, and let rise for 30 to 45 minutes. When the dough has doubled in height (it will tend to rise up but not outward), it is time to shape and bake the breadsticks.

Preheat the oven to 400 °F and oil your baking sheets or line them with parchment paper. Brush the dough with olive oil and sprinkle with salt. Cut the dough one piece at a time, about ¾-inch wide. Gently pick up each piece and stretch it to the length you want and that will fit either the width or length of your baking sheet. You can also twist the pieces to create spiraled breadsticks. Bake at 400°F for 15 to 20 minutes. The *grissini* should be browned and crisp, with no interior softness.

MAKES APPROXIMATELY 20 TWELVE-INCH *GRISSINI*

cornbread WITH CHILES & CHEESE

This moist cornbread is extra flavorful thanks to the addition of sweet corn, Cheddar cheese, and chiles. This recipe can also be made into muffins and works well with a bowl of chili at lunch, or eggs and home-cooked pinto beans at breakfast.

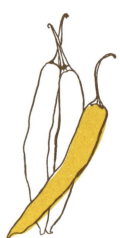

- **1 cup unbleached flour**
- **2 teaspoons baking powder**
- **1 teaspoon baking soda**
- **3 tablespoons sugar or honey**
- **1 teaspoon salt**
- **⅔ cup cornmeal**
- **3 eggs room temperature, separated**
- **1 cup buttermilk**
- **3 tablespoons vegetable oil or melted unsalted butter**
- **1 cup grated Cheddar cheese**
- **½ cup whole kernels of fresh corn, briefly blanched and cooled**
- **¼ cup canned Anaheim mild green chiles, chopped**

Preheat the oven to 375°F. Grease a 9-inch springform or round cake pan.

Sift the flour, baking powder and soda, sugar, salt, and cornmeal into a medium bowl.

In another bowl, combine the egg yolks, buttermilk, and oil or melted butter. Beat with a whisk until well-blended. With an electric beater, whip egg whites until soft peaks form.

Make a well in the middle of the dry ingredients. Add the wet to the dry, mixing just until moist. Stir in the cheese, corn, and chilies. Gently fold in egg whites until just blended. The egg whites should still be visible in the batter. Do not overmix. Pour the batter into the greased pan.

Bake for 45 minutes, or until golden brown and a toothpick comes out clean when inserted in middle. Cool briefly on racks before removing from the pan. Cut into wedges and serve.

MAKES 10 TO 12 SERVINGS

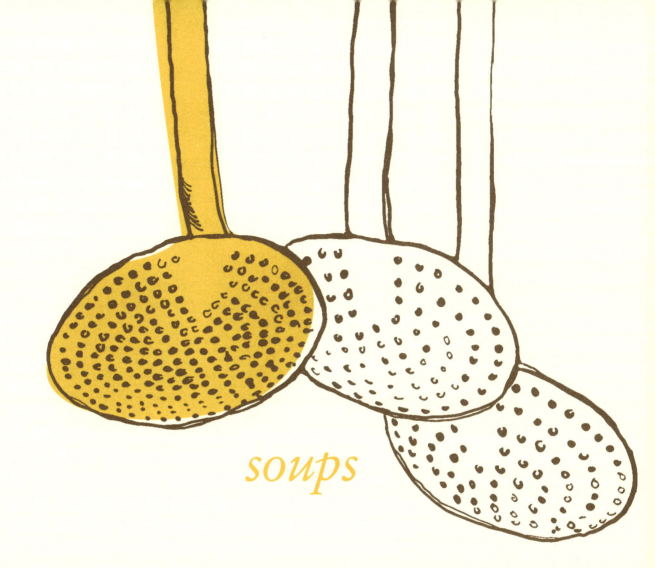

soups

Soups, along with salads, freshly baked breads, and cold cuts, are the mainstay of lunch at the Ranch. They add a homey touch that always satisfies and can be adapted to whatever is in season. Garnishes such as yogurt, crème fraîche, croutons, fresh herbs, or grated cheese give soups a touch of elegance. At home, a hearty soup can easily be the centerpiece of a simple dinner.

If you enjoy making soup, you should treat yourself to a good quality large pot with high sides. Make sure it is stainless steel to avoid a reaction with acidic foods. Your pot should also have a heavy bottom so that your soup won't burn while it is simmering away.

For some soups, a flavorful, rich stock is critical to add depth and flavor. But for many, especially spicy soups or those using ingredients with strong flavors, water can be substituted. Stock making can be done when you have some free time in the kitchen as all stocks freeze well. Here are a few tips for successful stocks:

- Use fresh vegetables that you would feel comfortable eating on their own. You don't want to ruin your stock with spoiled or moldy produce.

- Wash all ingredients. Peel carrots and onions.

- Roughly chop the ingredients to expose more surface area, which will release more flavor.

- Add salt sparingly to your stock because, if you reduce it later, the salt will become too concentrated. A small amount will help bring out flavors and give the stock color.

- Use ingredients that are compatible with the soup you are intending to make. For example, green onions or leeks could be used as part of the onion flavor. Avoid the brassica family (broccoli, Brussels sprouts, cauliflower, and cabbage) as their flavors are too strong.

- Strain stock soon after you have removed it from the stove. Some herbs and vegetables can turn your stock bitter as they sit.

Soups offer the perfect opportunity to experiment and be creative. Measurements can be approximate, so give yourself a little freedom to stray from the recipes.

vegetable STOCK

This basic stock recipe produces a flavorful and rich soup base and is wonderful to have on hand. It is possible to add more of one or another ingredient to pair this stock with a specific style of soup being made, but be sure not to add anything from the cabbage or brassica family (broccoli, Brussels sprouts, cauliflower, or cabbage) as their strong flavor and color will overpower the stock. With the addition of a bit of pasta and a few freshly cut up vegetables, you can have a quick and tasty dinner or lunch.

- 3 yellow onions, sliced
- 2 leeks, the white and very light green part, chopped
- 4 to 6 garlic cloves, chopped
- 4 carrots, peeled and chopped
- ¼ pound button mushrooms, sliced, or 2 dried shiitake mushrooms (optional)
- 4 celery ribs, sliced
- 6 parsley sprigs, chopped
- 6 fresh thyme sprigs or 1 teaspoon dried
- 2 bay leaves
- ½ teaspoon peppercorns
- 8 cups water

Add all ingredients to a large stockpot. Bring to a boil, reduce to a simmer, and cook uncovered, simmering gently, for about 1 hour. Pour stock through a sieve, pressing out the liquid with a spoon. Discard the vegetables. Use immediately or cool before refrigerating. The stock will keep for a week in the refrigerator or can be frozen for up to 3 months.

MAKES 4 CUPS

CHICKEN *stock*

For a rich stock, you should have about the same weight of chicken and vegetables. Using the whole chicken imparts the best flavor. If you want a light blond stock, do not brown the chicken or vegetables, and simmer the ingredients for just one hour. Follow the directions below if you want a deep, rich brown stock.

- 1 large chicken, and/or parts, approximately 5 to 6 pounds
- Olive oil, for sautéing
- 6 carrots, peeled, coarsely chopped
- 3 onions, peeled, quartered
- 6 celery ribs, coarsely chopped
- 3 bay leaves
- 1 teaspoon black peppercorns
- 2 to 3 garlic cloves, smashed
- 10 sprigs fresh thyme or 1 teaspoon dried
- ½ teaspoon salt
- ¼ cup coarsely chopped fresh parsley
- 2 tablespoons tomato paste
- 3½ quarts cold water

Preheat oven to 450°F. Cut up the chicken and roast in the oven until well browned, turning once. Meanwhile in a sauté pan, heat a small amount of oil and sauté the carrots, onions, and celery over high heat until browned.

When the chicken is browned, deglaze the pan with a little hot water. Place all the chicken, the browned vegetables, and all the remaining ingredients into a stockpot and bring to a simmer. Simmer for about ½ hour, skimming off any foam that appears. Continue simmering for 4 to 5 hours to extract maximum flavor.

Pour the stock through a colander lined with cheesecloth or a fine-meshed sieve. Let the stock cool in the pot in an ice bath. Skim off as much fat as possible, and then refrigerate or freeze. The stock will keep for 1 week refrigerated or 3 months frozen.

MAKES APPROXIMATELY 9 CUPS

fresh corn STOCK

This corn stock is very simple and freezes well. It is light yet robust with the distinct flavor of fresh corn.

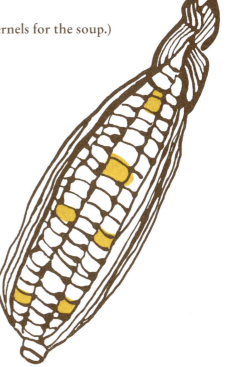

6 shaved corn cobs, broken into pieces. (Save the kernels for the soup.)
1 yellow onion, sliced
1 potato, sliced
1 celery rib, sliced
5 parsley sprigs, chopped
5 garlic cloves, smashed
1 teaspoon salt
½ teaspoon peppercorns
9 cups water

Add all of the ingredients to a large stockpot. Bring to a boil, reduce the heat, and simmer, uncovered, for about 30 minutes. Pour the stock through a fine-meshed sieve or through a colander lined with cheesecloth. Press out the liquid from the vegetables and discard them. Use immediately or let cool before storing. The stock will keep for a week in the refrigerator or can be frozen for up to 3 months.

MAKES APPROXIMATELY 7 CUPS

FISH *stock*

Because most markets receive their fish already trimmed, you might find it difficult to obtain fish heads and trimmings for making fish stock. If so, you can use fish fillets of a non-oily variety (avoid mackerel, bluefish, or salmon) to make your stock. You can also make a broth with half canned, low-salt, chicken stock and half water and simmer that with the following vegetables and herbs.

> 2 pounds (2 quarts) non-oily fresh or frozen fish heads, bones, and trimmings
> 1½ cups thinly sliced onion
> ½ cup thinly sliced celery stalk
> ½ cup thinly sliced leek, white part only (add a little more onion if leeks not available)
> 10 fresh parsley stems (no leaves, as they will color the stock)
> 1 cup dry white wine or ½ cup dry French vermouth (optional)
> ¼ teaspoon salt (no more, in case you need to reduce this stock)

Put all the ingredients into a large stainless steel pot and add cold water to cover by a good ½ inch, about 1½ quarts. Bring to a simmer and skim off the scum that will form on top for several minutes. Simmer uncovered for 30 minutes. Longer cooking will not improve the flavor. Strain the stock through a fine-meshed sieve into another stainless pot. Taste for strength and, if you think the flavor needs to be stronger, reduce the stock by boiling uncovered until the flavor is more concentrated.

Store in the refrigerator once cooled or freeze. The stock will keep for up to 5 days refrigerated or 3 months frozen.

MAKES 6 CUPS

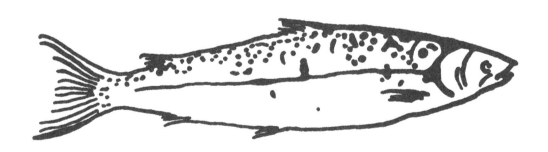

curried BUTTERNUT SQUASH SOUP

This is a delicious fall and winter soup, when squash is sweet and plentiful in the markets. Vegetarians can enjoy this flavorful soup by using vegetable stock instead of chicken stock. For vegans, we leave out the honey, use only oil, and omit the half-and-half. Any leftover baked squash can be used to make pumpkin pie filling.

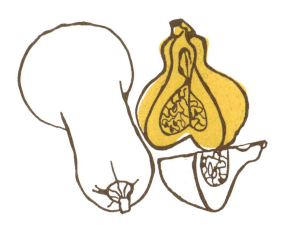

- 3 cups butternut squash, baked and puréed
- 3 cups yellow onions, chopped
- 2 tablespoons unsalted butter
- 1 tablespoon vegetable oil
- 6 cups chicken or vegetable stock
- 1½ tablespoons fresh curry powder, lightly toasted
- ¼ teaspoon nutmeg, freshly grated
- 1 tablespoon honey
- Salt and freshly ground white pepper
- 1 cup half-and-half
- ½ cup fresh shiitake mushrooms, chopped or 4 dried shiitake mushrooms (see Note)
- 3 tablespoons chives, minced

To prepare the squash, preheat oven to 375°F. Cut the squash in half, remove the seeds, and place skin-side down on a baking sheet. Bake for about 1 hour and 15 minutes or until very soft. Let cool and then scoop meat out of the shell and measure.

In a sauté pan, over low to medium heat, cook the onions with the butter and oil until very soft, but not brown. Let cool slightly. Combine the onions and squash in batches in the blender, using some of the stock if necessary to purée until smooth. Add this to a soup pot along with the stock, curry, nutmeg, honey, salt and pepper to taste and bring to a gentle simmer. Cook for 10 to 15 minutes.

Stir in the half-and-half, taste, and correct seasonings if necessary. Do not let the soup come to a boil after adding the half-and-half or it will curdle. Just before serving, stir in the shiitakes and sprinkle on the chives.

Note: If you choose to use dried shiitake mushrooms, first reconstitute them by pouring boiling water over them and allowing to soak for 15 minutes. Then chop the mushrooms finely, discarding the tough stems. You should obtain approximately ⅓ cup finely diced mushrooms.

MAKES 10 TO 12 SERVINGS

CORN, BEAN, AND SQUASH *stew*

We look forward to making this stew each fall with the last of the summer's red tomatoes, yellow corn, and autumn's newly harvested squash. Butternut and delicata squash or pumpkin work well in this recipe.

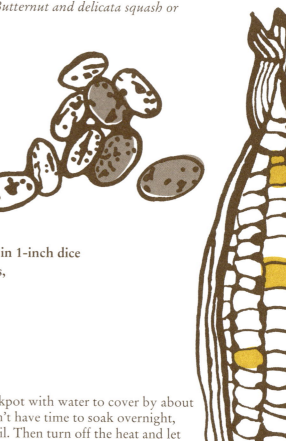

- 1 cup uncooked pinto beans
- 1 teaspoon cumin seed
- 1 teaspoon dried oregano
- ¼ cup vegetable oil
- 1 large onion, diced, approximately 2 cups
- 2 garlic cloves, minced
- 1 teaspoon ground cinnamon
- Large pinch of ground cloves
- 1 tablespoon paprika
- ½ teaspoon salt
- 2 cups water or vegetable stock
- 2 cups tomatoes, blanched, peeled, and cut in 1-inch dice
- 3 cups squash, peeled, cut into 1-inch cubes, 1¼ pounds squash, approximately
- 1½ cups fresh corn or frozen kernels
- 2 jalapeño peppers, seeded, finely chopped
- Cilantro for garnish
- Lemon or lime for garnish (optional)

Measure and sort the beans. Rinse and place in a stockpot with water to cover by about 4 inches. Soak overnight, rinse, and drain. (If you don't have time to soak overnight, you can cover the beans with water and bring to a boil. Then turn off the heat and let the beans rest in water for one hour. Rinse, drain, and continue.)

Cover the soaked, drained beans with fresh water. The water should be about 2 inches over the beans. Bring to a boil, then reduce heat and simmer uncovered, until beans are soft but not falling apart. This will take about 1½ hours. While they are cooking, proceed with the rest of the soup.

Toast the cumin seeds in a skillet until fragrant, then add oregano and toast briefly. Do not let them burn. Grind them in a blender or spice grinder and set aside.

Heat the oil in a skillet and sauté the onions until they are soft and translucent, about 5 to 8 minutes. Add the garlic, the toasted cumin and oregano, the cinnamon, cloves, paprika, and salt. Sauté another few minutes. Add the water or stock and the tomatoes. Cook for 10 minutes. Add the squash and cook for about 30 minutes or until it is about halfway cooked, but not falling apart. Add the corn and jalapeños. Drain the cooked beans, add to the soup, and cook until the squash is tender. If the stew is too thick, add some additional water or stock. Check for seasonings and add salt if necessary. Garnish with cilantro and a squeeze of lime or lemon if desired.

MAKES 4 TO 6 SERVINGS

POTATO CORN *chowder*

There are many variations on corn chowder, but this recipe is outstanding because of the stock, which provides a robust corn flavor. We only make this in the summer, when the corn is at its best. It's delicious paired with ripe summer heirloom tomatoes, freshly baked sourdough bread, and a mixed green salad. There is nothing difficult about this recipe, but you do need time to prepare the stock. You will need about one hour to make the stock and another hour for the soup itself.

- 7 cups corn stock (page 67)
- 2 tablespoons olive oil
- 1 yellow onion, diced, approximately 2 cups
- ½ teaspoon fresh thyme or ¼ teaspoon dried
- ½ teaspoon fresh basil or ¼ teaspoon dried
- ½ teaspoon salt
- ⅛ teaspoon white pepper
- 4 garlic cloves, finely minced
- 2 bay leaves
- 1 celery rib, diced, approximately ½ cup
- ¼ cup white wine (optional)
- 6 ears of corn, shaved, approximately 5 cups of kernels
- 1 pound of Yukon gold or white rose potatoes, ½-inch dice, approximately 3 cups
- Dash of cayenne pepper (optional)
- 2 tablespoons fresh basil, chiffonade

Make the corn stock. Then heat the oil in a stockpot and add the onions, thyme, basil, salt, and pepper. Sauté over medium heat for about 5 minutes or until the onions are soft. Add the garlic, bay leaves, and celery and continue to sauté another few minutes, being careful not to burn the garlic. Then add the wine and cook for 1 to 2 minutes, until the pan is almost dry.

Add the stock, corn kernels, and potatoes. Cook the soup over low heat for 20 minutes or until the potatoes are thoroughly cooked. Remove the bay leaves and discard. Measure out 3 cups of the soup, let cool slightly, and purée in batches in a blender or food processor. Return the puréed soup to the pot and reheat. Taste the soup, adding salt if needed and a dash of cayenne pepper to liven things up if desired. Stir in the basil right before serving.

MAKES 8 SERVINGS

potato leek soup

You can't find a recipe easier than this, yet this soup is delicious and extremely satisfying in spite of its simplicity.

- 4 cups potatoes, sliced
- 3 to 4 cups leeks, sliced
- 2 quarts water
- 1 tablespoon salt
- 4 to 6 tablespoons cream or 3 tablespoons unsalted butter
- 3 tablespoons chives, minced

In a soup pot, simmer the potatoes, leeks, water, and salt together, partially covered, for 50 minutes to 1 hour. Let cool slightly. In batches, blend the potato-leek mixture in a blender or food processor until smooth. Just before serving, bring to a light simmer and add the cream or butter. Remove from the heat and garnish with the minced chives.

MAKES 8 SERVINGS

vegetarian FRENCH ONION SOUP

Even though this is a vegetarian version of the classic French Onion soup, it has great richness and depth. This is achieved by making two rounds of the stock. Make the first batch a day ahead and then it will be easy to skim off the fat that rises to the top.

Stock:
⅓ pound unsalted butter
1½ pounds onions, sliced
3 tomatoes
3 sprigs basil
2 stalks celery, chopped
8 cups water

Onion Soup:
⅓ pound unsalted butter
1½ pounds onions, sliced
6 cups onion stock
2 teaspoons salt or tamari
1 tablespoon miso* (optional)
Freshly ground black pepper

Garnish:
2 cups croutons
1 cup (¼ pound) Gruyère cheese, grated
4 tablespoons Italian parsley, chopped

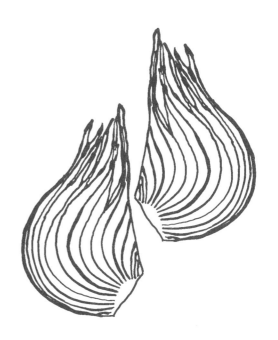

To make the stock: In a large, heavy-bottomed soup pot, melt the butter over medium-low heat and add the onions. Cook onions slowly, stirring occasionally, until they turn a deep, golden brown, ½ to 1 hour. Add the tomatoes, basil, celery, and water and simmer gently for about 30 to 45 minutes over medium heat. Strain the stock and reserve it for the soup.

To make the soup: Melt the butter, adding the onions and cooking until the onions are a deep, golden brown, stirring occasionally to prevent burning, about 1 hour. Add the stock to the onions, add salt or tamari, and again simmer for 45 minutes to 1 hour. Turn off the heat. Mix the miso with a bit of the stock in a small bowl first, as this will make it easier to incorporate into the soup. Add it to the soup. Check for seasoning, adding salt or more miso if desired. Garnish with croutons, cheese, and a sprinkling of parsley.

* Miso, a fermented soybean paste, is very salty and is used to add depth. Use sparingly to deepen the flavor if desired.

MAKES 6 TO 8 SERVINGS

WHITE BEAN SOUP WITH *rosemary toast*

This soup has amazing flavor and never fails to please. Make sure you cook the beans thoroughly. The soup should have a creamy texture when puréed and will not if your beans are not properly cooked.

Soup:
2½ cups white beans, cannellini or great Northern
1 fresh rosemary sprig
2 fresh sage leaves
2 bay leaves
1 medium onion, diced, approximately 1½ cups
1 tablespoon olive oil
½ teaspoon dried basil
Salt and freshly ground black pepper
6 garlic cloves, finely chopped
¼ cup dry white wine
1 cup Roma tomatoes, seeded and diced

Rosemary Toast:
2 to 4 tablespoons olive oil
2 garlic cloves, finely chopped
½ teaspoon fresh rosemary, finely chopped
½ of a 2-inch-wide baguette, sliced ¼-inch thick, approximately 16 slices

To make the soup: Spread the beans out on a baking sheet and sort. Rinse and soak in 2 quarts cold water overnight. Drain the beans and place in a soup pot with water to cover by 1 to 2 inches. Add rosemary, sage, and bay leaves. Bring to a boil, then reduce heat to medium-low and simmer, uncovered, stirring occasionally until the beans are soft and beginning to fall apart, about 1½ hours. Remove the herbs.

Purée about two-thirds of the beans in a blender or food processor and return to the soup pot.

In another pan, sauté the onions with the oil, basil, and salt until the onions are soft and translucent. Add the garlic, stir, and continue to sauté another few minutes. Then add the wine and tomatoes and simmer briefly, about 5 minutes. Combine the tomato mixture with the beans and cook over very low heat for about 30 minutes. Thin with a little water if necessary and add salt and pepper to taste.

To make the toasts: Preheat the oven to 375°F. Combine the oil, garlic, and rosemary and brush on the bread. Place on a baking sheet and bake for 8 to 10 minutes or until crisp and lightly browned.

Serve the soup with 2 rosemary toasts per bowl.

MAKES 8 TO 9 SERVINGS

hot and sour soup

This is a nourishing soup and it is easy to prepare. Add the bok choy at the very end to keep it nice and green.

4 cups vegetable or chicken stock
3 dried shiitake mushrooms, approximately ½ ounce
½ pound firm tofu, drained and cut into ¼-inch strips
2 tablespoons tamari or soy sauce
2 teaspoons dark sesame oil
1 tablespoon dry sherry (optional)
1 cup bok choy, cut into ribbons, or celery, thinly sliced
3 to 4 green onions, minced
1 teaspoon fresh ginger, grated
1 tablespoon cornstarch, dissolved in 2 tablespoons cold water
1 egg, beaten
2 tablespoons seasoned rice vinegar
¼ to ½ teaspoon black pepper or red pepper flakes, to taste
Salt

Boil one cup of the stock and combine with the dried mushrooms in a small bowl. Soak for 15 minutes. Place remaining 3 cups of stock in a medium-sized soup pot and bring to a light simmer. Cut the tofu into strips and marinate it in the tamari, sesame oil, and sherry. Drain the mushrooms and save the liquid. Add the mushroom soaking liquid to the stock on the stove, leaving any sediment behind in the bowl. Slice the mushrooms (throwing away the tough stems) and add to the stock. Bring to a simmer for 5 minutes. Add the bok choy, green onions, ginger, tofu, and the marinade. Let cook for 3 minutes. Add the cornstarch and water mixture. Bring back to a gentle boil. Drizzle the egg into the soup, stirring to form threads. When the soup is clear and a little thickened, remove from the heat, stir in the vinegar, and the pepper. Adjust to taste with salt and pepper. Serve hot.

MAKES 4 TO 6 SERVINGS

tomato soup

Liz's mother, Marion, returned from a stay at Findhorn in Scotland with the recipe for this soup. It originally was made with tomato paste, but we like to make it with tomato juice. This is a quick and easy soup to make and the ingredients are usually on hand.

- ¼ cup yellow onion, minced
- 1 tablespoon olive oil
- 1 garlic clove, minced
- 3 tablespoons flour
- 1 quart tomato juice
- 1 teaspoon salt
- 1 tablespoon chopped Italian parsley
- 2 teaspoons paprika
- 2 teaspoons fresh basil or 1 teaspoon dried basil
- ½ teaspoon ground cinnamon
- 2 cups milk
- 2 tablespoons Parmesan cheese, grated
- 1 tablespoon apple cider vinegar
- 1 teaspoon honey

In a medium-sized soup pot, sauté the onion in the oil until translucent and soft. Add the garlic and cook for a minute, being careful not to burn. Whisk in the flour and cook for a minute or two, stirring until the flour taste has cooked out and it is a light brown. Whisk in the tomato juice. Add the salt, parsley, paprika, basil, and cinnamon and bring to a simmer. Cook for 15 minutes, stirring occasionally.

Add the milk and cheese and bring back up to heat, but not to a boil. Turn off the heat and add the vinegar and honey. Let sit 5 minutes before serving. Check for seasoning.

MAKES 6 SERVINGS

BLACK BEAN *chili*

Credit is due to The Greens Cookbook *for this chili, which is a lunch staple at the Ranch. We serve this with cornbread or smoked chicken quesadillas and, of course, salad. We offer a variety of garnishes: crème fraîche spiked with chipotle purée, chopped pickled jalapeños, chopped green onion, grated Cheddar cheese, or chopped cilantro.*

- 2 cups black beans, uncooked
- 1 bay leaf
- 2 tablespoons olive oil
- 3 medium yellow onions, chopped, approximately 6 cups
- 4 teaspoons cumin seed
- 4 teaspoons dried oregano
- 4 teaspoons paprika
- ¼ teaspoon cayenne pepper (optional)
- 2 to 3 tablespoons chili powder
- 4 garlic cloves, chopped
- 1 teaspoon salt plus more to season
- 2½ cups tomatoes, peeled, seeded, and chopped or one 28-ounce can (including juice)
- Freshly ground black pepper
- 1 tablespoon seasoned rice vinegar
- ¼ cup cilantro, chopped

Measure and sort the beans. Rinse in a colander and put into a soup pot. Cover with water by at least 4 inches and let soak overnight.

The next day, drain the beans, rinse, and put back in the pot with the bay leaf and water to cover by 2 inches. Simmer, uncovered, until cooked through but not falling apart, approximately 1½ hours. Meanwhile, heat the oil in a large pot and sauté the onions until soft, about 10 minutes. While the onions are cooking, toast the cumin seeds in a small sauté pan for a few minutes, stirring. Add the oregano, paprika, cayenne, and chili powder and toast just until fragrant. Do not burn. Add these spices plus the garlic and salt to the onions and cook, stirring, for 5 minutes. Add the tomatoes and their juice and simmer for about 20 minutes.

Drain the cooked beans, reserving the liquid. Add the tomato and onion mixture to the cooked beans. There should be enough liquid just to cover. Add some of the reserved bean liquid or water if needed. Continue cooking until the beans are soft and the flavors have melded. Season to taste with salt, pepper, and the rice vinegar. Sprinkle or stir in the cilantro right before serving.

MAKES 8 SERVINGS

"MO-ROCKIN" *lentil soup*

Lentils cook quickly and give this soup a solid, earthy base. It is nutritious, yet truly "rocks," with tantalizing aromas of ginger and fragrant spices. For a Moroccan touch, serve with yogurt on the side or hummus and pita bread.

1⅓ cups baby French lentils
6 cups cold water
2 tablespoons olive oil
1 medium yellow onion, chopped, approximately 2 cups
Salt
Pinch of cayenne pepper
1 small carrot, peeled, ¼-inch dice, approximately ½ cup
1 celery rib, ¼-inch dice, approximately ½ cup
1 small red or yellow bell pepper, ¼-inch dice, approximately ½ cup
1 teaspoon cumin seed, toasted and ground
½ teaspoon coriander, ground
⅛ teaspoon turmeric
4 garlic cloves, finely chopped
1 tablespoon fresh ginger, peeled and grated
1 cup tomatoes, seeded and diced
Freshly ground black pepper
Cilantro for garnish

Sort and rinse the lentils. Put them into a soup pot and cover with the water. Bring to a boil, reduce the heat, and simmer until tender, about 20 minutes. Heat the oil in a sauté pan over medium heat, add the onions, salt and cayenne to taste, and cook until tender, about 6 to 8 minutes. Add the carrots, celery, pepper, and spices. Cook until tender, about 5 more minutes. Add the garlic and ginger and cook for 1 minute. Add this vegetable mixture and the tomatoes to the lentils. Cover and cook for 30 minutes, or until the lentils are soft but not falling apart. Season to taste with salt and pepper. Garnish with cilantro and serve.

MAKES 6 TO 8 SERVINGS

watermelon GAZPACHO

Refreshing and unusual, this soup is perfect for a hot summer day. Our friend, Lucy Kotter, created this soup after picking a surplus of heirloom tomatoes in her garden. Fully ripe and bursting with flavor, quality tomatoes make this soup special. If not available, it would be best to substitute canned tomato juice. We like it best when it is spicy.

- 6 to 8 medium to large ripe tomatoes, yielding 3 to 4 cups purée and 1½ cups diced
- 3 to 4 cups seedless red watermelon, yielding 1 cup purée and 2 cups, diced ¼ inch
- ½ medium red onion, finely diced, approximately ¾ cup
- 1 garlic clove, finely minced
- 2 teaspoons salt
- 2½ teaspoons chili powder
- ⅛ teaspoon ground cumin
- ¼ teaspoon cayenne pepper
- 2 tablespoons chopped cilantro
- 1 tablespoon balsamic vinegar

In a blender, purée about two-thirds of the tomatoes, one-third of the watermelon, and one-half of the onion. Pour into a bowl or non-reactive container. Dice the remaining tomatoes, watermelon, and onion and add to the purée. Stir in the garlic, salt, spices, cilantro, and balsamic vinegar. Taste and adjust the seasonings.

MAKES 5 TO 6 SERVINGS

spicy carrot soup

This spicy soup, adapted from Annie Somerville's Fields of Greens, *will warm you up on a winter day. If you make vegetable stock specifically for this soup, add 10 slices of fresh ginger to your stock for extra flavor.*

- 1 tablespoon olive oil
- 1 medium yellow onion, chopped, approximately 1½ cups
- 2 garlic cloves, chopped
- 2 teaspoons grated fresh ginger
- 1½ teaspoons cumin seed, toasted and ground
- 1 teaspoon coriander seed, toasted and ground
- Pinch of cayenne pepper
- 2 pounds carrots, peeled and thinly sliced, approximately 7 cups
- 1 medium potato, peeled and sliced
- 1 teaspoon salt plus more to season
- 5 cups vegetable stock or water
- ½ cup fresh orange juice
- Crème fraîche for garnish
- Cilantro for garnish

Heat the oil in a soup pot and add the onion and sauté until translucent. Add the garlic, ginger, cumin, coriander, and cayenne. Cook for a few minutes, stirring, and add a bit of stock if the garlic or spices begin to stick. Add the carrots, potato, salt, and enough stock to cover. Cook until the carrots are soft and then, in a blender or food processor, purée the soup until smooth. Add the remaining stock, thinning the soup to the desired consistency. Reheat the soup to serve and add the orange juice just before serving. Taste and add salt and a bit more cayenne if needed. Garnish with crème fraîche and cilantro.

MAKES 6 TO 7 SERVINGS

salads and dressings

This section contains recipes for salads of simple, mixed greens and also heartier salads that can be served as a main course.

Here at the Ranch, as throughout the West Coast, we are fortunate to live in an area where fresh salad greens, herbs, and vegetables are readily available. With such variety and abundance, it is easy to make delicious salads all year long.

In making salads, the care you use in handling the greens is important. All greens should be thoroughly washed, especially spinach and cilantro. Handle greens very gently to avoid bruising. If you are tearing lettuce into smaller pieces, do it with a light touch. Spin your greens dry in a salad spinner or put them in a large, clean dishtowel and give them a whirl . . . outside.

Fresh, homemade dressings are easy to make. Always taste the dressing with a piece of the greens to be used in the salad before you mix everything together.

Salads offer many opportunities for beautiful presentation. The bowl or platter you choose can complement or highlight the colors of the salad. There are also garnishes to consider; pomegranate, pumpkin, or sunflower seeds, bell peppers and many other vegetables and fruits can add color and interest to your dish. As with soups, salad making can be fun and a great outlet for your culinary creativity.

sesame-ginger VINAIGRETTE

This Asian-style vinaigrette livens up green salads, vegetables, pasta, fish, and grains. It is particularly delicious drizzled over steamed broccoli.

- 2 inches fresh ginger, peeled and chopped, yielding approximately ¼ cup
- ½ cup seasoned rice vinegar
- 3 tablespoons tamari or soy sauce
- 1 teaspoon dark, toasted sesame oil
- 3 garlic cloves, minced
- ¼ teaspoon freshly ground black pepper
- Juice of one lemon or orange
- ¾ to 1 cup light vegetable oil

Place all of the ingredients, except the vegetable oil, in the blender and purée until smooth. On low speed, slowly add the oil in a steady stream until emulsified. Keeps for at least 2 weeks, covered, in the refrigerator.

MAKES 1½ TO 1¾ CUPS

balsamic VINAIGRETTE

Balsamic vinegar takes its name from the Italian word meaning "health-giving" or "cure all" and is traditionally made in Modena, Italy. True, aged balsamic from this area is expensive. There are moderately priced vinegars available now that will be fine for this vinaigrette but avoid the really cheap imitations. If fresh herbs are unavailable, it is better to leave them out. We use this vinaigrette frequently with our mixed green or baby spinach salads.

½ cup medium grade balsamic vinegar
½ shallot minced, approximately 1 teaspoon
1 garlic clove, minced
¼ teaspoon Dijon-style mustard
1 tablespoon fresh basil, chopped
½ teaspoon fresh thyme leaves, minced
Salt and freshly ground black pepper
Pinch of brown sugar
1 cup olive oil

Put all of the ingredients, except the olive oil, in a bowl and stir to combine. With a whisk, add the oil slowly at first and then in a steady stream and continue whisking until the mixture is emulsified. Taste and adjust the seasoning if necessary. Store in an airtight container in the refrigerator.

MAKES 1½ CUPS

gorgonzola DRESSING

This dressing keeps well and is a good choice with butter lettuce, sliced pears, and caramelized walnuts. You can substitute a good quality blue cheese for the Gorgonzola. Go light on the garlic because the flavor intensifies as it sits.

1 cup sour cream
1 cup buttermilk
3 ounces Gorgonzola or blue cheese, crumbled
1 tablespoon apple cider vinegar
½ tablespoon Worcestershire sauce
1 to 2 small garlic cloves, pressed or finely minced
Salt and freshly ground black pepper

In a medium bowl, whisk the sour cream until softened. Add the buttermilk, cheese, vinegar, Worcestershire, garlic, salt, and pepper. Stir to combine, taste, and, if necessary, adjust the seasonings. Let the dressing sit in the refrigerator for about 1 hour before using.

MAKES 2 CUPS

buttermilk-herb DRESSING

Try this drizzled over a salad of Asian pear, Gorgonzola, and endive. In making this dressing, it is important to use only fresh herbs. If one of the herbs is not available, it is better to just leave it out.

¾ cup buttermilk
½ cup mayonnaise
1 small shallot or 1 green onion, minced (1 tablespoon)
1 to 2 medium garlic cloves, minced (1 teaspoon)
Salt and pepper to taste
Generous pinch curry powder
1 tablespoon fresh basil, minced
1 tablespoon fresh thyme, minced
Squeeze of lemon, approximately 1 teaspoon

Put all of the ingredients in a bowl and stir to combine. Taste, and adjust the seasonings if desired. Cover and place in the refrigerator for at least 1 hour before serving. This dressing will keep for up to 1 week.

MAKES 1½ CUPS

citrus VINAIGRETTE

Chipotle peppers are jalapeños that have been dried and smoked. They have a rich, complex flavor. They can be found dried or in sauce form in the Mexican section of your local supermarket. We use Búfalo brand chipotle sauce for this recipe.

1½ tablespoons zest of tangerine or orange
2 teaspoons zest of lime
½ cup plus 2 tablespoons freshly squeezed tangerine or orange juice
½ cup plus 2 tablespoons seasoned rice vinegar
2 tablespoons freshly squeezed lime juice
1 teaspoon chipotle sauce
½ teaspoon fresh oregano, minced
1 tablespoon fresh cilantro, chopped
¼ teaspoon ground cumin
½ teaspoon chili powder
¼ teaspoon salt
Pinch of black pepper
½ teaspoon honey (optional)
½ cup olive oil

Put all of the ingredients, except the oil, into a bowl and whisk to combine. Add the oil in a slow and steady stream, continuing to whisk until well blended. Taste for seasonings, and adjust if desired. Cover and store in the refrigerator. This vinaigrette will keep for up to 2 weeks.

MAKES 2 CUPS

fresh tomato DRESSING

This came to us from a wonderful natural foods restaurant in Juneau, Alaska, called the Fiddlehead. It is a refreshing summer dressing.

½ cup mayonnaise
⅓ cup chopped yellow onion
2 tablespoons apple cider vinegar
2 tablespoons vegetable oil
½ cup seeded, coarsely chopped red tomato
1 tablespoon chopped fresh parsley
Salt and freshly ground black pepper

Put mayonnaise, onion, vinegar, and oil into the food processor and pulse to mix well. The onion should still be visible and in small bits, as if grated. Then add the tomato and parsley and pulse a few more times, but make sure you leave a little texture to the dressing. Add salt and pepper to taste.

To mix by hand, mince the onion, tomato, and parsley and whisk in the remaining ingredients. Add salt and pepper to taste.

This dressing should be stored in the refrigerator and will keep for up to 1 week.

MAKES 1½ CUPS

champagne VINAIGRETTE

Champagne vinegar is delicate in flavor and traditionally made from the wine that comes out at the dégorgement stage of the Champagne process. This vinaigrette is light and works well with mixed greens or spring vegetables.

¼ cup Champagne vinegar
½ shallot, minced
1 teaspoon grainy or Dijon-style mustard
¼ teaspoon kosher salt
Freshly ground black pepper
⅓ to ½ cup light olive oil

In a medium-sized bowl, whisk together the first 5 ingredients. Whisk the oil into the vinegar mixture in a slow steady stream until thick and emulsified. Taste for salt and pepper and adjust if necessary.

MAKES ½ TO ¾ CUP

ariel's VINAIGRETTE

This is a simple, all-purpose dressing, using seasoned rice vinegar, which goes well with many types of greens.

- ¾ cup seasoned rice vinegar
- ¾ teaspoon dry mustard
- ½ teaspoon freshly ground black pepper
- ½ teaspoon sea salt
- 1 garlic clove, finely minced or smashed
- 1 tablespoon fresh basil, chiffonade
- 1½ cups canola or light olive oil

Mix together the vinegar, mustard, pepper, salt, garlic, and basil. Whisking continuously, add the oil in a slow steady stream until emulsified. Taste for seasoning and adjust if necessary.

MAKES 2 CUPS

bishop's ranch VINAIGRETTE

We named this after the Ranch because it was our favorite vinaigrette back in the late 1980s. This simple vinaigrette is perfect for drizzling over a light salad of greens or over baby steamed potatoes and asparagus.

- 1 teaspoon Dijon-style mustard
- 4 tablespoons red wine vinegar
- ½ teaspoon sugar or honey
- ¼ teaspoon salt
- Pinch of freshly ground black pepper
- 2 tablespoons chives, minced
- ½ cup olive oil

In a medium-sized mixing bowl, combine the mustard, vinegar, sugar, salt, pepper, and chives and whisk to combine. Add the oil in a slow and steady stream until emulsified. Taste and adjust the seasonings if desired.

MAKES ¾ CUP

BLACK BEAN SALAD WITH *Cumin* VINAIGRETTE

Ariel created this summer salad for a friend's wedding. The salad is attractive, easy to make, and excellent for large crowds. It is delicious paired with a quesadilla, steak, chicken, or fish. By itself, this salad is the perfect meal for a vegetarian, vegan, or non-dairy diet.

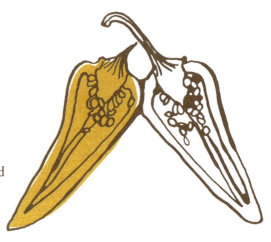

- 1 red bell pepper, seeded and diced
- 1 yellow bell pepper, seeded and diced
- ½ red onion, diced
- 1 jalapeño pepper, seeded and minced
- 2 cups fresh corn kernels, approximately 4 ears of corn
- 1 cup chopped cilantro, plus extra sprigs for garnish
- 6 cups canned, cooked, black beans
- 1 teaspoon cumin seed, toasted and ground or 1 teaspoon ground cumin
- Juice from 1 large or 2 small lemons, approximately 2 to 3 tablespoons
- 2 tablespoons soy sauce
- 2 teaspoons Dijon-style mustard
- 2 garlic cloves, minced
- ½ cup olive oil
- Salt and pepper

Prepare the bell peppers, onion, and the jalapeño pepper. Boil 4 ears of corn for about 3 minutes, remove from the water, and cool. Cut the kernels off the cob. Wash, spin dry, and coarsely chop the 1 cup of cilantro leaves. Set all aside.

Drain and rinse the black beans. Place the beans in a large bowl. In a smaller bowl, whisk together the cumin, lemon juice, soy sauce, mustard, and garlic. Slowly whisk in the oil until emulsified. Add this vinaigrette to the beans and toss to coat. Gently fold in the peppers, onion, corn, and cilantro. Taste the salad and add salt, pepper, and perhaps more lemon juice if needed. Cover and refrigerate for about half an hour before serving. Garnish with sprigs of cilantro.

MAKES 6 SERVINGS AS A MAIN DISH; 12 SERVINGS AS A SIDE DISH

romaine WITH RUBY GRAPEFRUIT, JICAMA, AND AVOCADO

This salad is great for a hot summer day or paired with spicy, hot foods that would benefit from the cooling contrast. Either toasted almonds or pickled red onions work well as a garnish for this salad.

> 2 hearts of romaine lettuce
> 1 ruby grapefruit, segmented, no pith
> ½ cup jicama, peeled, julienned or cut into matchsticks
> ¼ cup citrus vinaigrette (page 87)
> Salt and freshly ground black pepper
> 1 ripe but firm avocado, peeled, sliced
> ¼ cup sliced almonds, toasted or ¼ cup pickled red onions (page 181)

Cut the ends off the lettuce and remove any brown, wilted leaves. Wash the individual leaves carefully, and spin or towel dry. Combine the whole leaves of romaine, grapefruit, and jicama in a large mixing bowl. Toss gently with the vinaigrette to coat evenly. Season to taste with salt and pepper. Taste a leaf. Adjust seasoning if necessary. Sprinkle on the sliced almonds and avocado and serve.

MAKES 4 SERVINGS

Caesar SALAD

It is important that the lettuce for this salad be cold and crisp. You can cut or tear the romaine at the last minute into bite-sized pieces, but a more attractive presentation can be achieved by using whole leaves, dressing them, and assembling on individual salad plates or a large platter as directed below. Use fresh, quality ingredients for the dressing and make it just before serving, as the flavor is best when fresh. Below are instructions for mixing by hand, which creates a loose, lemon-colored dressing, and with a food processor, which produces a creamy dressing.

Croutons:
2 tablespoons mild-tasting olive oil
1 garlic clove, pressed
Pinch of salt
4 to 5 slices Italian- or French-style bread such as ciabatta, levain, or sourdough

Dressing:
2 medium-sized eggs, coddled
Juice of 1 large or 2 small lemons, approximately 3 tablespoons of juice, strained
¼ teaspoon Dijon-style mustard
Dash of Worcestershire sauce
2 teaspoons red wine vinegar
1 to 2 garlic cloves, pressed
6 to 8 oil- or salt-packed anchovies, rinsed and chopped
½ teaspoon salt
¼ teaspoon freshly ground black pepper
4 ounces Parmigiano-Reggiano cheese freshly grated, approximately 1¼ cups
⅔ to ¾ cup mild tasting olive oil

2 to 3 hearts of romaine, washed and dried

To make the croutons: Preheat the oven to 400°F. Combine the oil, garlic, and salt in a medium bowl and let sit for 5 minutes. Meanwhile, cut the bread into cubes. Add the bread to the oil and toss to coat. Spread the bread onto a baking sheet lined with parchment paper and bake, stirring occasionally, until golden brown, about 12 to 15 minutes. Set aside. You may also make the croutons in a heavy skillet on top of the stove by placing all of the ingredients over very low heat and toasting, stirring occasionally, for about 15 minutes or until crisp.

To coddle the eggs: Gently lower the uncracked eggs into boiling water to cover and simmer for 2 minutes. Remove and run cold water over them to cool. Crack across the middle with a knife and scoop the egg out with a teaspoon.

To make the dressing by hand: Whisk together the lemon juice, mustard, Worcestershire, vinegar, garlic, anchovies, salt, and pepper. Add the eggs and ¼ cup of the cheese and whisk just to emulsify. Whisk in ⅔ cup of the oil, in a slow and steady stream until emulsified. Add more oil if needed. Taste with a leaf of lettuce and adjust with salt or lemon juice. Chill in the refrigerator until serving.

To make the dressing with a food processor: Combine the lemon juice, mustard, Worcestershire, vinegar, garlic, anchovies, salt, and pepper in a food processor fitted with a steel blade. Pulse to combine. Add the eggs and ¼ cup of the cheese and pulse for about 30 seconds more. With the motor running, slowly add the oil in a slow and steady stream until emulsified. Taste with a leaf of lettuce and adjust with salt or lemon juice. Chill in the refrigerator until serving.

To assemble the salad: Wash and dry the lettuce. Separate the leaves into a large salad bowl, drizzle on enough of the dressing to coat, and toss. Sprinkle on some Parmigiano-Reggiano and toss to coat. Taste and add more dressing if needed. Arrange the leaves in an overlapping pattern on a plate or platter, sprinkle with more cheese, the croutons, and a grind of fresh pepper, and serve.

MAKES 1 CUP OF DRESSING AND 4 TO 6 SERVINGS

lemon-chicken
PASTA SALAD WITH GREENS

This is a summery dish that works well for lunch or dinner. The chicken and dressing can be made ahead, and it is an easy recipe to expand if you suddenly have company!

Dressing:
¾ cup light olive oil
⅔ cup fresh lemon juice
¼ cup plus 2 tablespoons buttermilk
1 tablespoon mayonnaise
1 tablespoon fresh dill, chopped
3 garlic cloves, minced
1½ teaspoons sugar
Salt and freshly ground black pepper

Salad:
2 large boneless, skinless chicken breasts yielding 4 cups chicken, cooked and sliced
½ pound uncooked fusilli pasta
1 teaspoon salt plus more, to season
2 tablespoons olive oil
1 red onion, thinly sliced
1 red bell pepper, thinly sliced
1 yellow bell pepper, thinly sliced
4 ounces feta cheese, crumbled, approximately ½ cup
¼ cup cilantro leaves, roughly chopped, plus sprigs for garnish
2 quarts mixed greens or lettuce
Freshly ground black pepper

To make the dressing: Place all the ingredients for the lemon dressing in a bowl and whisk until blended. Taste and adjust if necessary. You want it lemony and a bit creamy. Cover and refrigerate.

To make the salad: Cook the chicken by grilling, poaching, or baking in the oven according to directions on page 113. Cool and slice on the diagonal into strips. Refrigerate until needed.

Put a large pot of water on to boil. When the water boils, add the salt and the fusilli and cook until al dente, about 12 minutes. Drain and toss with half of the lemon dressing in a large bowl.

Meanwhile, heat a large sauté pan over medium heat. Add 1 tablespoon oil and sauté the onions until just tender, about 8 minutes. Put them into the bowl with the pasta. Add 1 more tablespoon of the oil to the pan and sauté the bell peppers until just tender, about 8 minutes. Combine with the onions and pasta.

Remove the chicken from the refrigerator and add it to the pasta mix, tossing to evenly distribute all the ingredients. Gently toss in the chopped cilantro leaves and the cheese. Season to taste with salt and pepper, adding more lemon juice if needed.

Place the greens in a large bowl and toss to coat with the reserved lemon dressing, using only as much as needed. Divide the salad greens onto 6 or 8 plates, then divide the chicken pasta mixture onto the greens. Garnish with the cilantro sprigs.

MAKES 8 TO 10 SERVINGS

chinese noodle salad WITH ROASTED EGGPLANT & GINGER-SOY DRESSING

This salad makes a tasty and satisfying lunch or dinner. It was adapted from The Greens Cookbook. *In spite of the many ingredients, it is quick and easy to make and keeps well. The noodles and dressing can be prepared ahead of the meal, and so can the vegetables, but it is best to mix them together at the last minute.*

Dressing and Noodles:
5 tablespoons toasted sesame oil
8 tablespoons soy sauce
3 tablespoons balsamic vinegar
3 tablespoons sugar
1 tablespoon chili oil
1 tablespoon fresh ginger, peeled and minced
1 garlic clove, finely minced
10 scallions, white part and some of the green, thinly sliced
4 tablespoons cilantro, chopped
14 ounces fresh Chinese egg noodles

Vegetables:
1 pound Japanese eggplant
2 medium carrots
1 cup snow peas, strings removed
¼ pound mung bean sprouts, approximately 2 cups
1 red bell pepper, roasted, peeled, seeded, and cut into ¼ by 2-inch strips

Garnish:
3 tablespoons sesame seeds
Cilantro sprigs

Combine the first 9 ingredients in a bowl and whisk together until the sugar has dissolved. Set aside. Bring a large pot of water to boil. Loosen the noodles with your fingers; add the noodles to the boiling water. Cook for 2 to 3 minutes, until al dente or slightly firm to the bite. Do not overcook. Immediately drain them and rinse in cold water. Drain out as much water as you can, then place them in a large mixing bowl. Add the dressing to the noodles and toss together. Cover and refrigerate if not using immediately.

Preheat the oven to 400°F. Pierce the eggplant with a fork, place on a baking sheet, and roast until soft, about 20 to 30 minutes. Cool, cut in half, and peel the skin off of the flesh. Throw away the skin and gently pull or cut the flesh into 1-to 2-inch strips. Set aside.

Peel and julienne the carrots and rinse the sprouts. Bring a quart of water to a boil and blanch the snow peas, just for a minute, until they are bright green. Remove and immediately drain and cool with cold water. Cut them into long, narrow strips. Roast the red bell pepper by setting it over a gas flame, turning with tongs as it chars, and then removing to a plastic bag to let it steam for at least 1 minute. Then peel and de-seed and cut into ¼ by 2-inch strips.

Briefly toast the sesame seeds in a pan on the stove over medium heat.

Add the eggplant, snow peas, sprouts, carrots, and bell pepper to the noodles and gently toss together, until evenly distributed. Taste and adjust the seasoning if necessary. Garnish with cilantro and toasted sesame seeds and serve.

MAKES 6 TO 8 SERVINGS

roasted vegetable salad
WITH LIME-HONEY DRESSING

This offbeat variation on potato salad is beautiful to look at and tangy to taste. Serve warm or at room temperature, as a side dish or vegetarian entrée.

Salad:
Olive oil to coat
1½ pounds red potatoes or Yukon golds, cut into ½-inch cubes, approximately 1 quart
1 medium eggplant, cut into 1-inch cubes, salted and drained
1 small yellow or red onion, sliced ¼-inch thick
1 medium red bell pepper, de-seeded and cut into 1-inch cubes, approximately 1½ cups
1 yellow bell pepper, de-seeded and cut into 1-inch cubes, approximately 1½ cups
1 pound green beans, cut in half, approximately 1 quart
1 head of garlic, cloves coarsely chopped, approximately ½ cup
Salt and freshly ground black pepper
6 ounces feta cheese, crumbled, approximately 1 cup

Dressing:
2 tablespoons fresh oregano, chopped
6 tablespoons fresh Italian parsley, chopped
2 tablespoons scallions, chopped
¼ cup fresh lime juice
2 tablespoons honey
¼ cup olive oil
Salt
Pinch of freshly ground black pepper

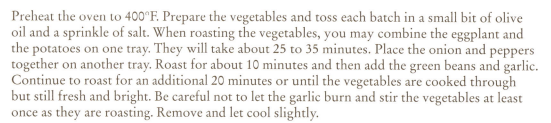

Preheat the oven to 400°F. Prepare the vegetables and toss each batch in a small bit of olive oil and a sprinkle of salt. When roasting the vegetables, you may combine the eggplant and the potatoes on one tray. They will take about 25 to 35 minutes. Place the onion and peppers together on another tray. Roast for about 10 minutes and then add the green beans and garlic. Continue to roast for an additional 20 minutes or until the vegetables are cooked through but still fresh and bright. Be careful not to let the garlic burn and stir the vegetables at least once as they are roasting. Remove and let cool slightly.

While the vegetables are roasting, make the dressing. In a large bowl, mix the herbs, scallions, lime juice, honey, and a pinch of salt and pepper. Whisking, add the oil in a slow and steady stream until emulsified. Set aside.

Add the dressing to the roasted vegetables and toss to coat. Sprinkle with the feta and gently toss, being careful not to break up the feta too much. Check seasonings and adjust with salt, pepper, or lime juice if necessary.

MAKES 8 SERVINGS

roasted potato salad
WITH BACON AND SPICY PECANS

This is a delicious salad that goes well with grilled meats. It is best eaten at room temperature or even slightly warm. Leftovers do not keep well so make just what you will use. We use applewood-smoked bacon which has a rich, hearty flavor and is leaner than regular bacon. If that is not available, use another thick-cut, good-quality bacon for this dish.

Potato Salad:
1½ pounds Yukon gold or red potatoes, approximately 5 medium-sized potatoes
Olive oil
Salt and freshly ground black pepper
3 strips of smoked bacon, cooked and coarsely chopped, yielding ¼ cup
¼ cup green onion, finely sliced

Pecans:
⅓ cup pecan pieces
½ teaspoon salt
Generous pinch cayenne pepper
Pinch of ground cinnamon
1 tablespoon melted unsalted butter

Dressing:
2 tablespoons apple cider vinegar
½ teaspoon mustard seed
2 teaspoons honey or brown sugar
2 tablespoons Italian parsley, coarsely chopped
2 tablespoons vegetable oil

Heat oven to 450°F. Cut potatoes into ¾-inch cubes. You should have about 4½ cups of cubes. Toss with a small amount of oil and lots of salt and pepper. Roast in the oven on a baking sheet lined with parchment paper. Rotate the pan and turn the potatoes at least once as they roast. They are done when the edges turn brown and they are cooked through. Taste one to check. It should take about 20 minutes. Set aside to cool.

Combine the pecans with the salt, cayenne, cinnamon, and butter. Place on a baking sheet and bake until lightly browned, being very careful not to burn them, about 8 minutes. Pull out and set aside to cool as soon as they are done.

In a small bowl, combine the vinegar, mustard seed, honey or sugar, and parsley. Whisk in the oil until emulsified. Add the dressing to the potatoes and taste for salt and pepper. Just before serving, gently fold in the bacon, pecans, and green onion.

MAKES 6 SERVINGS

middle eastern
PLATTER WITH PITA TRIANGLES

This Greek-style dish with its crunchy vegetables and lemony vinaigrette is a refreshing treat in the middle of summer. You can serve this as a platter with pita triangles or make the ingredients into sandwiches with the pitas cut in half to form pockets.

Lemon Vinaigrette:
5 teaspoons fresh lemon juice
2 teaspoons Champagne vinegar
1 teaspoon lemon zest
2 small garlic cloves, minced
Pinch cayenne pepper
2 teaspoons fresh mint leaves, julienne
6 tablespoons olive oil

Platter:
½ small red onion, thinly sliced
1 yellow or red bell pepper, thinly sliced
1½ cucumbers, peeled, seeded, and diced
3 ounces feta cheese, crumbled
15 to 20 kalamata olives, pitted, rinsed, and drained
Salt and freshly ground black pepper
8 to 12 washed and dried lettuce leaves
1 to 2 cups hummus (page 191)
4 to 6 whole pita breads
¼ cup olive oil
1 tablespoon kosher salt
2 tablespoons coarsely chopped cilantro leaves

Preheat the oven to 400°F.

To make the vinaigrette, put the ingredients into a small bowl and whisk to combine.

To make the platter, combine the onion, pepper, cucumber, and vinaigrette. Gently toss in the cheese and the olives, being careful not to overmix as the olives will discolor the dish and the feta will turn to mush. Check for seasonings and add more salt, pepper, or lemon juice if needed. Place the lettuce leaves on a large platter or divide onto individual salad plates. Spoon the salad mixture onto the leaves. Put the hummus into a bowl and serve with the salad or spoon onto individual plates. Cut each pita bread into 4 triangles, brush with oil, and sprinkle with salt and chopped cilantro. Place the triangles on a baking sheet and toast in the hot oven until crisped and a bit browned. Serve the pita triangles alongside the salad as scoops for the hummus.

To serve this as a sandwich, place the pita bread on a baking sheet, and heat slightly in the oven for 2 to 3 minutes, just until softened. Cut the pitas in half, spoon a tablespoon or two of hummus into the opening, slide in a lettuce leaf, and add a big spoonful of the salad mixture.

MAKES 4 TO 6 SERVINGS

HILLARY'S *salad*

This colorful salad is a meal in itself and is one of our favorites. Liz's daughter, Hillary, recreated this dish after having it at Jaffe's restaurant in Arcata, California.

- 1½ cups Sesame-Ginger Vinaigrette, divided (page 83)
- One 7-ounce package of udon noodles
- 1 box firm tofu, 14 ounces
- 1 cup cornstarch
- Vegetable oil, for frying
- Tamari or soy sauce
- 2 heads butter lettuce
- ½ cup grated carrot
- ½ to ¾ cup cilantro leaves
- 2 cups mung bean sprouts or sunflower sprouts
- 1 or 2 ears of corn, approximately 1 cup fresh corn kernels
- ⅓ cup green onion, cut diagonally
- 1 tablespoon black sesame seeds, for garnish (optional)

Make the Sesame-Ginger Vinaigrette.

Cook the udon noodles according to package directions and then drain and toss them with ½ cup of the Sesame-Ginger Vinaigrette. Place in the refrigerator until ready to assemble the salad.

Drain the tofu, then let it sit for 15 minutes with a weight to assist the draining. A plate with a heavy can of food on top works well for this operation. Drain again and pat dry with a paper towel. Cut the block into 20 small cubes. Put the cornstarch into a low-sided bowl and place the tofu cubes in the cornstarch, stirring gently to coat. Fry the cubes in hot oil until crispy and browned a bit. Drain on paper towels and sprinkle with tamari. Set aside.

Wash, spin dry, and tear the butter lettuce into pieces. Peel and grate the carrot. A fine long grate looks best. Wash the cilantro, spin dry, and pick off the leaves. A little stem is all right. Blanch the corn in boiling water for 2 minutes, remove, and cool. Cut the kernels off the cob.

To assemble the salad, toss the noodles, tofu, and prepared vegetables (reserving some of the tofu and carrot for the top) with the butter lettuce and about ⅓ cup dressing. Check to see if the amount of dressing seems adequate and add more if needed. Garnish with reserved tofu and carrot and sprinkle with black sesame seeds.

MAKES 6 TO 8 SERVINGS

jicama WITH LIME AND CHILI

This is a refreshing, low-fat appetizer or side dish.

> ½ medium-sized jicama, peeled and cut into 2-inch sticks, approximately 2 cups
> 3 tablespoons fresh lime juice
> 1 tablespoon sugar
> ¼ teaspoon chili powder
> 2 tablespoons finely chopped cilantro

Mix all of the ingredients together and then taste and adjust the seasonings. Cover and refrigerate for a few hours before serving. Gently stir a few times during this period to make sure that all the sticks have some exposure to the marinade.

MAKES 4 TO 6 SERVINGS

poultry and meat

poultry and meat

When purchasing poultry, beef, pork, and lamb, we suggest you try to find sources that are free-range, grass-fed, hormone-free, and organically grown. You will notice a big improvement in the flavor and texture and there is a greater chance that the animals led happy and healthy lives. They will thank you and your body and the earth will thank you as well.

Try to develop a relationship with your local butcher. Don't be afraid to ask lots of questions, such as what part of the animal the cut came from or how and where the animal was raised. Remember that success in cooking meat is the result of finding the right cut for the method of cooking. Look for meat that is labeled USDA choice or prime. Salting your poultry or meat before cooking, rather than after cooking, also helps create a more flavorful, well-balanced, and succulent dish. The salt has time to permeate and meld with the meat for a fuller flavor.

New trends occur in food preparation as people travel and cultures mix. Nowhere is this more apparent than in meat preparation. There has been a growing interest in ethnic foods, which has brought a rich diversity of tastes home to our tables. This is further driven by the rise in popularity of cooking shows on television.

Lifestyle changes and health concerns are also contributing to the changing world of meat cookery. Fish and chicken have become more popular. The taste and juiciness of meat has changed as the industry selects and breeds for animals with less fat. This has affected methods of preparation, with marinades and brining becoming popular as a way to maintain succulence and juice. Spice rubs have become important to add flavor in grilling.

In this section, we have included recipes that use a variety of cooking techniques, including roasting, braising, grilling, and baking. Some recipes are for simple meals for two and some will feed a crowd. Most of the recipes are easy to prepare, and the more elaborate ones have been divided into several steps, which allows for some prepping ahead. Enjoy.

ORANGE CHICKEN WITH
olives and thyme

In this attractive dish the chicken is set off by bits of orange and flecks of parsley. The sauce is especially good with white rice. This can be made using all thighs. If you choose to do so, substitute more thigh meat for the breasts and put all of it into one baking pan. The preparation and sautéeing take at least a half-hour, and the oven time will be about an hour, so you should allow around 1½ to 2 hours for this recipe.

- 1 cup fresh orange segments
- 10 pieces of chicken, thighs and breasts
- Olive oil, for sautéeing
- 4 teaspoons sea salt
- 1 teaspoon pepper
- 2 teaspoons paprika
- 2 cups unbleached flour
- 3 large yellow onions, peeled, sliced
- One 6-ounce can frozen orange juice concentrate, thawed
- ½ cup honey
- ¼ cup fresh lemon juice
- 2 teaspoons ground ginger
- 1 teaspoon ground nutmeg
- 12 fresh thyme sprigs
- 1 cup pitted whole black kalamata olives, rinsed
- Italian parsley, coarsely chopped

To prepare the orange segments, use a sharp knife to slice off the bottom and top of each orange. Place the orange flat-side down on a board and peel by cutting from top to bottom just inside the skin. Do not leave any white pith. Then place the orange on its side and cut down toward the center against the side of the membrane to remove each segment. Set aside.

Preheat the oven to 400°F. Wash and dry the chicken. Separate the chicken breasts from the thighs. Combine the salt, pepper, paprika, and flour in a shallow pan. Dredge the chicken in the flour mixture, shaking off any excess flour.

In a heavy skillet, heat the oil, but not to smoking. Sauté the chicken on both sides until crispy and golden brown. Remove the pieces to two small roasting pans or Pyrex casseroles, one for breasts, one for thighs. Do not crowd. In the same skillet, sauté the onions over medium heat until tender. Spread them evenly over the chicken pieces. In the same pan again, combine the orange juice concentrate, honey, lemon juice, and spices. Stir to combine. Bring the mixture to a simmer. Immediately pour mixture evenly over the chicken, dividing it between the two pans. Turn the chicken over in the sauce, making sure the meat is well-coated. Nestle the thyme sprigs between the chicken pieces. Cover the pans with foil or a lid. The thighs need to cook for around 50 minutes total and the breasts around 35 minutes, so put the thighs in the oven first and let them bake for 20 minutes. Then put the breasts in and continue baking all for an additional 20 minutes. Remove the foil from the pans and add the olives and orange segments. Continue baking, uncovered, for about 10 to 15 minutes longer, or until meat is done and the juices have reduced a bit. Remove from the oven, arrange chicken on a large platter, pour remaining sauce over it, sprinkle with parsley, and serve.

MAKES 6 TO 8 SERVINGS

korean-style
CHICKEN WITH BLACK SESAME SEEDS

This recipe is very fast and easy to make, great for both kids and adults. The marinade can be used with chicken wings for an easy appetizer. It also works well with thinly sliced beef. The black sesame seeds can be found in the Asian section of your local supermarket. They are an attractive garnish but certainly are optional. The amount of marinade here is enough for up to 5 pounds of chicken wings or wing-drumettes.

Marinade:
1 cup tamari or soy sauce
⅓ cup sugar
1 tablespoon dark sesame oil
1 tablespoon shallot or white onion, peeled and minced
3 green onions, chopped
1 tablespoon garlic, minced
1 tablespoon fresh ginger, peeled and minced (optional)
¼ cup cilantro stems and leaves, minced (optional)
½ teaspoon freshly ground black pepper

10 pieces of chicken thighs and drumsticks, washed and patted dry
Black sesame seeds for garnish
Cilantro sprigs for garnish

In a large bowl, stir together the first 9 ingredients, until the sugar has dissolved. Add the chicken pieces and toss to coat. Let sit, covered, for about 4 hours or overnight in the refrigerator.

Preheat the oven to 400°F. Place the chicken, skin-side up, on a baking sheet lined with parchment paper. Bake until the chicken is a dark golden brown and the juices run clear, about 50 to 60 minutes. Garnish with cilantro sprigs and sesame seeds and serve.

MAKES 6 TO 8 SERVINGS

CHICKEN BREAST WITH
lemon-caper sauce

The chicken breast in this recipe is soaked in buttermilk overnight, encrusted with flavorful breadcrumbs, baked in the oven, and drizzled with a piquant lemon-caper sauce. Lightly pounding the chicken breast will ensure even and quick cooking, resulting in a juicy and tender piece of meat. This dish is ideal for company, as it can be prepped well in advance with minimum effort at the last minute.

Chicken:
1 cup buttermilk
1 bay leaf, crumbled
6 sprigs fresh thyme
10 whole peppercorns
1 teaspoon salt
8 boneless, skinless chicken breast halves
4 cups fine breadcrumbs
1 tablespoon fresh thyme leaves
1 teaspoon kosher salt
½ cup unsalted butter, melted

Sauce:
½ cup unsalted butter
1 tablespoon lemon juice
2 tablespoons capers
Pinch of sugar
Italian parsley, chopped

To make the chicken: Combine the buttermilk, bay leaf, thyme, peppercorns, and salt in a medium-sized container or bowl. Place the chicken breasts one at a time into a heavy plastic bag or between two pieces of parchment paper and lightly pound the chicken with a meat tenderizing mallet, flattening the breast to be about one-third wider in size. Add the pounded chicken breasts to the buttermilk mixture and toss to coat. Cover and refrigerate overnight.

The following day, when ready to proceed, put the breadcrumbs, thyme, and salt in a food processor. Pulse briefly to combine. Set aside in a shallow dish.

Preheat the oven to 425°F. Remove the chicken from the buttermilk. Dip the chicken breasts into the melted butter and then into the breadcrumbs. Press the crumbs onto the chicken or roll the pieces of meat to get an even coating. Place the chicken on a baking sheet lined with parchment paper. Bake for 10 minutes for small pieces and 15 to 20 for larger pieces. They should be golden brown and firm to the touch. Remove from the oven and set aside to rest, lightly covered.

To make the sauce: Melt the butter in a saucepan. Remove from the heat and stir in the lemon juice, capers, and sugar. Transfer the chicken to a warm platter and pour the sauce over. Sprinkle with parsley and serve.

MAKES 6 TO 8 SERVINGS

ROASTED CHICKEN WITH
rosemary and garlic

This tasty chicken has been our simple standby for many years. It is appropriate in all seasons. We usually serve this dish with mashed potatoes or soft polenta and a gravy made from the pan drippings.

¼ cup olive oil
1 tablespoon balsamic vinegar
¼ cup soy sauce
½ head of garlic, slivered
Small handful of rosemary sprigs, chopped
Freshly ground black pepper
8 pieces of chicken, washed, rinsed and patted dry
1 teaspoon kosher salt

Preheat the oven to 400°F. Mix together the first 6 ingredients in a bowl. Add the chicken to the marinade and let sit for at least 2 hours. Remove the chicken from the marinade, place in a shallow pan, sprinkle with the salt. Bake the breast for 20 to 30 minutes and the thighs and legs for 45 minutes to 1 hour, until the juices run clear and the chicken is browned on the outside. Alternatively, light the grill and cook the chicken breast for about 25 to 30 minutes and the thighs and drumsticks for about 40 to 45 minutes or until the juices run clear.

MAKES 4 TO 6 SERVINGS

grilled CHICKEN BREAST WITH ADOBO SAUCE, CITRUS BUTTER, & TROPICAL FRUIT SALSA

This richly spiced chicken is accented by sweet fruit salsa. We serve this with white rice and a seasonal vegetable. Adobo sauce can be found in the Mexican food section of your local supermarket. The citrus butter can be made up to one week ahead and the salsa can be made earlier in the day.

Citrus Butter:
½ cup salted butter, room temperature
Zest of ½ lemon, minced
Zest of ½ lime, minced
½ shallot, minced
1 small garlic clove, minced
1 tablespoon chives, minced

Tropical Fruit Salsa:
1 medium shallot, minced
1 small garlic clove, minced
½ jalapeño pepper, seeded and minced
½ cup red or yellow bell pepper, very small dice
1 mango, peeled, seeded, and cut into small dice, approximately 1 cup
¼ cantaloupe, peeled and cut into small dice, approximately 1 cup
¼ medium papaya, peeled, seeded, and cut into small dice, approximately 1 cup
¼ cup fresh cilantro, chopped
Salt and freshly ground black pepper
Juice of 1 lime
Splash of seasoned rice vinegar

Chicken:
6 large chicken breasts, boneless, skinless
Salt and pepper
2 tablespoons canned adobo sauce
2 tablespoons vegetable oil

To make the citrus butter: Put all of the ingredients into a small bowl and mix with a fork until combined. Put the mixture onto a sheet of waxed paper or plastic wrap and roll into a log. Let sit in the refrigerator until needed.

To make the salsa: Combine all of the ingredients in a small bowl. Season to taste with the salt and pepper, lime, and rice vinegar. Cover and set aside.

To make the chicken: Season the chicken with salt and pepper on both sides. Combine the adobo sauce and the oil together in a small bowl. Rub this mixture on the chicken breasts to coat. Refrigerate until ready to grill.

Preheat a charcoal grill. Remove the chicken and the citrus butter from the refrigerator. Cut the butter into 6 equal pieces. Grill the chicken until almost done, turning occasionally. The time will vary depending on how hot your grill is, but you will probably need at least 6 minutes per side. When almost done, place 1 piece of butter on the top side of each piece of chicken and let sit, covered, until the butter has partially melted. Remove from the grill onto a plate. Spoon the salsa over the top of each breast and serve over a bed of rice.

MAKES 6 SERVINGS

BRAISED CHICKEN WITH
thyme and apple cider

This is a delicious, comforting dish for fall, winter, or spring. Serve with soft polenta and seasonal vegetables on the side. There is nothing difficult about this recipe, but it takes at least 2½ hours for the slow braising so allow yourself plenty of time.

Salt and pepper
8 each chicken legs and thighs (attached if possible)
2 tablespoons olive oil
1¼ cups yellow onion, chopped
1¼ cups celery, sliced
1 cup carrots, peeled and cut into ½-inch chunks
4 large garlic cloves, minced
2 tablespoons apple cider vinegar
6 sprigs of fresh thyme, leaves removed and coarsely chopped
Pinch of red pepper flakes
2 cups chopped tomatoes or one 28-ounce can, drained
1 cup apple juice or cider
5 cups chicken stock
Parsley, for garnish

Preheat oven to 425°F. Salt and pepper the pieces of chicken and lay them out on a baking sheet. Bake in the hot oven until beginning to brown, 20 to 30 minutes, turning once. If you have a convection oven, use it because the fan will help speed the browning. When the chicken is browned, remove it from the oven and turn down the temperature to 400°F.

Meanwhile, heat the oil in a large sauté pan and cook the onion, celery, and carrots until soft. Remove the vegetables and set aside. In the same pan, briefly sauté the garlic. Add the vinegar, thyme, pepper flakes, tomatoes, apple juice, and stock. Bring to a boil. This is your braising liquid. There might seem to be more than you need, but you will use the extra to replenish as noted below.

Once the chicken is browned, place the pieces in a large roasting pan. Try to keep the chicken in one layer. Distribute the sautéed vegetables over the chicken and pour in the braising liquid until it reaches halfway up the chicken. Cover the pan and braise in the hot oven for 1 hour. Remove the cover, add more liquid if necessary, and continue braising uncovered about 1½ to 2 hours.

At this point, your liquid might be reduced enough that it is perfect to serve. If it could use some further reducing to make it thicker, remove the chicken from the oven and pour off the braising liquid into a pan on the stove. Add any extra braising liquid that was set aside, if necessary. Bring to a rapid boil over high heat. Continue boiling until slightly reduced. Arrange the chicken on a serving platter and pour the reduced braising liquid over it. Garnish with parsley and serve.

MAKES 6 TO 8 SERVINGS

ENCHILADA MOLE *con pollo*

These rich and tasty enchiladas are a favorite of everyone at the Ranch. They go well with a green salad tossed with orange and avocado slices and Citrus Vinaigrette (page 87). And, of course, fresh salsa. This is a good dish for a dinner party, as the enchiladas can be made ahead, refrigerated, and baked when needed. It is important to obtain Mexican chocolate, such as Ibarra, for this recipe. It can be found in the Mexican section of your supermarket and is a special combination of sugar, cacao, almonds, cinnamon, and lecithin. The sauce does take a few hours to cook, so it should be started early or done the day before.

Mole:
½ cup vegetable oil
3½ teaspoons unbleached flour
2½ teaspoons chili powder
3 cups water or chicken stock
½ teaspoon ground cloves
½ teaspoon ground cinnamon
2 tablespoons ground cumin
1 round (3 ounces) Mexican chocolate, grated, approximately ½ cup

Enchiladas:
2 tablespoons vegetable oil
2 cups diced yellow onion
2 garlic cloves, minced
1 quart (1½ pounds) cooked chicken meat, diced
One 14-ounce can whole tomatoes
2 teaspoons dried oregano
1 tablespoon ground cumin
2 tablespoons Dijon-style mustard
1 tablespoon salt
1 teaspoon black pepper
10 flour tortillas, 8½ inches in diameter
4 cups grated Cheddar cheese
1¼ cups green onions, chopped
1 cup crème fraîche or sour cream
Fresh tomato salsa

To make the mole: Heat the oil in a 3 to 4 quart heavy-bottomed pan. Mix the flour and chili powder together, add it to the oil, and cook, stirring frequently, until it starts to darken. Be careful not to let it burn. Remove from the heat and add the water or chicken stock. Stir until smooth. Add the cloves, cinnamon, cumin, and chocolate and stir well. Cook for 2 to 3 hours over low heat, stirring occasionally, until the sauce is thick and velvety. This can be done ahead and kept refrigerated until needed to complete the recipe.

To assemble the enchiladas: Heat the oil in a large skillet and sauté the onion until transparent. Add the garlic and continue cooking another minute. Add the chicken. Stir. Add the tomatoes, oregano, cumin, mustard, salt, and pepper. Stir and cook for 15 minutes over low heat to develop the flavors.

Preheat the oven to 350°F. Grease a 9 by 13-inch baking pan. Heat up some of the mole sauce in a skillet. The sauce should be about ½-inch deep in the pan. Dip the tortillas briefly, one at a time, in the warm sauce to soften them. After dipping a tortilla, fill it with about ½ cup of the chicken mixture, ¼ cup cheese, and 2 tablespoons green onions. Roll up each filled tortilla and place it in the baking pan. Pour the remaining mole sauce over the filled and rolled tortillas and top with the remaining cheese. At this point, the enchiladas can be refrigerated until ready to bake. Bake in a 350°F oven until bubbling, approximately 1 hour. Serve topped with crème fraîche or sour cream with salsa on the side.

MAKES 5 TO 6 SERVINGS

FOCACCIA SANDWICH *with* CHICKEN, ROASTED EGGPLANT, RED BELL PEPPER, AND BASIL AIOLI

This is the sandwich Ariel and her partner, Chris Russi, developed from dinner leftovers while snowboarding in Tahoe. Apparently, Chris was miraculously able to perform 360s after this meal. The Grilled Pork Tenderloin would work well as an alternative to the chicken (page 118). You can make your own focaccia for this sandwich, using the recipe on page 58, or purchase it ready-made at your local bakery. Ciabatta bread would also work as a substitute. All of the components can be made a day ahead, and then you have a wonderful lunch ready for the beach or the slopes!

Chicken:
4 boneless chicken breasts, washed, rinsed, and dried
Olive oil, for brushing
Salt and pepper
2 teaspoons fresh herbs, Italian parsley, basil, or thyme, chopped (optional)

Relish:
2 medium-sized globe eggplants
Kosher salt
2 red bell peppers
2 yellow or red onions, thinly sliced
2 tablespoons olive oil, plus more to coat pan
Dash of sugar
Balsamic vinegar
Freshly ground black pepper

2 cups Basil Aioli (page 180)
1 recipe Ariel's Focaccia, cut into twelve
  4 by 4-inch pieces (page 58)
1 bunch arugula, washed and spun dry (optional)

Preheat the oven to 450°F.

To prepare the chicken: Place the breasts on a baking sheet lined with parchment paper. Brush oil on both sides, sprinkle with salt and pepper and herbs if using. Bake for 20 minutes or until firm to the touch and the juices run clear when cut with a knife. Alternatively, grill the chicken. If using immediately, thinly slice on the diagonal and set aside. If making ahead, refrigerate.

To make the relish: Peel and cut the eggplant into ½-inch cubes. Place them in a medium bowl and salt liberally. Let sit for 30 minutes. Drain off liquid and pat dry with a paper towel. Toss the eggplant with the oil and place on a baking sheet lined with parchment paper. Bake until tender and lightly browned, about 20 to 30 minutes. Set aside in a bowl and let cool.

Meanwhile, roast the peppers. Turn the gas stove flames on high and evenly char the peppers over the flames. Or, roast in a 450°F oven for about 20 minutes, until blistery. Place in a bowl, cover with plastic wrap or foil and let sit 10 minutes to "sweat." Remove covering and let cool. Pull off the charred skin, slice open, and remove the seeds. Do not rinse. Slice into thin strips and add to the eggplant.

Heat a heavy-bottomed pan over medium heat. Add oil to coat the pan and add the onions. Cook until the onions are transparent, about 8 to 10 minutes. Sprinkle on a dash of sugar, a splash of vinegar, and a pinch of salt and pepper. Stir to combine and turn the heat down to low. Let cook until the onions are soft, lightly browned, and caramelized, about 25 to 30 minutes. Add this to the eggplant and pepper mixture and set aside or place in the refrigerator until assembly.

Make the basil aioli.

To assemble, line up all of your ingredients. Cut the focaccia into pieces and then split them. Slather basil aioli on both sides of the focaccia. Place a dollop of the relish on the bottom side of the bread, spread evenly. Place two slices of chicken on the relish, add two or three pieces of arugula, and replace the top side of the bread. Repeat with the rest of the ingredients. Keep these at a cool temperature if not eating immediately, as the aioli is made with uncooked egg.

MAKES 8 TO 12 SANDWICHES

CORNISH GAME HENS WITH
butternut squash and sage

These small birds are the result of crossing a Cornish gamecock and Plymouth Rock hen. The meat is more tender and flavorful than chicken and, split, the bird is perfect for two people. Cornish hens are usually found in the frozen meat section of stores. Delicata squash may be substituted for butternut and, in that case, the skin may be left on.

- 4 Cornish game hens, approximately 1 to 2 pounds each
- ½ cup unsalted butter, softened
- 2 teaspoons fresh sage, finely chopped or 1 teaspoon dried, plus 12 sprigs fresh sage
- Kosher salt and freshly ground black pepper
- 6 to 8 garlic cloves
- 1 tablespoon olive oil
- 2 cups onion, chopped
- 4 cups butternut squash, peeled and cubed into ½-inch pieces
- ½ cup dry white wine
- ½ cup homemade chicken stock or low salt canned chicken stock
- 2 tablespoons butter

Heat the oven to 400°F. Remove any extra fat from the bird cavity. Rinse and pat the hens dry. Combine the softened butter with the chopped sage. Carefully loosen the skin from the breast meat and stuff about 2 teaspoons of the butter-sage mixture under the skin. Repeat with the remaining hens. Rub the rest of the softened butter over the entire surface of the hens, season with salt and pepper, and place 2 cloves of garlic and a sprig of sage in each cavity.

Heat the oil in a roasting pan and sauté the onions over medium heat on the stove, until lightly browned. Remove from heat and add the squash and the remaining sage sprigs. Add the wine and the stock.

Arrange the hens on the vegetables, breast-side down, and roast in the oven for 15 minutes. Turn the hens breast-side up, baste with the juices, and roast for about 30 to 35 minutes longer, until they are browned and the juices run clear from the thigh when pierced with a knife.

Remove the hens and the vegetables to a platter and cover to keep warm. Place the roasting pan with the remaining juices on the stove over high heat and reduce for about 3 minutes or more to thicken. Whisk in the butter, adjust the seasoning to taste, pour the sauce over the hens, and serve.

MAKES 6 TO 8 SERVINGS

BISHOP'S RANCH TURKEY *meatloaf*

This is a flavorful, firm, and juicy meatloaf, but with half the fat! Part of the beauty of this entrée is the little flecks of vegetables scattered throughout. We serve this with Yukon gold mashed potatoes. Chopping the vegetables in a fine, ¼-inch dice will help the meatloaf hold together.

- 1 onion, finely chopped
- 2 celery ribs, finely chopped
- 1 large carrot, peeled and finely chopped
- 3 tablespoons olive oil
- 2 garlic cloves, minced
- 1 green apple, peeled and finely chopped
- ½ cup Italian parsley, chopped
- 1 tablespoon fresh thyme, chopped
- 2 eggs, beaten
- 1 cup breadcrumbs
- 2 pounds ground turkey
- 1 teaspoon salt
- 2 pinches freshly ground black pepper
- Barbeque sauce (page 186) or ketchup, to brush on

Preheat the oven to 375°F. Line a baking sheet with parchment paper or lightly grease.

Sauté the onion, celery, and carrots in the oil for about 5 minutes or until tender and limp, stirring occasionally. Add the garlic and apple and sauté for a minute or two longer. Remove the vegetables from the heat and let cool for a few minutes. Put the vegetables and the rest of the ingredients into a medium-sized bowl and mix well to combine. Shape the meat into one free-form loaf, approximately 5 by 12-inches, and place on the baking sheet. Brush with the barbeque sauce or ketchup. Bake for about 45 minutes to 1 hour or until the meat is firm to the touch or a thermometer inserted into the center of the loaf reads 160°F. Let stand for 5 minutes, tented with foil, before slicing.

MAKES 8 TO 10 SERVINGS

TURKEY *mole*

We serve this with white rice, romaine lettuce with jicama, avocado and citrus, and plenty of corn and flour tortillas. The mole sauce freezes well, so you might double the recipe to have sauce on hand for an easy meal another day.

4 dried pasilla or ancho chiles
4 dried negro chiles (ancho may be substituted if this variety is not available)
1 medium yellow onion, diced
¼ cup vegetable oil
3 garlic cloves, minced
½ teaspoon ground cinnamon
½ teaspoon ground coriander
⅛ teaspoon ground cloves
1 teaspoon pepper
3 tablespoons raw, skinless peanuts or whole almonds
3 tablespoons dark or golden raisins
4 Roma tomatoes, peeled, seeded, and chopped or ½ cup drained canned tomatoes
1 small corn tortilla, lightly toasted and broken into small pieces or 2 pieces white bread
3 tablespoons sesame seeds, lightly toasted, plus more, for garnish
2 to 3 cups chicken stock
½ round (1.5 ounces) Mexican chocolate, grated, approximately ¼ cup
1-ounce square bittersweet chocolate, coarsely chopped, approximately ¼ cup
1½ teaspoons salt
Salt and pepper
8 pieces of turkey thighs (chicken may be substituted)
Vegetable oil, to sauté
¼ cup chopped cilantro, for garnish

Devein and remove the seeds from the dried chiles. Roast them in a large, heavy skillet, stirring occasionally, until their aroma is released, about 2 minutes. Place the chiles in a bowl, pour boiling water, to cover, and set aside to cool for about 30 minutes. When cool, transfer the chiles and the liquid to the blender in small batches and process until very smooth. Set aside.

Sauté the onion until soft and golden. Add the garlic and sauté for about 1 minute longer, being careful not to burn. Stir in the cinnamon, coriander, cloves, and pepper. Cook about 2 minutes longer, stirring occasionally. Add the nuts, raisins, tomatoes, and tortilla or bread and cook until soft, about 5 minutes. Add 3 tablespoons of the toasted sesame seeds.

In small batches, add the onion mixture and the chicken stock to the blender and blend until smooth.

Pour the onion and spice purée into the pan that was used to sauté them. Pour in the blended dried chile mixture, chocolates, and the salt and cook over medium heat for about 10 minutes to blend the flavors. This sauce keeps well and can be made a day ahead.

Salt and pepper the turkey on both sides. Heat the oil in a large, heavy-bottomed Dutch oven over medium heat and fry the turkey on both sides until golden brown. Set aside. Heat the mole sauce. Add the browned turkey and cook, covered and over low heat for about 1 hour, or until the turkey is very tender and falling off the bone. The end consistency of the sauce should be like heavy cream. If it is too thick, thin it with a bit of water or stock. Serve the turkey thighs sprinkled with sesame seeds and chopped cilantro and over white rice. Serve extra sauce on the side.

MAKES 8 SERVINGS

GRILLED PORK *tenderloin*

Pork tenderloins are ideal for grilling because they have little fat and are easy to handle. If a grill is not available, the tenderloins can be seared on top of the stove and then finished in the oven. You will find that brining creates a meat that is moist and tender. The marinade furthers this process and punches up the flavor. If you have time only for one process, do the marinade. Pork tenderloin goes well with anything from a fruit salsa to an Italian salsa verde. Serve this with polenta or roasted baby potatoes and green beans or wilted greens. We use any leftovers from this dish for focaccia sandwiches (page 112) or tacos the next day.

Brine:
3 quarts water
¼ cup salt
½ cup sugar

4 pounds pork tenderloin

Marinade:
½ bunch fresh sage
2 tablespoons cumin seed or fennel seed, roasted and ground
6 to 8 garlic cloves, chopped
Salt and pepper
2 tablespoons olive oil
½ cup orange juice or white wine or apple juice

The day before cooking, place the ingredients for the brine in a plastic container or non-reactive shallow pan. Pull off the silver skin from the pork and discard. Trim off any excess fat. Add the tenderloins to the brine, cover, and refrigerate overnight. If it is necessary to brine the same day, allow 2 to 3 hours in the brine.

Two hours before serving time, make the marinade for the pork. Place all of the ingredients for the marinade in a blender or food processor and blend until emulsified, 1 or 2 minutes.

Pull the pork out of the brine and pat dry. Discard the brine mixture. Place the tenderloin in a long shallow pan and add the marinade. Turn the pork to coat. Let sit in the refrigerator for 1 hour.

Meanwhile, make a fire for the grill, turn on your gas grill, or preheat the oven to 400°F. Fifteen minutes before the coals are ready, take the pork out of the refrigerator, gently wipe off the excess marinade, and discard the marinade that the pork was in. Let the meat sit at room temperature until you are ready to proceed with the grilling.

When the coals are hot, grill the pork, searing evenly, about 7 minutes per side, 12 to 14 minutes total. Turn off the grill and leave the tenderloins inside for an additional 5 minutes or remove to an ovenproof platter and place it in the oven to finish cooking, for about 10 minutes. The internal temperature should register 145 to 150°F. Do not overcook. The meat will continue to cook after it is removed from the oven. Remove it from the oven or grill, place it on a board for slicing, and let it rest for 10 minutes, covered, to allow the juices to redistribute. Slice the meat on the diagonal, arrange decoratively on a plate or platter, spoon on the pan juices, and serve.

MAKES 8 TO 10 SERVINGS

SLOW-ROASTED PORK WITH
sage and garlic

Porchetta, arista, slow-roasted shoulder of pork, Tuscan pork—there are many names for essentially the same technique. Italians will roast a whole pig over a pit-rotisserie and then sell the succulent, herb-infused meat at their farmers' markets. This is an easier version using the shoulder or Boston butt. The slow roasting, coupled with a low oven temperature, concentrates the flavor and melts the meat. Serve with Yukon gold mashed potatoes or soft polenta and roasted spring asparagus or wilted greens.

- 1 pork shoulder butt or Boston butt, boneless, approximately 6 to 7 pounds
- 8 to 10 garlic cloves, coarsely chopped
- 2 tablespoons fennel seed, toasted over medium heat until aromatic
- 1 teaspoon red pepper flakes
- 2 handfuls fresh sage leaves, coarsely chopped
- 2 teaspoons freshly ground black pepper
- 4 to 6 tablespoons kosher salt
- Olive oil
- 2 lemons, quartered (optional)

Make long ¼-inch deep slashes in a crosshatch pattern over the surface of the fatty skin of the pork butt. Combine the garlic, fennel, pepper flakes, sage, pepper, and salt in a food processor and pulse until just combined and very coarsely chopped. Add oil until a loose paste forms, scraping down the sides of the bowl between pulses. Rub this mixture into the incisions and over the entire roast. Cover with plastic wrap and refrigerate overnight.

Preheat the oven to 450°F. Remove the meat from the refrigerator and let come to room temperature, about 30 minutes. Place the pork, skin- and fat-side up in a roasting pan and roast for about 30 minutes or until the top is brown and the skin is crackling. Turn the heat down to 300°F and roast 3 to 4 hours, basting with the rendered fat occasionally, or until the meat is very tender and falls apart when pushed with your finger.

Remove the meat from the oven and let rest for about 15 minutes before slicing. Pour the juices and fat into a container. Skim off the fat with a ladle and discard. Pour the pan juices over the meat and serve with the lemon wedges.

MAKES 8 TO 10 SERVINGS

MOROCCAN *lamb kabobs*
WITH YOGURT MINT SAUCE

These kabobs are easy to prepare and release a tantalizing aroma as they grill. Serve with saffron rice or couscous, the yogurt-mint sauce, and sautéed vegetables. Toasted pita triangles and hummus (page 191) also go well with this meal. Beef can be used in place of lamb if desired.

- 1½ teaspoons ground cinnamon
- 1½ teaspoons ground coriander seed
- 1½ teaspoons kosher salt
- ½ teaspoon freshly ground black pepper
- ¾ teaspoon ground cumin
- ½ teaspoon ground nutmeg
- 1 teaspoon ground paprika
- 3½ pounds boneless leg of lamb or tender cut of beef, cut into 1-inch cubes
- 15 to 20 wooden skewers, soaked in water for 45 minutes

Combine all the spices in a large shallow dish. Place the cubes of lamb in the spice mixture and toss to coat. Thread the lamb onto the skewers, 4 or 5 per skewer. Preheat the grill or oven pan broiler. Grill the kabobs for about 10 to 15 minutes, turning occasionally. The length of time will depend on how hot your grill is and how well-done you prefer the meat. Transfer to a platter and serve with yogurt-mint sauce.

MAKES 8 TO 12 SERVINGS

YOGURT MINT SAUCE

1½ cups plain whole-milk yogurt
2 tablespoons fresh lemon juice
1 garlic clove, pressed or minced
1 teaspoon kosher salt
¼ teaspoon freshly ground black pepper
3 tablespoons fresh mint leaves, minced
3 tablespoons fresh Italian parsley leaves, minced

Put all of the ingredients into a small bowl and stir to combine. Cover and refrigerate until ready to use.

MAKES APPROXIMATELY 1½ CUPS

GRILLED *hanger steak*

Hanger steak is a very flavorful cut that, while not always on the supermarket shelves, can be ordered from a butcher. Similar to skirt steak, it is a tenderloin and benefits from marinating. It is best cooked briefly over high heat. Hanger steak comes in varying sizes, so, if what you have is not all the same dimensions, be prepared to leave some on the grill longer to finish cooking. We serve this with Gorgonzola butter (page 185) or a tangy herb sauce such as salsa verde (page 189), chimichurri, or salmoriglio (page 190).

3 pounds hanger steak or skirt steak
Freshly ground black pepper

Marinade:
½ cup tamari or soy sauce
1 cup balsamic vinegar
¼ cup Worcestershire sauce
2 tablespoons olive oil
6 garlic cloves, mashed

If the butcher has not already done it, remove the silver skin and tendons from the hanger steak. This will leave you with 2 tenderloins of hanger steak. Dust the steak with black pepper. Mix the marinade ingredients in a bowl and place the steak along with the marinade in a glass baking dish or a heavy plastic bag to marinate overnight, or at least 4 hours.

Take the meat out 1 hour before you plan to grill to bring it to room temperature. Prepare your grill. Remove the meat from the marinade and grill it about 3 to 4 minutes per side. Timing will vary according to the heat of the coals and the distance of the meat from the coals or flame. If not cooked through, you can place the meat on an upper rack and close the lid of a gas-fired grill or finish the cooking in a 350°F oven. Let the meat sit for 15 minutes before slicing. After sitting, the meat should be at 135 to 140°F for medium rare or 140 to 150°F for medium. Slice on the diagonal for larger slices, or straight across for smaller but less chewy, pieces. Serve with a sauce on the side.

MAKES 6 SERVINGS

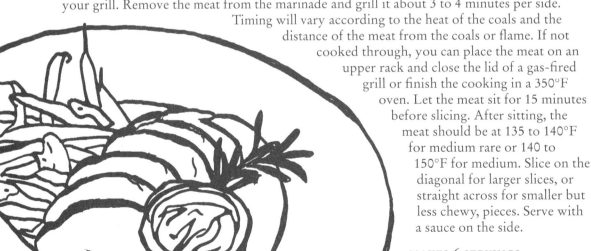

BEEF SHORT RIBS BRAISED IN
barbeque sauce

Short ribs are full of flavor and lend themselves to a long, slow braise in the oven. They are quite fatty, so it is necessary to find a way to get rid of the excess fat. Typically this is done by a hot sauté or roasting in a hot oven, followed by a slow braise. In this recipe, we remove some of the fat by first simmering the ribs; this also serves to soften the connective tissue. Because the fat will rise to the top of the liquid and harden if left in the refrigerator overnight, this recipe is best done as a two-day process. Beef short ribs come in two cuts: English-style, as rectangles, or flanken-style, which are long and cut across the rib bones. For hearty eaters, allow two ribs if English-style or one if cut in the larger flanken-style. These succulent ribs are good served with brown rice, mashed potatoes, or polenta and they heat up well if any are leftover. Make sure you have lots of the sauce on hand!

3½ to 4 pounds of short ribs
1 tablespoon salt
2 yellow onions, chopped, plus 1 large yellow onion, cut into 1-inch chunks
4 bay leaves

Barbeque Sauce (enough for up to 5 pounds of ribs):
½ cup firmly packed brown sugar
½ cup apple cider vinegar
½ cup Worcestershire sauce
1 cup ketchup
2 teaspoons dry mustard
2 teaspoons paprika
1 teaspoon salt
2 cups meat broth plus more if needed

Trim the ribs of any excess fat on the outside. Place the ribs in a large pot with salted cold water to cover. Add the chopped onions and bay leaves. Bring to a boil, then turn down to low and gently simmer for 2 hours. Cool the pot in an ice bath or let cool overnight in the refrigerator. When the fat has risen and congealed, skim off and discard. Strain the meat from the liquid, discarding the onions and bay leaves but SAVING THE LIQUID or broth.

To make the barbeque sauce, put all the ingredients in a bowl and whisk together. Because of the meat broth, it will be thin, but will thicken as the ribs bake.

Preheat the oven to 350°F. Place the ribs in a baking pan and scatter the chunks of onion over the top. Pour the barbeque sauce over the ribs and onions and bake, covered, for 45 minutes to 1 hour. Remove from the oven and give the ribs a stir, and add a bit more broth if much sauce has evaporated. Put back in the oven, uncovered this time, and bake another hour, allowing the sauce to thicken and get darker. The ribs can be held for a while once they are cooked, but don't let all the sauce evaporate.

MAKES 4 TO 5 SERVINGS

BEEF STEW WITH CABERNET AND
hoisin sauce

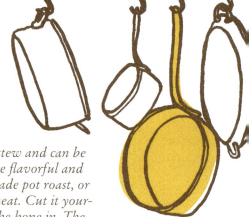

Our guests love this tasty stew. Hoisin sauce adds complexity to the stew and can be found in the Asian section of your supermarket. You will obtain more flavorful and tender meat if you purchase a piece of boneless beef chuck roast, a blade pot roast, or even trimmed English-cut short ribs instead of buying precut stew meat. Cut it yourself or ask your butcher to do it for you. If you use short ribs, leave the bone in. The stew reheats well if you wish to make it a day ahead.

- 3½ pounds boneless beef chuck roast, cut into 2½-inch pieces
- Salt and freshly ground black pepper
- 4 tablespoons olive oil, divided
- 3½ cups onion, chopped into 1-inch pieces
- 2 cups Cabernet Sauvignon, divided
- One 14.5-ounce can of diced tomatoes, juice included
- ½ cup hoisin sauce
- 2 bay leaves
- 1 pound carrots, approximately 5, peeled and cut diagonally into 1-inch pieces
- 1 tablespoon cornstarch mixed with 1 tablespoon cold water
- 4 tablespoons chopped fresh Italian parsley

Sprinkle the meat with salt and pepper. Heat 2 tablespoons of the oil in a heavy, large pot over high heat and add the meat to the pot. Sauté until it is browned on all sides. Remove the meat from the pot and set aside. Reduce the heat to medium and add the remaining 2 tablespoons of the oil to the pot. Add the onions and sauté until golden brown, about 10 minutes. Return the meat to the pot, add 1 cup of the wine, tomatoes with their juice, hoisin sauce, and the bay leaves. Bring to a boil. Reduce heat to low, cover the pot, and simmer 45 minutes, stirring occasionally.

Add the carrots and the remaining 1 cup of wine. Cover again and simmer 30 minutes, stirring occasionally. Uncover, increase the heat and bring to a boil, and cook until the sauce is slightly thickened, stirring occasionally, about 15 minutes longer. Now reduce the heat, add the cornstarch mixture, and simmer until the sauce thickens, stirring occasionally, about 10 minutes. Discard the bay leaves and taste for salt and pepper. Ladle into a serving dish and garnish with parsley.

MAKES 6 TO 8 SERVINGS

fish and shellfish

fish and shellfish

Fish is best purchased fresh, and wild fish is better for you (and the environment) than farm-raised. We treat fish as a seasonal product, looking forward to the Pacific king salmon season from late spring to the end of summer. Unless you have caught it yourself, most fish is already a few days old when you buy it, so try to purchase fish on the same day you plan to cook it. Fish keeps best at 32 to 34°F, which is colder than the average 40°F refrigerator. To maintain the quality of your fish, store it in a pan with ice or ice packs.

The best thing about fish is that it is delicious and easy to prepare. Any simple broiled, baked, or grilled fish can be served with a variety of flavored butters or sauces. You can choose from tomato salsa, salsa verde, a lemon vinaigrette, or beurre blanc to name just a few. And don't forget the wedge of fresh lemon!

ROCK SHRIMP AND
sweet corn fritters

This is a special treat in the summertime, when the corn is fresh, crunchy, and sweet. Serve with a salad of mixed greens for a light, yet complete, meal. Prawns may be substituted for the rock shrimp, just cut them into smaller pieces. You may also use frozen shrimp. Thaw them completely and omit the soaking procedure from the recipe, just rinse off and dry. Note that the partially mixed batter needs to rest in the refrigerator for 1 hour, so plan your time with that in mind.

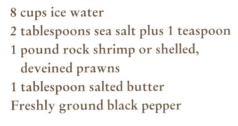

8 cups ice water
2 tablespoons sea salt plus 1 teaspoon
1 pound rock shrimp or shelled, deveined prawns
1 tablespoon salted butter
Freshly ground black pepper

Batter:
1 tablespoon sugar
2 cups unbleached flour
1 teaspoon baking powder
4 large eggs, separated

4 tablespoons salted butter, melted and cooled
2 cups whole milk
4 cups fresh corn kernels, cut off the cob, approximately 6 ears
½ cup fresh basil chiffonade, approximately ½ bunch fresh basil
Light olive oil or vegetable oil, for frying

Chipotle Red Chile Cream, garnish, page 188

Combine 2 tablespoons of the sea salt with the ice water and soak the rock shrimp in the mixture for 20 minutes (to remove any sand or rock), then drain and pat dry. In a medium-sized pan, sauté the shrimp with 1 tablespoon butter, until just cooked through, about 1 to 2 minutes. Drain off any liquid and add a pinch of pepper. Spread the shrimp onto a baking sheet to cool. Refrigerate.

In a bowl, whisk together the sugar, flour, baking powder, and the remaining salt. In a separate bowl, whisk together the egg yolks, butter, and milk and add to the flour mixture, mixing just enough to make a smooth batter. Do not overmix or it will become tough. Cover and let rest in the refrigerator for at least 1 hour.

While the batter rests, shave the kernels from the corncobs. Toss the kernels with your fingers to separate them. Set aside. In a clean, dry bowl, beat the egg whites until soft peaks form. Remove the batter from the refrigerator and gently stir in the corn and basil. Then gently fold in the egg whites. Do not overmix. You should still be able to see some of the egg white in the mixture.

Heat a griddle or skillet over medium heat, until the pan is hot enough that a drop of water sizzles and evaporates when dropped on it. Add 2 tablespoons oil to the pan and drop the batter by large spoonfuls onto the griddle. They should be about 5 inches in diameter. Sprinkle 5 to 6 of the rock shrimp onto the batter. Check with a spatula and, when the undersides are a golden brown, turn the fritters over and cook until golden. Repeat with the remaining batter. Transfer the fritters to a platter and keep warm in the oven until you are ready to serve. Do not stack them on top of each other or they will steam. Drizzle with Chipotle Red Chile Cream before serving.

MAKES APPROXIMATELY TWENTY 5-INCH FRITTERS, 8 TO 10 SERVINGS

FETTUCCINE WITH *rock shrimp*, SUN-DRIED TOMATOES, BASIL, AND CREAM

Rock shrimp is similar to lobster in flavor and in texture. If you can't find rock shrimp at your local supermarket, substitute prawns. In the summer, we add fresh corn kernels and Sun Gold cherry tomatoes to this dish.

8 cups ice water
2 tablespoons sea salt plus 1 teaspoon for pasta water
1¼ pound rock shrimp
2 tablespoons light olive oil
1 large yellow onion, quartered and thinly sliced
Pinch of red pepper flakes
2 cups heavy cream
½ cup oil-packed sun-dried tomatoes, chopped
¾ pound dried fettuccine pasta
2 tablespoons salted butter
3 garlic cloves, minced
¼ cup fresh basil, chiffonade
Freshly ground black pepper
1 tablespoon Italian parsley, chopped
Fresh Parmesan cheese, grated

Combine 2 tablespoons of the sea salt with the ice water and soak the rock shrimp in the mixture for 20 minutes (to remove any sand or rock), then drain and pat dry.

Heat the oil in a large skillet and sauté the onions and pepper flakes on medium heat until very soft and beginning to color, approximately 10 to 15 minutes. Add the cream and bring to a boil. Let the cream reduce, at least 15 minutes, until it coats the back of a wooden spoon, and then add the sun-dried tomatoes. Remove from the heat.

Set a large pot of water on the stove to boil. When the water is boiling, add the remaining 1 teaspoon of salt and cook the pasta until al dente, about 8 to 10 minutes. Drain and keep warm.

Heat the butter in a small skillet and sauté the rock shrimp until just cooked through. Add the garlic and cook for another minute. Transfer to a mixing bowl and pour the cream sauce over the shrimp. Stir in the basil and correct the seasoning by adding salt and pepper to taste.

Add the cooked pasta to the sauce and toss. Garnish with the parsley and serve with the cheese.

MAKES 6 TO 8 SERVINGS

pescado CON JUGO DE NARANJA

This recipe was gathered by Liz's son-in-law, Bradley Hoessle, on a trip to Baja. We like to call it by its Mexican name, rather than Fish with Orange Juice. It is easy to make and light. Serve with rice and a green salad and you have a simple, healthy dinner.

¼ cup light olive oil

2 tablespoons salted butter

1 red onion, sliced

1 red bell pepper, sliced into thin strips

1 yellow, orange, or green bell pepper, or a combination, sliced into thin strips

1 to 2 cups fresh white mushrooms, quartered

6 garlic cloves, minced

Freshly squeezed orange juice or reconstituted from frozen, enough to cover, approximately 4 cups.

2½ pounds fresh white fish, such as orange roughy, halibut, rock cod, or snapper, cut into serving-size pieces

3 green onions, sliced diagonally

¼ bunch cilantro, chopped

2 jalapeño or serrano peppers, seeded and finely minced

Orange slices, for garnish

Heat the oil and butter in a large sauté pan big enough to hold all of the ingredients. Sauté the red onions, bell peppers, mushrooms, and garlic until cooked yet crisp. They will cook more when you poach the fish. Add the orange juice, fish, green onions, cilantro, and jalapeños. Poach until the fish flakes, turning the pieces once during cooking. Remove from the heat as soon as done. Garnish with the orange slices and serve immediately.

MAKES 6 SERVINGS

BAKED COD WITH
basil and parmesan

The fish stays moist in its crisp crust of flavorful Parmesan cheese, basil, and garlic. We usually make this with rockfish, lingcod, or sea bass.

- ½ lemon, peeled and seeded
- ½ cup olive oil
- 2 large garlic cloves, pressed
- 3 tablespoons fresh basil, finely chopped or 1 tablespoon dried
- 2 cups breadcrumbs
- ⅓ cup freshly grated Parmesan cheese
- Generous pinch of black pepper
- Salt
- 2 pounds fish fillets
- ¼ cup Dijon-style mustard, approximately

Preheat the oven to 400°F. Purée the lemon in a blender with the oil. Pour the lemon mixture into a heated skillet and let cook for a minute. Then add the garlic and basil and continue sautéeing until aromatic, for another minute or so. Stir in the breadcrumbs and mix until they are well coated with oil. Continue sautéeing them, stirring often, until they are dry. Remove the mixture to a bowl and stir in the cheese and pepper. Taste and add salt if needed.

Wash and dry the fish fillets. Cut them into serving-size pieces. Lightly brush each piece with the mustard and then roll the fish in the seasoned breadcrumbs. Place each piece in an oiled baking pan. If you have some crumb mixture left, you can spoon a little extra on the top if needed. Bake for 20 to 25 minutes or until the fish turns white and flakes easily with a fork. If the fillets are thick, it could take as long as 30 minutes.

MAKES 5 TO 6 SERVINGS

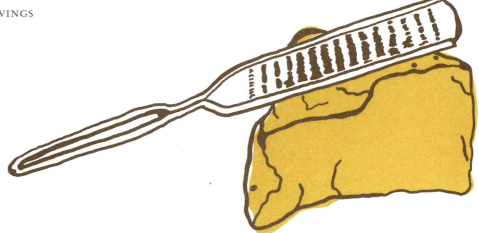

GRILLED SALMON WITH
italian salsa verde

This is a simple preparation for salmon. In the summer, we usually grill the salmon, but it can also quickly be seared on each side on the stovetop and then finished with three to five minutes in a 450°F oven.

> 2 tablespoons light olive oil
> Zest and juice of one lemon
> 6 fresh salmon steaks or pieces of fillet
> Salt and freshly ground black pepper
> 1 cup salsa verde (page 189)

At least one hour before grilling, put the oil in a non-reactive 9 by 13-inch pan. Sprinkle the zest of the lemon over the oil and add the juice. Place each steak in the marinade, sprinkle with salt and pepper, and turn over. Salt and pepper the other side that is now facing up. Cover and refrigerate until ready to grill.

Heat the grill and cook the fillets, turning once until done. The amount of time will depend on how hot the grill is. When the salmon is done, remove to plates or a platter and put a dollop of salsa verde on top of each one.

MAKES 6 SERVINGS

fish stew WITH GARLIC ROUILLE

This is a vibrant fish stew, spiked with a garlic rouille. It comes together faster than it might look at first glance. Use a non-oily, firm white fish such as cod, lingcod, halibut, sea bass, monkfish, catfish, or snapper. Variety will add to the flavor of the stew. Make sure you look over the ingredients for the fish stock recipe before going shopping because you will need fish for that too. The stock can be made ahead and even freezes well, thus making this a quick and easy meal to prepare.

Soup Base:
2 tablespoons olive oil
2 onions, sliced
8 large garlic cloves, roughly chopped
3 cups chopped fresh tomatoes or 2 cups canned plum tomatoes
½ teaspoon dried thyme
¼ teaspoon fennel seed
2 pinches saffron threads
1 two-inch piece of fresh orange peel
½ teaspoon black peppercorns
1 six-inch doubled piece of cheesecloth
2 quarts fish stock (page 68)
½ teaspoon salt, depending on how salty your stock is

Rouille:
6 large garlic cloves, minced and mashed to a paste
¼ teaspoon salt
⅓ cup roasted red bell pepper, skinned and seeded or canned roasted red bell pepper
½ cup fresh basil, approximately 12 large leaves
¼ cup soup base
¾ cup bread crumbs
3 egg yolks
¾ to 1 cup olive oil
Pinch of cayenne

Stew:
2 to 2½ pounds white fish, deboned and cut into 2-inch chunks
3 quarts soup base

Garnish:
1 cup Italian parsley, chopped
4 cups croutons

fish and shellfish

To make the soup base: Heat the oil in a stockpot. Over medium heat, sauté the onions until soft and translucent. Add the garlic and sauté until tender. Do not burn or brown. Add the tomatoes and simmer for 5 minutes. Put the thyme, fennel seed, saffron, orange peel, and pepper into the cheesecloth and tie into a bag. Add this to the pot along with the stock. Simmer slowly for 45 minutes uncovered. It can simmer a bit longer if you aren't ready to proceed, but you should partially cover the pot and make sure the heat is low. Before using, remove the cheesecloth bag with the herbs and spices. Taste and add salt if needed.

To make the rouille: Place the garlic in a blender with the salt, the roasted red bell pepper, and the basil and blend to a paste. Add the hot stock, bread crumbs, and egg yolks and blend until sticky and smooth. Add the oil in a slow stream until all is incorporated and the rouille is the consistency of mayonnaise. Taste and add cayenne pepper if desired. Scrape the rouille into a serving bowl. Cover and refrigerate until just before serving.

Prepare the fish and chop the parsley. Heat up the soup base until steamy and hot. Fold in the chunks of fish, bring back to a simmer, and cook for 2 to 3 minutes or just until the fish turns opaque rather than translucent. Do not overcook!

Serve the stew in shallow soup bowls, as the fish sinks to the bottom. Garnish with a dollop of the rouille, freshly chopped parsley, and croutons. Serve extra rouille and croutons on the side.

MAKES 10 TO 12 SERVINGS

FISH KABOBS WITH *citrus marinade*

The citrus marinade keeps the fish moist and punches up the flavor. We like to serve the kabobs with rice, a cabbage slaw, a drizzle of Chipotle Red Chile Cream and the Tropical Fruit Salsa on the side. These kabobs also make great fish tacos.

Marinade:
Zest of 1 lime, 1 orange, and 1 lemon
2 tablespoons each of lime, orange, and lemon juice
1 cup cilantro, chopped
¼ cup vegetable oil
6 garlic cloves, pressed or minced
2 teaspoons tamari or soy sauce
½ teaspoon ground cumin
1 teaspoon sugar
2 teaspoons salt
3 pinches freshly ground black pepper
2 jalapeños, seeded and finely minced

2 pounds firm-fleshed fish such as halibut, swordfish, shark, mahi mahi, or seabass
1 recipe Tropical Fruit Salsa, page 193
1 recipe Chipotle Red Chile Cream, page 188
1 small green cabbage, finely shredded, approximately 6 cups
½ red bell pepper, diced into ¼-inch pieces
2 tablespoons lime juice
2 tablespoons seasoned rice vinegar
12 to 14 wooden skewers, soaked in water for approximately 45 minutes

Mix the marinade ingredients together and place in a glass bowl. Cut the fish into 1¼-inch chunks and place in the marinade, tossing to immerse all sides of the fish. Cover and marinate for at least 15 minutes or up to 2 hours.

Make the Tropical Fruit Salsa and the Chipotle Red Chile Cream. Set aside.

Shred the cabbage and dice the red bell pepper. Toss with the lime juice and vinegar. Taste and adjust seasonings. Set aside.

Turn on the grill and thread the fish on the skewers. Grill, turning once, until the fish is done, approximately 6 minutes. Remove the fish from the skewers and serve on a bed of the cabbage, with Tropical Fruit Salsa on the side and a drizzle of Chipotle Red Chile Cream.

MAKES 12 TO 14 SKEWERS; 4 TO 6 SERVINGS

vegetarian main dishes

vegetarian main dishes

It seems that tofu is no longer the terrible "T" word and that, in the last decade, vegetarianism has become mainstream. Vegetables, which in the past were used primarily as side dishes, now take center stage. And there are many reasons why they should. Vegetarian meals can be satisfying and beautiful and contain ample protein. Often the elimination of the dominant meat entrée frees up one's creativity and, as a result, interesting combinations suddenly take place. Meatless dishes can easily provide the central focus and drama that is expected to hold a meal together. Vegetarian meals also offer endless variety, including dishes such as stuffed crêpes or enchiladas, stews, frittatas, hearty salads, gratins, tarts, pastas and pizzas. The recipes that we have included in this section are quite varied and, of course, some of them can serve as side dishes for a meal that includes meat.

cheese and nut LOAF

This recipe, which we adapted from The Greens Cookbook, *is one of our most requested. It is even good cold. You can use white rice instead of brown, but it is not as chewy or flavorful in the loaf. The ingredients should be finely chopped to help the loaf hold together.*

- 1½ cups cooked brown rice (a large ½ cup of raw rice will produce this amount)
- 6 dried shiitake mushrooms
- 1½ cups walnuts
- ½ cup pecans or almonds
- 1 tablespoon salted butter
- 1 tablespoon olive oil
- 1 medium yellow onion, finely chopped
- 2 garlic cloves, finely minced
- ½ cup mushrooms, chopped
- 2 tablespoons fresh parsley, finely chopped
- 1 tablespoon fresh thyme leaves, chopped or ½ teaspoon dried thyme
- 1 tablespoon fresh marjoram, chopped or 1 teaspoon dried marjoram
- 4 eggs
- 1 cup cottage cheese
- 12 ounces (1 quart) coarsely grated cheese (make sure you include some with a bit of sharpness, such as a sharp Cheddar or Gruyère along with a milder Jack, Muenster, etc.)
- Salt and pepper

If you do not have cooked rice available, begin by cooking the rice. Preheat the oven to 350°F. Grease a large, 5 by 9-inch loaf pan. In addition, line it with parchment paper. It is adequate to use just one strip of parchment to line the larger sides and bottom, leaving the ends free. This will help you to turn out the nut loaf, as it tends to stick a little. Grease the parchment.

Boil a cup of water and pour it over the dried mushrooms. Let soak for 20 minutes. Then drain and finely chop, throwing away the tough pieces of stem. Toast the nuts for 7 to 10 minutes in the oven. Remove, cool, and then chop. Set aside.

Sauté the onions in the butter and oil in a medium-sized saucepan until translucent, then add the garlic, the fresh and dried mushrooms, and the herbs. Cook until the liquid released by the mushrooms is almost completely reduced.

In a large bowl, whisk the eggs. Add the cottage cheese, grated cheese, rice, nuts, and the onion and mushroom mixture. Stir to combine. Season to taste with salt and pepper.

Spoon the mixture into the prepared pan and bake until the top is golden brown and rounded, about one hour and 15 minutes. If the top is getting too brown, you can cover it with foil during the last minutes of cooking. The loaf should be firm, so leave it in a little longer if needed. Remove from the oven and let sit 10 minutes before turning it out. Remove the parchment paper and carefully slice.

MAKES 6 TO 8 SERVINGS

WINTER *curry*

This yellow curry is a wonderful way to showcase the beauty of fall and winter vegetables as well as warm your body with invigorating Indian spices. The curry is delicious served over a bed of hot, steaming basmati rice with our Red Tomato Chutney (page 182), chopped peanuts, and a drizzle of crème fraîche or yogurt.

- 2 teaspoons yellow mustard seed
- 2 teaspoons cumin seed
- 2 teaspoons coriander seed
- 1 teaspoon fenugreek seed
- ½ teaspoon ground turmeric
- ¼ teaspoon cayenne pepper plus more to season (optional)
- 1 pound fresh tomatoes, seeded and chopped, approximately 2 cups, or canned and diced tomatoes, with their juice
- 1½ cups water
- 1 teaspoon salt plus ¼ teaspoon
- 3 tablespoons fresh ginger, peeled and grated
- 1 stalk broccoli, separated into approximately 2 cups florets
- 1 tablespoon vegetable oil
- 1 medium yellow onion, cut in a ½-inch dice, approximately 2 cups
- 4 garlic cloves, finely minced
- 2 carrots, peeled and sliced on the diagonal, 2-inches thick, approximately 2 cups
- 1 pound potatoes, cut into 1-inch cubes, approximately 4 cups
- 1 medium fennel bulb, trimmed and cut into 1-inch pieces
- One 13.5-ounce can coconut milk
- 1 small (or ½ large) red bell pepper, seeded and thinly sliced into strips
- Salt and freshly ground black pepper to season
- 2 tablespoons cilantro, chopped

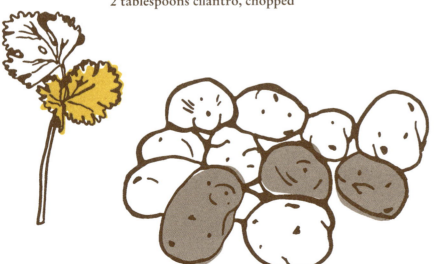

vegetarian main dishes . PAGE 138

In a small pan, over medium heat, toast the mustard seed until fragrant. Set aside.

In the same pan, toast the cumin and coriander seeds for a few minutes, until aromatic. Be very careful not to burn the spices, taking care to shake pan frequently while toasting. Combine the cumin and the coriander with the fenugreek and grind together in a spice grinder or with a mortar and pestle. Add the turmeric and cayenne to the spice mixture and set aside.

In a saucepan, combine the tomatoes, water, 1 teaspoon salt, spice mixture, mustard seed, and the ginger. Simmer uncovered, over low heat, for 15 to 20 minutes while sautéing the vegetables.

Bring a pot of water to boil, add ¼ teaspoon salt, and blanch the broccoli for about 1 minute or until al dente and bright green. Rinse with cold water, drain, and set aside.

Heat a large sauté pan over medium heat. Add the oil and heat. Then add the onions and sauté for about 5 minutes or until soft and translucent. Add the garlic, carrots, potatoes, and fennel and cook for approximately 10 minutes.

Add the tomato mixture and the coconut milk; simmer uncovered, over low heat, for about 30 minutes. Gently stir in the broccoli and bell peppers and cook for another 3 minutes, until heated through. Season with salt, cayenne, and freshly ground pepper to taste. Sprinkle with the cilantro just before serving.

MAKES 6 SERVINGS

vegetarian main dishes. PAGE 139

spanakopita

This one-pan meal is a traditional Greek dish. It keeps well and takes about one hour to assemble and then another hour or so to cook.

Filling:
- Two 10-ounce packages frozen, chopped spinach, thawed or 2 pounds fresh spinach
- 3 tablespoons olive oil
- 1 large yellow onion, finely chopped
- ½ pound fresh mushrooms, sliced
- 2 garlic cloves, minced
- Salt and pepper to taste
- 6 eggs
- ½ pound feta cheese, crumbled
- ½ cup Parmigiano-Reggiano cheese, grated
- ½ cup Italian parsley, chopped
- 2 teaspoons fresh oregano, minced

Filo:
- ¼ pound salted butter, melted
- ½ cup olive oil
- 1 pound filo dough, thawed

Preheat the oven to 350°F. Place the thawed spinach in a colander and squeeze the water out with your hands to remove any excess liquid. If you are using fresh spinach, steam it briefly to wilt, allow it to cool, then place in a colander and squeeze out the excess liquid. Heat a large sauté pan over medium heat. Add 3 tablespoons of the oil and the onions and cook until soft and translucent. Add the mushrooms and garlic and cook for about 15 minutes, or until most of the liquid has evaporated and the mushrooms are lightly browned. Season with salt and pepper to taste. Set aside to cool.

Whisk the eggs together in a large bowl. Then stir in the cheeses, spinach, cooled onion mixture, parsley, and oregano.

Blend the melted butter with the remaining oil and brush a thin layer onto a 10 by 15-inch glass baking dish. Gently unroll the filo dough on a dry work surface. Cover the filo with a dry towel and then cover the dry towel with a damp towel, so the filo dough will not dry out. Gently lay one sheet of filo dough in and up the sides of the pan and brush with the butter mixture. Repeat with 9 more layers, lightly brushing each one with the butter mixture, up and over the sides.

Spread the spinach mixture evenly over the layered dough. Fold the edges of dough over the spinach and layer 10 more sheets of dough, brushing each successive layer with the butter and oil. Tuck in the sides of the overhanging dough and cut into square or triangular pieces. Precutting the spanakopita helps keep the filo from shattering after it is baked. Be careful not to cut through to the bottom or the filling will leak out. Bake for 60 to 75 minutes or until golden, crispy, and slightly puffed. Let sit for 10 minutes before cutting pieces all the way to the bottom and then serve.

MAKES 10 TO 12 SERVINGS

chilaquile casserole

Where did we ever find this recipe? We have been making it for more than 15 years and it is still a big favorite of staff and guests alike. We like to serve it with black beans and a green salad, sliced tomatoes when in season, fresh salsa, and guacamole. It is a good way to use up slightly stale tortillas and, of course, the ever present zucchini.

12 corn tortillas
2 tablespoons olive or vegetable oil
1 yellow onion, diced
1 green, yellow, or red bell pepper, diced
1½ cups diced zucchini, approximately 2 squashes
3 garlic cloves, minced
Salt and pepper
¼ cup chopped cilantro
½ teaspoon toasted cumin seed, ground
1 cup diced green chiles, canned
2 cups grated Monterey Jack cheese or Muenster or mozzarella
4 large eggs
2 cups buttermilk

Preheat oven to 375°F. Grease a 9 by 13-inch glass pan or the equivalent. Tear or cut the tortillas into pieces. This is easily done by cutting them as a stack into 8 triangles. Spread half of the tortilla pieces evenly onto the greased pan.

Heat the oil in a large skillet and sauté the onions until soft. Add the bell peppers, zucchini, and garlic and sauté just a few minutes, until almost cooked but not soft. Add the spices and the chiles to the vegetables.

Spread the vegetable mixture and the grated cheese over the tortillas, then arrange the remaining tortillas on top. Beat the eggs and the buttermilk until well blended and slowly pour over the top of the casserole. Bake for approximately 1 hour, until set and nicely puffed and browned on top.

MAKES 8 TO 10 SERVINGS

pizza dough

This pizza dough is quite versatile. It can be used for its original purpose or it can be rolled out for bread sticks, folded over for calzones, or disguised as naan bread at an Indian meal. If you have extra dough, it can be refrigerated for use the next day or frozen before the first rise for another day. Simply oil and place it in a ziplock bag and freeze for up to a month. To use, thaw by pulling from the freezer and leaving overnight in the refrigerator. Remove from the refrigerator about one-half hour before rolling out and baking. When making lots of pizza for big crowds, we keep the dough from over-rising by placing the already rolled out dough in the refrigerator on sheet pans until we are ready to add the toppings and bake. We have also included instructions for mixing the dough in a food processor.

1⅓ cups lukewarm water
½ teaspoon honey or sugar
1 tablespoon active dry baking yeast
¼ cup olive oil
2 teaspoons salt
4 cups unbleached flour plus more as needed

To make the dough by hand or with a stand mixer: Combine the water, honey or sugar, and yeast in a medium-sized mixing bowl or the bowl of a stand mixer fitted with a dough hook. Let it sit for 10 minutes or until the yeast is active. Add the oil and salt. Stirring with a wooden spoon or on the low setting of the mixer, slowly incorporate the flour, ½ cup at a time, until it is too difficult to stir or mix. The dough will be pulling away from the sides of the bowl. For hand-mixing, turn the dough out onto a flat surface that has been sprinkled with flour. Knead the dough for about 8 minutes, lightly dusting the dough with flour only as needed to prevent the dough from sticking. Knead until a soft, shiny, elastic ball of dough has formed. For finishing in the mixer, continue to add the flour ¼ cup at a time at first, and then by the tablespoon, until the dough is a shiny, smooth, and elastic ball. This will take about 8 to 10 minutes. Transfer the dough to a clean, oiled bowl, cover with plastic wrap or a damp dishtowel, and allow it to rise for 1 hour or until doubled in size.

To make the dough in a food processor: Add the yeast and the sugar to the water in a bowl or a glass measuring cup. Let it sit 10 minutes until active. Meanwhile, in a food processor fitted with a metal blade, pulse the flour and salt together. Add the oil to the yeast mixture and then, with the machine running, pour in the liquids and process until the mixture forms a soft dough. Scrape the dough out of the processor and onto a lightly floured surface. Briefly knead the dough until it is a shiny, smooth, and elastic ball, adding only as much flour as needed. Transfer the dough to a clean, oiled bowl, cover with plastic wrap, and allow to rise for 1 hour or until doubled in size.

Garlic-Olive Oil:

We like to brush our rolled pizza dough with a mixture of garlic and olive oil. So we have this mixture on hand as we are forming and topping the pizza.

> **Garlic-Olive Oil:**
> **¼ cup olive oil**
> **2 garlic cloves, minced**

Baking the Pizza:

Preheat the oven to 450°F. You are now ready to roll. Punch down the dough, cut into 2 to 4 pieces, and shape into balls. Let rest for 5 to 10 minutes. On a lightly floured surface, roll out the dough into 9- or 14-inch rounds, ¼-inch or slightly less thick. Place on a pizza stone, an oiled baking sheet, or on a baking sheet lined with parchment and sprinkled with polenta. Brush with the olive oil mixture. Add your toppings of choice to the dough and bake for about 15 minutes. To get the bottoms crisp, rotate your pizzas by placing the first one on the lowest rack for 5 to 10 minutes and then on the top rack while the next pizza is started on the bottom rack. We often leave the pizza on the actual floor of the oven without a rack for a few minutes. Watch carefully!

MAKES TWO 14-INCH CRUSTS OR FOUR 9- TO 10-INCH CRUSTS

ROASTED EGGPLANT, RED BELL PEPPER, RED ONION, FONTINA, & ROSEMARY *pizza*

MAKES 12 TO 15 SERVINGS

There are no rules with pizza. It's fun to experiment and see what kind of unusual pizzas you can put together. The combinations are endless. This is one of our favorites.

- 1 medium-sized eggplant, cubed, salted, and drained, approximately 4 cups
- ¼ cup olive oil
- 2 red bell peppers, roasted, seeded and sliced (page 97}
- 1 recipe pizza dough, rolled out and ready to "top" (page 142)
- Garlic-infused olive oil (page 143), for brushing on
- 1 sprig fresh rosemary, leaves only, minced
- 2 cups tomato sauce (page 187)
- 6 ounces fontina cheese, grated
- 1 large red onion, thinly sliced
- 3 ounces Parmigiano-Reggiano cheese, freshly grated

Preheat the oven to 400°F. Coat the eggplant with ¼ cup of the olive oil. Place on a baking sheet lined with parchment paper and bake until softened. Set aside. Prepare the bell peppers and set aside.

Turn oven up to 450°F. Brush the entire pizza dough, out to the edge, with the garlic oil. Sprinkle on the rosemary. Spread on the sauce and then layer with fontina, eggplant, bell peppers, red onion, and Parmigiano-Reggiano. Bake in the oven until the crust is brown and the cheese is bubbly, about 10 to 12 minutes.

MAKES TWO 12- TO 14-INCH PIZZAS

vegetarian main dishes . PAGE 144

greek-style pizza
WITH SPINACH, FETA, AND OREGANO

There are purists who refuse to touch Greek Pizza but we love the combination of flavors. It works well with or without tomato sauce, just make sure the spinach is well drained.

- 2 tablespoons olive oil
- 1 red or yellow onion, thinly sliced
- 4 garlic cloves, finely minced
- 1 pound washed and trimmed spinach, approximately 8 cups
- 1 teaspoon lemon zest (optional)
- 1 tablespoon chopped fresh oregano or 1 teaspoon fresh rosemary leaves, chopped
- Salt and pepper
- ½ recipe pizza dough (page 142)
- Garlic-infused olive oil (page 143)
- 1½ cups tomato sauce (page 187)
- 1 cup crumbled feta cheese, approximately 3 ounces
- 2 cups grated mozzarella cheese, approximately ½ pound
- ¼ cup grated Parmesan cheese

Preheat the oven to 450°F. Heat a heavy-bottomed skillet and add the oil and the onion. Sauté the onion until it is translucent and starting to turn golden, about 10 minutes. Add the garlic and sauté another minute being careful not to burn. Add the spinach and wilt for a minute, just until reduced in volume but still green. Remove from the pan and place in a colander to drain. Press out the excess moisture and toss with the lemon zest, herbs, and salt and pepper to taste. Set aside.

While the spinach is draining, roll out the dough and place it on a pizza stone, an oiled baking sheet, or a baking sheet lined with parchment paper and sprinkled with polenta. Brush the dough with the garlic-infused olive oil. Assemble the pizza by spreading on the sauce, leaving a ½-inch edge free of sauce around the outside. Spread the spinach mixture on top, then the feta, then the mozzarella, and finally the Parmesan. Bake the pizza for about 15 minutes, or until the bottom is browned and crisp and the cheese is bubbling and golden.

MAKES ONE LARGE 14-INCH OR TWO SMALL 9-INCH PIZZAS

pizza with caramelized onion, smoked chicken, and gorgonzola

White pizzas, which are actually more common in Italy than here in the United States, are made without a red sauce. This white pizza is delicious. For a vegetarian version, we substitute lightly toasted walnuts in place of the chicken. We often vary this recipe by adding roasted red bell pepper.

- 1 tablespoon olive oil
- 2 medium red or yellow onions, thinly sliced
- 1 garlic clove, minced, approximately 1 teaspoon
- Salt and pepper
- ½ recipe pizza dough (page 142)
- Garlic-infused olive oil (page 143)
- 1½ to 2 cups smoked chicken, shredded or ½ cup toasted walnut pieces, coarsely chopped
- 3 ounces Gorgonzola cheese, crumbled, approximately 1 cup
- 4 ounces mozzarella cheese, grated, approximately 1½ cups
- ½ ounce Parmesan cheese, grated, approximately 3 tablespoons

Heat the oil in a large sauté pan. Add the onions, a sprinkle of salt, and a few pinches of pepper. Sauté slowly over medium heat, stirring frequently, until the onions are caramelized and golden brown, about 30 minutes. Add the garlic and sauté for about 3 minutes, being careful not to let the garlic burn.

Preheat the oven to 450°F. Roll out the dough and place on the prepared pan. Brush the dough with the garlic-infused oil. Spread the caramelized onion mixture on the dough and then sprinkle on the chicken or the walnuts. Then sprinkle over the Gorgonzola, the mozzarella, and the Parmesan. Bake the pizza for about 15 minutes or until the crust is golden and crisp.

MAKES ONE LARGE 14-INCH PIZZA OR TWO SMALL 9-INCH PIZZAS

SHIITAKE MUSHROOM *ragoût*

This goes well with mashed potatoes or soft polenta (page 172). If fresh shiitake mushrooms are not available, substitute another wild mushroom or simply use more domestic, white mushrooms.

- 4 dry shiitake mushrooms
- 3 tablespoons olive oil
- 1 large onion, finely chopped, approximately 2 cups
- 4 garlic cloves, minced
- 1 teaspoon chopped fresh rosemary or ½ teaspoon dried rosemary
- 1 pound domestic or cremini mushrooms, thinly sliced
- ½ pound fresh shiitake mushrooms, thinly sliced
- 1 tablespoon tomato paste
- 1 cup dry red wine
- 1 tablespoon cornstarch
- 1⅓ cups cold beef broth, vegetable stock, or water
- 2 teaspoons Worcestershire sauce
- Salt
- Freshly ground black pepper

Pour a small amount of boiling water over the dried mushrooms and set aside to soak. After twenty minutes, drain them and save the liquid for part of the stock. Remove the tough stems and finely chop the mushrooms. Set the mushrooms aside until needed and add the liquid to the stock.

Heat the oil in a large skillet and sauté the onion, garlic, and rosemary over medium heat until the onion is translucent and softened. Add the fresh mushrooms and a sprinkling of salt and cook, stirring, for about 10 minutes or until most of the mushroom liquid has evaporated. Stir in the reconstituted dried mushrooms, the tomato paste, and the wine and simmer until most of the liquid is evaporated.

In a small bowl, whisk the cornstarch into the broth, stock, or water. When dissolved, add this and the Worcestershire sauce to the onion and mushroom mixture and bring all to a boil, stirring. Simmer this ragoût for 2 to 4 minutes and season with salt and pepper to taste.

MAKES 5½ CUPS; 4 TO 6 SERVINGS

BAKED *polenta* LAYERED WITH SPINACH, MUSHROOMS, FONTINA, AND GORGONZOLA

Tender, golden polenta oozing with nutty cheese and earthy mushrooms. This is almost a complete meal in itself. All you need is a salad and a bottle of wine. It is helpful to make the polenta early in the day so that it has time to cool and become firm.

Polenta:
4½ cups water
1½ teaspoons salt
1½ cups polenta

Filling and Garnish:
2 tablespoons olive oil
Salt and freshly ground black pepper
½ pound chanterelle, porcini or domestic mushrooms, approximately 2½ cups, sliced
4 cups fresh spinach, chopped into 3-inch pieces, briefly sautéed just to wilt, drained
2 to 3 cups tomato sauce (page 187)
½ pound fontina cheese, sliced
5 ounces Gorgonzola cheese, crumbled
Italian parsley, coarsely chopped, approximately 2 tablespoons
Basil, coarsely chopped, approximately 2 tablespoons

Place the water in a large saucepan with the salt. Bring to a boil and slowly add the polenta with a whisk to keep lumps from forming. Lower the heat and let it cook for about 15 to 20 minutes, stirring often with a wooden spoon. Pour into a 9 by 13-inch Pyrex pan. Cover and refrigerate until cool and firm, at least 1 hour. When the polenta is firm, turn it out onto a cutting board. It will slide out easily if you just turn the pan upside down. With a long knife, cut the polenta into ⅜-inch-wide strips and set aside until assembly.

Meanwhile, heat the oil in a sauté pan. Add the mushrooms and a sprinkle of salt and pepper and sauté until they are beginning to brown. Remove them from the pan and set aside. Add the spinach to the same pan and sauté briefly, just enough to wilt. Drain off any extra liquid and set aside.

Preheat the oven to 400°F. Spoon a thin layer of tomato sauce on the bottom of the 9 by 13-inch pan. Place one-half of the polenta slices flat on top of the sauce. Place a layer of the mushrooms, the spinach, and then the sliced fontina on top of the polenta. Place the remaining layer of polenta on top of the cheese, spoon sauce over the top layer, and bake in the oven, uncovered, for approximately 20 minutes. Remove from the oven and sprinkle on the crumbled Gorgonzola. Bake for another 10 to 15 minutes or until lightly browned and bubbly. Let cool about 5 minutes. Before serving, sprinkle the polenta with the freshly chopped herbs.

MAKES 4 TO 6 SERVINGS

VEGETABLE *egg foo yong*

For people who are emphasizing protein and vegetables in their diet, this is a good choice. We make these with lots of vegetables. With the exception of the sprouts, the vegetables need to be finely chopped to ensure that the pancake doesn't fall apart. If the mixture is difficult to hold together when you flip the pancake, add an additional egg or make your "foo" a little smaller. These are good any time of the day and are even delicious cold.

½ medium yellow onion, finely diced, ¾ cup
5 green onions, finely chopped, ½ to ¾ cup
2 ribs of celery, finely diced, 1½ cups
½ red, yellow or green bell pepper, finely diced, ½ cup
½ pound mung bean sprouts, coarsely chopped, approximately 1 quart
6 eggs
¼ teaspoon freshly ground black pepper
½ teaspoon sea salt
1 tablespoon tamari or soy sauce
6 tablespoons (or as needed) olive or vegetable oil

Egg Foo Yong Sauce:
¾ cup vegetable stock or water
½ teaspoon salt
1 teaspoon tamari or soy sauce
1 tablespoon oyster sauce (optional)
2 teaspoons cornstarch
2 tablespoons cold water

Prepare the vegetables. Crack the eggs into a large bowl, whisk to blend, and add the black pepper, salt, and tamari. Whisk again. Add the chopped vegetables and stir together.

Heat a large, heavy skillet and add 1 tablespoon of the oil. When the oil is hot and a drop of water sizzles and dances when flicked onto the skillet, give the vegetable-egg mixture a stir and pour 1 cup into the middle of the pan. With a wide spatula, push the vegetables into a flat pancake and scrape the egg that flows out the edges back to the side of the pancake. Lift the underside, after 2 to 3 minutes, with the spatula, loosening the pancake and checking if it is brown and ready to be turned. Adjust the heat if needed. When the pancake is nicely browned, flip it over and fry the other side. Remove to a platter in a warm oven and repeat with the rest of the egg mixture. Serve plain or with sauce.

To make the sauce, heat the stock in a small saucepan, then stir in the salt, tamari, and oyster sauce. Blend the cornstarch with the cold water. Stir this into the stock mixture and cook to thicken, for about 2 minutes, stirring occasionally. Spoon the sauce over the egg foo yong.

MAKES FIVE TO SIX 5-INCH PANCAKES

SUMMER PESTO AND TOMATO *lasagna*

This elegant vegetarian dish is bursting with the flavors of summer in Sonoma County. We make this when our garden is bountiful with sweet, heirloom tomatoes and savory basil. Lasagna construction may be quite time-consuming, so the béchamel sauce, pesto, and cheese grating can be done the day before. If fresh basil is unavailable, frozen pesto may be used.

Béchamel Sauce:
5 cups whole milk
¼ cup onion, peeled and chopped
2 bay leaves
4 peppercorns
1 to 2 sprigs fresh thyme
1 sprig parsley
4 tablespoons salted butter
¼ cup plus 1 tablespoon flour
Sea salt and pinch of freshly ground white pepper

Pesto:
4 cups basil leaves, tightly packed
¼ cup walnuts, lightly toasted and rubbed in a towel to remove any bitter skin
4 garlic cloves, coarsely chopped
½ cup Parmigiano-Reggiano cheese, freshly grated
¾ cup olive oil
Sea salt and pinch freshly ground black pepper

Combine the first 6 ingredients in a saucepan and simmer for 20 minutes, over medium to low heat. Pour the infused milk and herbs through a fine-mesh-strainer. Save the milk and discard the herbs. Return to low heat.

In a separate pan, melt the butter over medium to low heat. Whisk in the flour and cook for at least 3 minutes, stirring occasionally, until frothy and starting to turn golden brown. Slowly whisk in the hot milk and cook, stirring, for about 8 to 10 minutes, until the mixture is thick and coats the back of a spoon. Season to taste with salt and pepper. Set aside or refrigerate until time for assembly.

Combine the basil, walnuts, garlic, cheese, and ½ cup of the oil in a food processor or blender and blend until it forms a smooth purée, adding more oil if necessary. The pesto needs to be easy to spread. Season to taste with salt and pepper. You should have approximately 3 cups.

- 18 extra-wide lasagna noodles, cooked until al dente
- 2 cups fontina cheese, grated
- 2 cups vine-ripened tomatoes, skinned, seeded, and chopped or canned Roma tomatoes
- 1 cup Parmigiano-Reggiano cheese, freshly grated
- 1 cup toasted breadcrumbs, from Italian-style bread such as ciabatta or pulgliese, sautéed with a very small quantity of olive oil, over low heat, until lightly toasted

Preheat the oven to 375°F.

To assemble the lasagna: Place a layer of noodles (4 should be enough but it is good to cook a few extra in case they stick or break) in the bottom of a 9 by 13 by 2-inch buttered Pyrex baking dish. Trim the ends of the lasagna noodles to fit the pan if necessary. Ladle one-quarter of the béchamel over the noodles, spreading evenly with a spatula. Dollop one-half of the pesto, in little blobs, over the noodles. Cover with 1 cup of the fontina. Put down another layer of noodles, spread the tomatoes over the noodles, drizzle one-quarter of the béchamel over the tomatoes, and sprinkle with a handful of Parmigiano-Reggiano. Cover with the third layer of noodles. Ladle one-quarter more of the béchamel over the noodles, dollop on the rest of the pesto, sprinkle with the rest of the fontina and lay down the last layer of noodles. Spread the top layer evenly with the last of the béchamel, top with the toasted breadcrumbs, and then, finally, top with a handful of Parmigiano-Reggiano. Bake, uncovered, for 45 minutes to 1 hour, until lightly brown and bubbly.

MAKES 6 TO 8 SERVINGS

TART AND GALETTE *dough*

We use this crunchy dough for tarts, turnovers, and galettes. The fillings that follow will work equally well in whatever form you choose. Remember, the secret to a flaky crust is cold ingredients and a light hand. Once you add the liquids, do not mix too much or the gluten in the flour will overdevelop, resulting in a heavy, tough dough. This dough can be frozen. Take it out at least one hour before using. If you wish to make one large galette, the amounts in the following recipe should be doubled.

> 3 tablespoons sour cream, yogurt or buttermilk
> ⅓ cup ice water
> 1 cup unbleached flour
> ¼ cup cornmeal
> 1 teaspoon sugar
> ½ teaspoon salt
> 7 tablespoons cold unsalted butter, chopped into small cubes

To make the dough by hand: Stir the sour cream and water together in a small bowl and set aside. Put the flour, cornmeal, sugar, and salt into a large bowl and whisk together. Add the butter to the dry ingredients and, with a pastry blender, work the butter into the flour until the pieces of butter are the size of small peas. Sprinkle the cold sour cream mixture over the dough, 1 tablespoon at a time, while stirring with a fork. After all of the sour cream and water have been added, the dough should be moist enough to stick together when pressed. If not, add additional cold water, 1 teaspoon at a time, checking after each addition. With your hands, gather the dough together, form into a disk, and wrap in plastic film. Chill for at least 1 hour.

To make the dough in a food processor: Stir the sour cream and water together in a small bowl and set aside. Put the flour, cornmeal, sugar, and salt into a food processor and pulse a few times to mix the ingredients. Add half of the butter and pulse a few times. Add the remaining butter and pulse until the butter is evenly distributed and the size of small peas. Add the cold sour cream mixture and blend with short pulses, until the dough starts to stick together and pull away from the sides of the bowl. Immediately turn the pastry out into a bowl or a lightly floured work surface and press the dough together. Wrap in plastic film and chill in the refrigerator at least 1 hour.

To roll out the dough: Unroll the dough. If it is too cold to roll out, let it sit for a few minutes at room temperature until it is a bit softer. Lightly flour a work surface and your rolling pin. Roll the dough out with even strokes, turning it over at least once, and sprinkling more flour as needed to prevent sticking. Continue rolling until you get the desired size.

To make tarts: Roll the dough into a large circle, lift onto the tart pan, tuck down the dough along the sides, and then roll the pin over the top of the pan edge to cut off the excess dough. To prebake the tart shell, heat the oven to 400°F and bake approximately 15 minutes, or until the shell is starting to puff and turn golden. Fill the tart and continue according to the recipe you are following.

MAKES ONE 9-INCH OR 10-INCH TART

To make turnovers: Divide the dough into 2 pieces. Roll out each piece into a 10-inch circle. Place the desired filling a little off to one side of the center of the circle of dough. Brush the edges of the turnovers lightly with water, then fold the dough over the filling and press the edges together. Crimp the edges like you would a pie shell and place the turnovers on a baking sheet lined with parchment paper. Brush lightly with an egg wash*. Bake at 400°F for 25 to 30 minutes, until the pastry turns a golden brown.

MAKES 2 LARGE TURNOVERS

To make galettes: Roll out the doubled recipe of dough to 18-inches diameter. Lift onto a baking sheet lined with parchment paper. Arrange the desired filling in the middle of the circle of dough, leaving at least 4 inches free all around the edge. Fold in about one-third of the edge toward the center, pleating as necessary, leaving the middle of the galette open with the filling displayed. Brush the dough with an egg wash* if desired and bake at 400°F for 30 to 35 minutes, until the pastry is golden brown.

MAKES ONE 12-INCH GALETTE; YIELDS 12 TO 16 SLICES

*For the egg wash, combine 1 egg and 2 tablespoons of water.

BUTTERNUT SQUASH *galette*

We make these delicious galettes in the fall and winter when butternut squash is in season and plentiful. Because of the cornmeal in the crust, these travel well and are still good the next day, making them an excellent choice for picnics. Made into tiny galettes, they can be cut into small pieces and make nice appetizers. When we use this filling for turnovers, we cube the squash instead of slicing it and throw in a little thyme while it is roasting.

2 pounds butternut squash, peeled and sliced into ⅜-inch-thick half-moons
Olive oil for brushing plus 1 tablespoon, to sauté
Salt and freshly ground black pepper
1 tablespoon olive oil
1 large red onion, thinly sliced
3 large garlic cloves, minced
2 teaspoons fresh thyme leaves, chopped
1 double-recipe galette dough (page 152)
1½ cups grated Gruyère cheese
½ cup grated Parmesan cheese

Preheat the oven to 400°F. Prepare the squash and lay it out on a baking sheet lined with parchment paper. Brush the squash with just a touch of oil and lightly salt and pepper it. Roast the squash in the oven for approximately 20 minutes or until just tender. Remove and cool.

Heat the 1 tablespoon of oil in a sauté pan. Add the onions and sauté over medium to low heat, until the onions are soft and translucent, about 10 minutes. Add the garlic and thyme and cook for another few minutes. Remove from the heat and cool.

Roll out the dough to around 18 inches for a large galette, according to the directions on page 153. To assemble, place the dough on a baking sheet lined with parchment paper. Distribute half of the cheese over the middle of the dough circle, leaving about one-third free around the edge, which you will be folding inward over the filling. Then place half of the onion mixture on top of the cheese. Next arrange all the squash on top of the cheese and onions. Repeat with the remaining onions and then finish with the remaining cheese. Bake the galette at 400°F until golden brown, approximately 30 to 35 minutes.

MAKES ONE LARGE 12-INCH GALETTE

CHEESE AND TOMATO *galette*

Here's the perfect picnic food. The cornmeal pastry will stay crunchy and crisp at room temperature, even if the galette is made a day ahead. Gruyère cheese is a nice substitute for one or both of the cheeses, if you prefer. We like to pre-roast the tomatoes to deepen the flavor and to evaporate off some of the extra juice. If you skip this step, you will need to squeeze out the extra juice.

4 to 5 medium to large tomatoes, sliced ¼-inch thick
¼ teaspoon salt
2 pinches of freshly ground black pepper
1 double-recipe galette dough (page 152)
4 ounces of Monterey Jack cheese, shredded, approximately 1 cup
4 ounces of mozzarella cheese, shredded, approximately 1 cup
1 tablespoon flour
¼ cup fresh basil, chiffonade

Preheat the oven to 425°F. Place the tomatoes on a baking sheet lined with parchment paper. Sprinkle with salt and a little pepper. Roast in the oven for about 20 minutes, until the tomatoes have lost some of their liquid and show signs of browning. Remove and cool.

Roll out the dough to around 18 inches for a large galette, according to the directions on page 153. Place the dough on a baking sheet lined with parchment paper.

In a bowl, toss together the cheeses, flour, and basil. Reserve ½ cup for the top and strew the remaining mixture over the bottom of the circle of dough, leaving the outer ⅓ edge free to fold inward over the filling. Arrange the tomatoes on top of the cheese mixture. Sprinkle the reserved cheese mixture over the top of the tomatoes. Then fold the uncovered border of dough over the filling, pleating the dough as you go. It can be rustic!

Turn the oven down to 400°F and bake until the galette is golden brown, about 30 to 35 minutes.

MAKES ONE LARGE 12-INCH GALETTE

chard TART

This filling works well for tarts, turnovers, or galettes. White-stemmed chard is fine, or you can give your pastry a shot of color by mixing in yellow and red chard. If you are making a tart, prebake the shell in a 425°F oven for ten to fifteen minutes, just until it is set and lightly golden. You might have to prick the shell as it is baking if bubbles develop.

- 2 tablespoons olive oil
- 1 red onion, finely diced
- 1 pound chard, stems removed and leaves chopped into 1-inch ribbons
- 2 garlic cloves, chopped
- 2 tablespoons chopped fresh basil or 1½ teaspoons dried basil, crumbled
- ¼ teaspoon salt
- ⅛ teaspoon freshly ground black pepper
- Pinch of cayenne pepper
- 3 large eggs, lightly beaten
- ½ cup heavy cream or half-and-half
- 1 cup grated Parmesan cheese
- 1 single-recipe 10-inch, prebaked, tart shell (page 152)

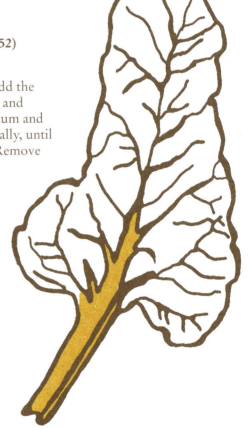

Preheat the oven to 375°F. In a large skillet, heat the oil and add the onions. Sauté over medium to low heat until the onion is soft and translucent, about 10 to 15 minutes. Increase the heat to medium and add the chard and garlic. Continue cooking, stirring occasionally, until the chard is tender. Add the basil, salt, pepper, and cayenne. Remove from the heat and let cool.

In a bowl, combine the eggs, cream, and cheese. Add the chard mixture and stir all together. Then spoon the mixture into the prebaked tart shell. Bake until the filling is golden and firm, about 25 to 35 minutes.

MAKES 1 LARGE 10-INCH TART

side dishes and vegetables

side dishes and vegetables

This section includes side dishes that complement meat or fish entrées. Some of them, such as the Roasted Summer-Vegetable Ragoût or Fiesta Rice, are also adequate as meals in and of themselves. Our rice dishes are usually made with brown or basmati rice. Basmati, a Himalayan variety, is extremely fragrant and flavorful and is especially tasty with Asian and Indian food.

Vegetables are inspiring in their extraordinary variety and versatility. Of course, they are best used in season when they are at the peak of their flavor. Both for health and taste, here at the Ranch we prefer organic produce. We buy as much as possible from local growers, at the farmers' market, and from our local organic grocer. We also have a summer garden at the Ranch for herbs and tomatoes. There is usually no shortage of kiwis or persimmons in the fall.

The freshest vegetables will be those you grow yourself. Even if it is impossible to grow a full garden, consider just a few pots of herbs, such as thyme, sage, basil, and parsley. Often a sprig or a handful is all that is needed, and it is convenient to have fresh herbs just outside the door or on a sun porch.

Roasting vegetables has become popular recently. It is easy, little attention is required, and the process concentrates and intensifies flavors. In addition to winter vegetables, we use the roasting process for tomatoes, green beans, and asparagus.

Vegetable dishes offer opportunities for experimentation and creativity. There is a lot to play with: color, taste, texture, and flavor. This is especially true now as new varieties are becoming available with greater frequency. Growers are bringing back heirlooms and introducing vegetables from other countries. We encourage you to let this abundance add a new dimension to your cooking.

roasted brussels sprouts
WITH SAGE AND SQUASH

This delicious combination of squash and Brussels sprouts is simple to prepare and cooks effortlessly in the oven. It pairs well with chicken, pork, or specialty sausages. We make it with butternut squash, but you can also use a fine-grained orange squash or delicata.

- 2 pounds of butternut squash, peeled and diced into ½-inch cubes, approximately 1 quart
- 1 pound Brussels sprouts, cut in half
- ¼ cup firmly packed brown sugar
- ¼ cup salted butter, melted
- ¼ cup olive oil
- 2 tablespoons chopped, fresh sage
- 1 tablespoon kosher salt
- ½ teaspoon freshly ground black pepper

Preheat the oven to 400°F. Mix all the ingredients together in a large bowl, then spread them out onto a baking sheet. Roast in the oven, turning occasionally, until the sprouts are beginning to brown and the squash is tender when pierced with a fork, about 30 to 45 minutes.

MAKES 6 SERVINGS

ROASTED SUMMER-VEGETABLE *ragoût*

This vegetable stew, often called ratatouille, dates back to 18th-century France. Traditionally, it is cooked slowly, but in our version, the vegetables are roasted separately and then combined for the last 10 minutes to maintain their brightness and character. This dish can be served hot or cold and is lovely served over soft polenta, rice, or pasta. You could experiment with any combination of seasonal vegetables in this recipe. Asparagus and fennel bulb are delicious additions in the springtime. This dish keeps well and can be made a day ahead.

2 medium eggplants (1½ pounds), cut into 1-inch cubes, approximately 2 quarts
Salt
Olive oil
1½ pounds tomatoes, approximately 4 medium tomatoes, yielding 2 cups after prepping
2 each red or yellow bell peppers, seeded and cut into 1-inch squares, yielding 3 cups
1½ pounds zucchini, cut into 1-inch cubes or half-moons, yielding 6 cups
1 large yellow onion cut into ½-inch pieces, approximately 2 cups
1½ tablespoons coarsely chopped garlic
1 tablespoon fresh oregano, chopped
¼ cup fresh basil, chiffonade
1 teaspoon fresh thyme, minced
Pepper
Pinch of red pepper flakes
Splash of balsamic vinegar (optional)

Preheat the oven to 450°F. Place the cubed eggplant in a bowl, salt liberally, and let it sit for about 15 minutes. Place in a colander to drain. Gently push on the eggplant to remove excess moisture and pat dry with a paper towel. Coat the eggplant lightly with oil and place on a baking sheet lined with parchment paper.

Meanwhile, place the whole tomatoes on a separate baking sheet lined with parchment paper. Toss the zucchini and the peppers with a bit of the oil and a sprinkling of salt and place on the baking sheet with the tomatoes.

Put all of these vegetables into the oven and roast for 15 minutes. Then, pull out the tomatoes and place in a bowl to cool. Turn the remaining vegetables with a spatula and return to the oven for a bit of further browning, 5 or 10 minutes longer. Remove the eggplant, zucchini, and bell peppers from the oven and set aside.

When the tomatoes are cool enough to handle, cut out the stems and pull off the skin, saving all the juice in the bowl. Cut the tomatoes into quarters and leave in the bowl.

Heat a large sauté pan over medium heat; add the olive oil and the onions and sauté until translucent and beginning to brown, about 3 to 4 minutes. Add the garlic, oregano, basil, thyme, and pepper flakes and sauté for 1 minute, stirring. Add the eggplant, zucchini, peppers, and tomatoes to the onions and cook over medium heat for about 10 minutes, to combine the flavors. Add a few grindings of black pepper. Do not let all the tomato juice cook off.

Check for seasoning, adding salt and pepper if needed. Add a tiny splash of balsamic vinegar if you wish to sharpen the flavor. Stir and serve.

MAKES 8 TO 10 SERVINGS

MAPLE-GLAZED *carrots*

You must use real maple syrup for this recipe. We serve these carrots with pork tenderloin, pork chops, or roast chicken.

> 1½ pounds carrots, approximately 8
> 2 tablespoons unsalted butter
> 1½ tablespoons pure maple syrup
> 1 teaspoon kosher salt

Peel and cut the carrots on the diagonal into 1½-inch pieces. Try to keep the pieces similar in size so they cook uniformly. Put the carrots into a sauté pan large enough that they are close to a single layer. Add enough water to come halfway up the sides of the carrots. Add the butter, maple syrup, and salt and bring to a boil over high heat. Cover the pan, but with the lid off a bit to let some of the steam out, and reduce the heat to medium. Shaking the pan occasionally, simmer the carrots until they are tender but not soft, about 10 minutes. There should be a slight resistance to a paring knife inserted into a carrot. Uncover the pan and continue to boil until the liquid evaporates and forms a syrup, and the carrots start to caramelize and become slightly brown. Roll the carrots around to evenly glaze them. Taste and add more salt if needed.

MAKES 4 TO 6 SERVINGS

HERB-BAKED TOMATOES *provençal*

Use fully ripe, heirloom tomatoes for the best flavor. These are attractive on a platter and may be prepared ahead of time.

> 4 medium, firm, ripe tomatoes
> 2 garlic cloves, finely minced, approximately 2 teaspoons
> 1 cup Italian parsley, approximately ⅓ cup chopped
> 3 tablespoons basil, chopped
> ¾ cup breadcrumbs made from day-old ciabatta or firm white bread
> Salt and freshly ground black pepper
> Olive oil, to drizzle

Preheat the oven to 400°F. Lightly oil a gratin dish. Cut the tomatoes in half and gently remove the seeds with your fingers or a teaspoon. Mix together the garlic, parsley, and basil. Combine this with the breadcrumbs and season to taste with salt and pepper. Fill the tomato halves with this mixture, set them in the gratin dish, and drizzle a small bit of oil over the top. Bake for 30 minutes. The tomatoes will be soft, so use a spatula to carefully remove them from the baking dish.

MAKES 4 TO 8 SERVINGS

CHINESE-STYLE *broccoli* WITH OYSTER SAUCE

Oyster sauce is a concentrate of oysters cooked in soy sauce and brine. It is used as a seasoning and also to make sauces smooth, rich, and velvety. It is easy to find in the Asian section of supermarkets. Steaming the broccoli retains its color and appearance and makes for an attractive presentation. If you would like a vegetarian version, substitute vegetable stock for the chicken stock and use hoisin sauce in place of the oyster sauce. This recipe is best done just before serving.

> 1 pound broccoli crowns, cut into small florets
> 1 tablespoon vegetable oil
> 3 garlic cloves, finely minced
> 1 tablespoon peeled and minced fresh ginger
> ¼ teaspoon red pepper flakes
> ¼ cup chicken stock
> ¼ cup oyster sauce
> 3 to 4 drops toasted sesame seed oil

Steam the broccoli florets until they are done but still retain a slight crunch and their bright green color. Remove from the heat at this point so as not to overcook.

Meanwhile, in a skillet, heat the vegetable oil and add the garlic, ginger, and pepper flakes. Stir-fry for just a few seconds, being very careful not to let the garlic brown. Stir in the stock and the oyster sauce. Cook for 1 minute, stirring.

When the broccoli is done, and just before serving, add it to the skillet with the sauce and stir all together, cooking just enough to heat through. Drizzle a few drops of toasted sesame seed oil over the top and serve.

MAKES 3 TO 4 SERVINGS

side dishes and vegetables . PAGE 164

roasted green beans
WITH SHALLOTS AND HAZELNUTS

If you prepare the ingredients ahead of time, this is an easy last-minute way to cook green beans.

¼ cup coarsely chopped Italian parsley
¼ cup toasted almonds or hazelnuts, coarsely chopped
1 teaspoon lemon zest
1 pound green beans, trimmed
6 medium shallots, minced
3 tablespoons olive oil
1 teaspoon salt
½ teaspoon freshly ground black pepper
5 garlic cloves, coarsely chopped

Preheat the oven to 400°F. Combine the parsley, nuts, and lemon zest in a small bowl and set aside.

Put the green beans and shallots into a bowl and toss with the oil, salt, and pepper. Put this mixture in a thin layer on a sheet pan and roast for about 10 minutes. Take the beans out of the oven, add the garlic, stir, and put back into the oven for another 8 to 10 minutes. Test periodically for doneness, being careful not to overcook. Remove beans from the oven and toss with the parsley, nuts, and lemon zest. Serve immediately.

MAKES 4 SERVINGS

MARINATED VEGETABLES WITH *fresh herbs*

This is a tasty side dish that is great for a party as it can be made ahead and is attractive on a large platter. We often serve it with lasagna, in which case we use oregano and basil in place of the dill and tarragon.

Marinade:
Juice of 1 lemon, approximately 2 tablespoons
½ cup apple cider vinegar
1 garlic clove, pressed
2 teaspoons Dijon-style mustard
½ teaspoon dried or fresh tarragon or
   1 teaspoon dried oregano
½ teaspoon dried marjoram
1 teaspoon chopped fresh dill or
   1 tablespoon chopped fresh basil
Sea salt and freshly ground pepper to taste
1½ cups olive oil
½ sweet red onion, sliced in thin rounds

Vegetables:
1 small cauliflower, broken into small florets
4 red potatoes, cut into 1½-inch cubes
½ red bell pepper, cut into ¼-inch-wide strips
½ green or yellow bell pepper,
   cut into ¼-inch-wide strips

Make the marinade by combining the lemon juice, vinegar, garlic, mustard, herbs, and seasonings. Slowly pour in the oil, whisking to emulsify. Taste and add more salt and pepper or lemon juice if needed. Stir in the sliced onions and set aside.

Prepare the vegetables. Steam the cauliflower and the potatoes until al dente, cooked but with a slight crunch left. Taste one of the potato cubes to make sure they are cooked through. Pour some of the marinade over the potato and cauliflower mixture while they are still warm and then let cool. Add the sliced peppers and a little more marinade just before serving.

MAKES 6 TO 8 SERVINGS

WILTED *greens*

These wholesome greens have a hearty flavor that complements almost any meal, plus they provide a bounty of vitamins and minerals. Keep the greens in separate bowls prior to sautéing, as they cook at different rates. Purchasing prewashed spinach will cut down your prep time.

- 1 tablespoon dried currants
- 1 tablespoon pine nuts, toasted (optional)
- 6 cups kale leaves (2 large bunches)
- 6 cups chard leaves plus stems (2 large bunches)
- 6 cups spinach leaves (2 large bunches)
- 1 tablespoon olive oil
- 1 garlic clove, minced
- ¼ cup water
- Salt and pepper

Cover the currants with a small amount of hot water to plump them and set aside. Lightly toast the pine nuts in a small sauté pan over low heat. Stir them occasionally and remove when slightly toasted, about 3 minutes. Set aside.

Strip the leaves from the kale stalk and discard the fibrous stalk. Layer the leaves and cut into ½-inch ribbons. Wash, drain, and set the kale aside in a bowl.

Cut the stems off the chard and chop them into small pieces, about ¼-inch thick. Wash them well and set aside in small bowl. Layer the chard leaves and cut into ½-inch ribbons. Wash, drain, and set the leaves aside in a bowl, separate from the stems.

If you haven't purchased prewashed spinach, wash the spinach leaves very carefully in fresh water. If using mature, large-leaved spinach, cut it into smaller pieces.

Have everything ready and close at hand, as this dish cooks quickly. Heat a large, wide-bottomed pan or pot with fairly high sides over medium heat. Add the oil, garlic, and a pinch of salt and pepper. Sauté for a minute, then add the water and the chard stems and continue cooking until the stems are just tender.

Add the kale leaves to the pan and, using tongs to toss the greens, sauté for 1 to 2 minutes, until the kale has wilted a bit. (The pot will be overflowing at first as you add the greens, but they will quickly cook down.) Add the chard leaves and a pinch of salt and toss over medium heat for about 3 to 5 minutes, or until the kale and chard have wilted and are just tender to the bite.

Lower the heat and add the spinach and currants. Cook until the spinach is just wilted and still bright green. Season with salt to taste. Serve immediately with the pan juices, scattering the toasted pine nuts over the top.

MAKES 4 TO 6 SERVINGS

CREAMED *swiss chard*

The history of chard has been traced back to the gardens of Babylon. This green has long, flat stalks which taste a little bit like celery, and large, curly, green leaves up top which taste more like spinach. Chard is now available with red or yellow stalks, in addition to the more familiar white. For this recipe, we recommend the white- or yellow-stemmed chard, as the red can bleed into the white sauce. This dish is comfort food at its best. We serve it with potato pancakes (page 171), Braised Sweet and Sour Red Cabbage (page 169), and chicken-apple sausages.

- 2 bunches Swiss chard, approximately 2 pounds
- ¼ cup unsalted butter
- ¼ cup unbleached flour
- 2 cups milk, warmed
- ½ teaspoon kosher salt
- Generous pinch of freshly ground black pepper
- Pinch of ground nutmeg
- 1½ cups shredded Gruyère or Jarlsberg cheese

Preheat the oven to 375°F. Wash and drain the chard. Run a chef's knife down the stem on each side of the leaves until you reach the area where the stem is approximately ¼-inch wide. Discard the larger stem piece and cut the leaves and smaller stems into 1-inch ribbons. You should have about 4 quarts of chard. Place it in a steamer with water and cook until just wilted, about 5 minutes. Set aside to cool. You will now have about 2½ to 3 cups of chard.

Make the white sauce by melting the butter in a heavy saucepan. Before it starts to brown, add the flour with a whisk and cook, stirring occasionally, until frothy and lightly browned, approximately 2 minutes. Add the milk to the flour mixture, whisking to prevent lumps. Cook over low heat, stirring occasionally, until the sauce thickens and coats the back of a spoon, about 3 to 4 minutes. Season with salt, pepper, and nutmeg. Remove from the heat and stir in 1 cup of the cheese, leaving the rest to sprinkle on top before baking.

Drain and squeeze any excess liquid from the chard. Add the chard to the sauce, stirring until thoroughly coated. Pour this mixture into a 7½ by 11¾-inch Pyrex baking dish, sprinkle the top with the remaining cheese, and bake in the oven for 30 to 45 minutes or until brown and bubbly. Let sit a few minutes before serving.

MAKES 4 TO 6 SERVINGS

BRAISED SWEET & SOUR *red cabbage*

This winter vegetable is completely transformed by a fast sauté, followed by a slow, covered simmer. Select cabbages that are heavy for their size and that have bright crisp leaves. We like to pair this dish with a roasted pork loin or chicken sausages and potato pancakes (page 171). For a vegetarian meal, this would work well paired with sautéed portobello mushrooms and mashed potatoes.

1 medium red cabbage
3 tablespoons vegetable oil or salted butter
2 tart apples, peeled and sliced
5 whole cloves
Salt
4 tablespoons apple cider vinegar
2 to 4 tablespoons brown sugar
Freshly ground pepper to taste

Quarter the cabbage and remove the core. Slice the cabbage into thin shreds or ribbons, about ¼-inch thick. Rinse the ribbons with cold water and drain. In a wide, heavy-bottomed pan, heat the oil or butter. Add the cabbage, apples, cloves, and a pinch of salt. Stir to combine and sauté for a few minutes, stirring. Turn the heat down to medium-low. Cover and cook for 20 minutes, or until the cabbage is tender and limp, stirring occasionally. Add the vinegar and sugar and cook for about 10 more minutes. Season to taste with salt and pepper, adding a bit more sugar and vinegar if necessary. Cook for about 5 more minutes to allow the flavors to meld.

MAKES 6 TO 8 SERVINGS

ROASTED *winter vegetables*

We often roast Yukon gold potatoes with nothing more than olive oil, rosemary, salt, and pepper. But delicata squash, rutabaga, or turnips are possibilities, in addition to some of the choices in the following recipe. You can use the procedure below for any combination of vegetables, figuring about 1½ cups of vegetables per person and adjusting the seasonings for that amount. We include the procedure for preparing the beets as they need a special treatment.

- 3 medium carrots, peeled and cut into 2- to 3-inch chunks
- 3 medium red or Yukon gold potatoes, cut into quarters
- 2 large parsnips, cut into 3-inch chunks
- 4 large garlic cloves, coarsely chopped
- Olive oil to coat
- Sea salt and freshly ground black pepper
- Fresh thyme sprigs, approximately 8
- 3 sprigs fresh rosemary
- 6 beets, red or golden, golf-ball size, tops trimmed off

Preheat the oven to 425°F. Combine the carrots, potatoes, parsnips, and 3 cloves of the garlic in a baking dish. It is important not to crowd the vegetables in the pan or they will not brown. Add a splash of oil and toss to coat. Season generously with salt and pepper. Nestle 6 of the thyme sprigs and 2 sprig of the rosemary in the vegetables. Cover with foil.

To prepare the beets, place them in a separate baking dish with a splash of oil, the rest of the garlic, and salt and pepper to taste. Nestle the remaining thyme and rosemary sprigs in the beets and cover with foil.

Place both of the pans in the oven and roast for 20 minutes. Remove from the oven and take off the foil covers. Gently stir the vegetables and return the pans, uncovered, to roast for 20 more minutes, or until tender to the bite. Check each variety at this time and return any that are not done to the oven. When tender, remove from the oven.

When the beets are cool to the touch, gently remove their skins with your fingers. Use gloves if you don't want pink hands. If you cooked red beets, keep them separate until serving, as the juice will turn all of the vegetables red. Strip some of the leaves off the thyme and rosemary sprigs, sprinkle them on the vegetables, and discard the stems. Taste for seasoning, adding salt and pepper if necessary.

Arrange all of the vegetables on a platter and serve.

MAKES 4 TO 6 SERVINGS

POTATO *pancakes*

Use russet or Idaho potatoes for this recipe as they have a high starch-to-moisture ratio. The starch helps the pancake hold together. For a change, try substituting a root vegetable, such as parsnip or celery root, for one-quarter of the potatoes. You could also make tiny, two-inch pancakes, using a one-tablespoon measure, and serve them as appetizers topped with crème fraîche, smoked salmon, and chives. At the Ranch, we serve potato pancakes as a hearty fall or winter dish with chicken or turkey sausages, sweet and sour cabbage, sour cream, applesauce, and freshly baked rye bread.

- ½ cup unbleached flour
- ¼ teaspoon baking powder
- 2 teaspoons salt
- 1 quart packed, grated potato (2 pounds) approximately 8 medium or 4 large russet potatoes
- 4 medium eggs, beaten
- ½ cup yellow onion, finely chopped
- ¼ cup Italian parsley, chopped
- Canola oil, for frying

Whisk together the flour, baking powder, and salt and set aside. Wash, peel, and then coarsely grate the potatoes. Wrap the shredded potato in a dishtowel and wring out as much liquid as possible. In a large mixing bowl combine the potatoes, eggs, onions, parsley, and dry ingredients. Mix only until the ingredients are just moistened.

Heat a heavy-bottomed, cast iron skillet or grill over medium heat. It should be hot enough to cause droplets of water tossed on the pan to sizzle and dance. Coat the pan with oil. Using a ½- or ¼-cup measure, depending on the size desired, pour the potato mixture onto the skillet and form into round pancakes, about ¼-inch thick. If eggy liquid seeps out, push it back into the pancake with your spatula. Fry until the bottom side is a deep golden brown. Then turn it over and fry the other side until golden brown and crispy, about 3 to 5 minutes per side. Transfer to a platter lined with paper towels to absorb any extra oil. Put the platter in a warm oven while frying the rest of the pancakes. Add more oil to your griddle or pan as needed.

½-CUP MEASURE: MAKES APPROXIMATELY TEN 4-INCH PANCAKES

¼-CUP MEASURE: MAKES APPROXIMATELY TWENTY 3-INCH PANCAKES

1-TABLESPOON MEASURE: MAKES APPROXIMATELY FORTY 2-INCH APPETIZERS.

soft *polenta*

The word "polenta" is used interchangeably for both the cooked product and the uncooked, coarsely ground cornmeal. It cooks into a thick corn porridge and is a staple in northern Italy. This is comfort food at its best. It can be served as a vegetarian entrée with Roasted Summer-Vegetable Ragoût (page 160) or Shiitake Mushroom Ragoût (page 147). Soft polenta also makes a tasty accompaniment to grilled chicken or sausages. If desired, chopped fresh herbs may be added just before serving.

- 1 teaspoon olive oil
- 2 garlic cloves, finely minced
- 2 medium shallots, chopped
- 2 cups chicken stock or water
- ⅔ cup polenta
- ¼ cup cream
- ¼ cup soft, mild, goat cheese or grated Parmesan cheese
- 1 tablespoon salted butter
- Salt and pepper
- 1 tablespoon chopped herbs: basil, thyme, or rosemary (optional)

In a large saucepan, heat the oil. Add the garlic and shallots and sauté 2 to 3 minutes, being careful not to burn. Add the stock and bring to a boil. Pull the pan off the heat and gradually whisk in the polenta. Return to medium heat and continue to cook, stirring to keep lumps from forming, until the polenta is thick. It should cook at least 10 minutes.

Remove from the heat and add the cream, cheese, and butter. Season to taste with salt and pepper. The polenta can be kept warm for up to an hour if kept in a double boiler over hot water and covered. If you wish to add the herbs, stir them in just before serving.

MAKES 4 TO 6 SERVINGS

side dishes and vegetables . PAGE 172

soft polenta
WITH RED PEPPER & ORANGE

This polenta dish is delicious served with grilled chicken, sausages, pork tenderloins, or portobello mushrooms.

6 cups chicken stock or water
1 small onion or shallot, minced
¼ cup red bell pepper, minced
1 bay leaf
1 teaspoon salt
2 teaspoons jalapeño pepper, seeded and minced
1½ cups polenta
¼ cup salted butter
Zest of 1 orange, minced
¼ cup green onion, minced
Salt and pepper

In a large, thick-bottomed saucepan, combine the stock or water, onions, bell peppers, bay leaf, salt, and jalapeño pepper. Bring to a boil and, in a slow and steady stream, add the polenta, whisking constantly to keep the mixture smooth. Turn the heat to low and cook, stirring frequently, for 10 to 15 minutes until the color has turned to a creamy, light-yellow, or until the spoon stands up straight in the pan. Pour the polenta into the top pan of a double boiler and add the butter, orange zest, and green onions. Season with salt and pepper as necessary. Let cook for another 10 minutes in the double boiler over medium heat. Turn off the heat and serve. The polenta can be kept warm in the double boiler for up to 1 hour.

MAKES 6 TO 8 SERVINGS

HOMEMADE *pinto beans*

Beans are an excellent source of protein, minerals, and vitamins, have a high fiber content, and are low in calories. Pinto beans fall into the red bean category, along with kidney, pink, small red, and cranberry beans. Each variety has a different personality. Pintos are meaty, but thin-skinned and well-suited for thick chilies and burritos. These beans are so tasty that they make a fine simple dinner, served with salad or wilted greens and a pan of cornbread. Remember, the salt doesn't get added until the beans are fully cooked. Adding the salt to the beans as they cook will retard their softening.

1 pound pinto beans, approximately 2 cups
1 large yellow onion, diced, approximately 2 cups
6 garlic cloves, minced
1 dried pasilla or Anaheim chili pepper, seeded and torn into pieces
1 teaspoon cumin seed
½ cup chopped cilantro, some stems fine
Salt

Spread the beans out on a baking sheet and clean them. Rinse under cold water and drain. The beans must be presoaked. You can either cover them with several inches of cold water and let them sit overnight, draining and rinsing them in the morning, or you can do the "quick soak" method*.

To cook the beans, cover the rinsed beans with 2 inches cold water. Add the onions, garlic, chili pepper, cumin seed, and cilantro. Bring all to a boil over high heat. Skim off any foam that rises to the surface. Turn down to low, and simmer for 1 to 2 hours, stirring and skimming occasionally, until very tender but not falling apart. You might need to add a bit more water as they cook. Taste for seasoning and add salt to taste after the beans are fully cooked.

MAKES 6 CUPS

*To quick soak, put the beans in a pot, cover with cold water to 2 inches above the beans, and bring to a boil. Turn off the heat and allow the beans to stand for at least 1 hour, or until they have swelled to double their original size. Drain the beans and rinse.

FRAGRANT *rice*

Basmati is the famous aromatic rice of Pakistan and northern India that is prized for its long slender grains and its nutty flavor. The aromatics in this dish are subtle and add a wonderful element to the already fragrant basmati rice. You might want to remove the whole spices before serving. We serve this with Indian, Thai, and sometimes Mexican dishes. This easy stovetop method of cooking rice will consistently yield satisfactory results with basmati or with long-grained varieties of rice. If plain rice is desired, simply leave out the ginger, garlic, and allspice.

- 1 cup basmati rice or other long-grained white rice
- 1 tablespoon olive oil or vegetable oil
- 3 garlic cloves, coarsely chopped, approximately 1 tablespoon
- 2 to 3 whole allspice berries
- 3 slices fresh ginger, peeled
- ½ teaspoon sea salt
- 1½ cups chicken stock, vegetable stock, or water
- 1 teaspoon toasted sesame oil (optional)
- ¼ cup cilantro, coarsely chopped (optional)

Cover the rice with cold water and rinse 2 or 3 times, until the water appears clear. Transfer to a sieve and drain briefly. Heat a heavy-bottomed saucepan over medium heat. Add the oil and the rice and stir constantly, sautéing for about 1 minute, until it turns milky-white. Add the garlic, allspice, ginger, and salt and sauté, stirring, about 1 minute, until the rice pops and the garlic is just starting to color. Be very careful not to burn the garlic. Remove from the heat and add the stock, then cover and return to heat. Bring to a boil, then turn down to a very low simmer for 15 minutes. After 15 minutes, turn off the heat and allow the rice to rest, covered in the pot, for at least 10 minutes. Do not open the lid while it is resting and absorbing the rest of the water. (You can open the lid quickly to cover the rice with a terry towel; right away replace the lid. This will aid in the absorption of the water.) Before serving, fluff briefly with a fork. If using the sesame oil and/or cilantro, gently fold it in. Serve warm.

MAKES 3 CUPS

FIESTA *rice*

In the past, this dish was titled Green Rice. One day we added fresh corn and red peppers and decided it was much more fiesta-like! A combination of cheeses works well in this recipe, one that melts well and another to add some sharp flavor. This comforting dish can be served as a vegetarian entrée and also works well as a side dish.

- 3 cups cooked white rice (1 cup uncooked)
- ½ cup yellow onion, diced
- 2 garlic cloves, minced
- 1 cup milk
- 1 egg, beaten
- 1¼ cups cheese, grated: sharp Cheddar, fontina, Asiago and Monterey Jack work well
- ½ large red or yellow bell pepper, seeded and diced into ¼-inch cubes
- ½ cup fresh corn kernels, cut off the cob (optional, only if in season)
- ½ cup chopped Italian parsley
- ¼ cup cilantro, chopped (optional)
- Salt and pepper
- 3 tablespoons olive oil

Preheat the oven to 350°F. If you do not have cooked rice available, cook 1 cup of white rice following the directions for the plain version of basmati rice on page 175.

Sauté the onion and garlic. Mix all of the ingredients except the oil in a large mixing bowl to combine. Scoop this mixture into an oiled 9 by 13-inch Pyrex pan. The rice mixture should be about 1½ to 2 inches thick. Drizzle the oil over the top. Bake for 1 hour or until set and nicely browned on top.

MAKES 6 TO 8 SERVINGS

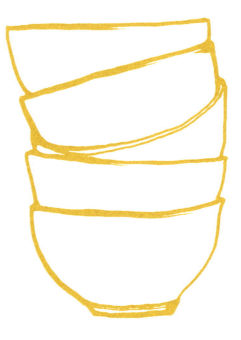

condiments and sauces

condiments and sauces

There are many ways that sauces, condiments, salsas, and chutneys work to enhance a dish. Swirled into a soup or drizzled over a dessert, they add an easy touch of elegance. A dab of colorful salsa or sauce can brighten the appearance of the meal and these extras can also heat up or cool down a dish. Crunch and textural contrast comes with adding condiments such as toasted nuts, sunflower or pumpkin seeds. Most importantly, they add a boost in flavor, either by pulling the dish together or by offering a contrast.

With salsas and sauces, remember that compatibility of flavor with the dish is essential. Sometimes a sauce can simply be a distraction or redundant. For example, it is difficult to improve on a freshly caught piece of wild salmon; a complex sauce might end up detracting from the full flavor that is already there. A raspberry sauce sets off a piece of chocolate torte or lemon pound cake perfectly, but a sauce would be redundant and confusing served with a layer cake that already had a filling and frosting. So, in deciding whether or not to use a sauce, we consider the overall complexity of the dish and of the entire meal.

CILANTRO *pesto*

This bright and flavorful sauce can be spread on chicken as it comes off the grill, drizzled on pizzas after they are baked, tossed with braised tofu, or used on sandwiches or pasta. It must be added right before serving or the bright green color will be lost. The pesto will keep in the refrigerator for a few days if kept in an airtight container and covered with a thin film of olive oil to prevent oxidation.

- **3 cups tightly packed cilantro leaves and upper part of stems**
- **4 garlic cloves, minced**
- **½ cup Parmesan or Asiago cheese, freshly grated**
- **1½ cups light olive oil**
- **¼ cup toasted pine nuts**
- **Splash of rice vinegar**
- **Salt and pepper**

Place the cilantro and garlic in a food processor fitted with a metal blade or in a blender. Pulse a few times until the cilantro is coarsely chopped. Add the cheese and then, with the motor running, add the oil in a slow steady stream until it is incorporated. Add the pine nuts and pulse a few times until the nuts are very coarsely ground, but still visible. Add the vinegar and the salt and pepper to taste. Pulse to combine. Check the seasoning and serve.

MAKES 2 CUPS

basil AIOLI

This tasty mayonnaise is very versatile. We use it as a spread for our focaccia sandwiches and also serve it with grilled salmon, roasted vegetables, or steamed artichokes. It also makes a delicious dressing for chicken salad.

- 1 cup light olive oil
- 1 cup fresh basil leaves
- 2 egg yolks
- 1 tablespoon lemon juice, Champagne vinegar, or white wine vinegar
- 1 teaspoon sea salt
- 1 garlic clove, finely minced

Place the oil and basil in a food processor and purée. Scrape into a bowl and set aside. In the same processor, pulse the egg yolk with a few drops of the lemon juice until the color begins to lighten. Add the basil oil, drop by drop at first, then a little faster as the mixture begins to emulsify. Season with salt and the minced garlic. Add the remaining lemon juice or vinegar.

Refrigerate immediately or place in a bowl over ice if using for service. This will keep in the refrigerator for up to two days but not longer because of the uncooked egg yolk.

MAKES APPROXIMATELY 1 CUP

PICKLED *red onions*

The tart flavor and striking color of these bright pink onions can enhance many sandwiches and salads. We serve these as a condiment with tacos, black bean chili, or spinach salad. They will keep in the refrigerator for several weeks.

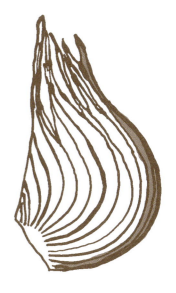

1 pound red onions, cut in half and thinly sliced
1 quart boiling water
⅔ cup seasoned rice vinegar
⅔ cup cold water
10 peppercorns
2 to 3 bay leaves

Separate the pieces of sliced onions and place them in a medium-sized glass or stainless steel bowl. Pour the boiling water over the onions, making sure that they are all equally covered. Allow the onions to sit for 1 minute in the water. Drain into a colander, place the onions back in the bowl, and add the vinegar, cold water, peppercorns, and bay leaves. Cover and refrigerate at least 1 hour before serving.

MAKES 2 CUPS

RED TOMATO *chutney*

This Indian-style chutney, inspired by Madhur Jaffrey, is an invaluable recipe both at home and in our kitchen at the Ranch. It can be made when tomatoes are at the peak of their season or with canned tomatoes in the winter. The chutney also cans well if you have lots of extra tomatoes to use. Fenugreek seed can be found in the bulk section of your local health food store and while the original recipe called for black mustard seed, yellow or brown mustard seed works fine and is more easily obtained. Try this chutney with roasted chicken, curries, and as a delicious condiment for stir fries.

2 tablespoons vegetable oil

½ teaspoon panchphoran (an Indian spice mix consisting of equal amounts of black or brown mustard seed, cumin seed, and fenugreek seed)

1-inch piece of fresh ginger, peeled and finely diced

1 whole, small, dried red chile

6 garlic cloves, minced

1 pound tomatoes, chopped, approximately 2 cups

1 teaspoon salt

⅓ cup sugar

4 dried apricots, cut into ½-inch pieces

2 whole fresh jalapeño peppers, seeded and finely diced

In a heavy-bottomed saucepan, heat the oil over medium heat. When hot, add the panchphoran and cook until the seeds pop, being very careful as they burn easily. Add the ginger and sauté for a minute, stirring. Turn the heat down to medium-low and add the rest of the ingredients. Simmer until the mixture is thick, stirring occasionally, for about 1 hour. Store in an airtight container in the refrigerator and bring to room temperature before serving.

MAKES 3 CUPS

tamari SUNFLOWER SEEDS

These crunchy and lightly salted seeds are a nutritious addition to salads and also great as a snack. Tamari is made from fermented soybeans, a by-product of the miso-making process. It is similar to soy sauce but has a stronger flavor. You can find tamari in the Asian section of your supermarket or at natural foods stores. If unavailable, soy sauce may be substituted. This recipe also works well with almonds and pumpkin seeds.

> 4 cups hulled sunflower seeds
> 1½ tablespoons vegetable oil
> 3 to 4 tablespoons tamari

Preheat the oven to 375°F. Spread the sunflower seeds on a large baking sheet. Pour the oil over the seeds and stir until the seeds are evenly coated. Bake in the oven, checking frequently, until they turn a very light golden brown, about 10 to 15 minutes. Remove from the oven and sprinkle on the tamari and stir to coat evenly. Return to the oven. Watch carefully, stirring every 5 minutes, until the seeds are a little darker and the tamari has been absorbed by the seeds. This will take approximately 10 minutes. The seeds should be on the dry side and medium-brown in color. When they are done, remove them from the oven and cool.

Store in an airtight container in the refrigerator. The seeds will keep for a month or more this way. It is best to sprinkle them on a salad at the last minute or serve them on the side as a condiment because, once on the salad, they absorb moisture and lose their crunch.

MAKES 4 CUPS

CARAMELIZED *nuts*

Try these as an addition to salads or as appetizers. We offer two versions here, both good. The second recipe is drier, and perhaps easier to make.

Caramelized Nuts 1:
¼ cup sugar
Pinch of salt
1 cup shelled pistachios, pecans, almonds, or walnuts

Heat the oven to 350°F and lightly toast the nuts for 5 to 8 minutes. Rub together in a towel to remove some of the outer skin if using walnuts or pistachios.

Put a small sauté pan over medium heat. Add the sugar and salt and let the mixture dissolve without stirring, until it turns caramel-brown. Do not let it smoke. Immediately take the pan off the heat and add the nuts, stirring with a wooden spoon until coated. Scrape the caramelized nuts out of the pan onto a plate or bowl. When cool, break the nuts apart or coarsely chop them with a knife.

Store in a tightly sealed plastic container in a dry place. Use within a few days. If any moisture gets in, the caramel will slowly melt.

MAKES 1 CUP

Caramelized Nuts 2:
2 cups shelled walnuts
½ cup water
3 tablespoons sugar or brown sugar
1 teaspoon salt
½ teaspoon cayenne pepper
Pinch of ground cinnamon or ½ teaspoon Chinese five-spice powder

Heat the oven to 350°F and toast the walnuts for 5 to 8 minutes. Rub together in a towel to remove some of the outer skin.

Cook the water, sugar, and salt together to form a semi-thick simple syrup, about 7 to 10 minutes. Add spices and stir to mix. Toss the nuts in the syrup to coat and spread onto a sheet pan, and bake at 350°F for 15 to 20 minutes. Watch carefully so they don't burn.

MAKES 2 CUPS

gorgonzola BUTTER

This compound butter is the finishing touch for steaks. It can be stored in a covered container in the refrigerator for up to three days. If you want to store it longer, roll the butter into a log about one-and-a-half inches in diameter, wrap, and freeze for up to two months.

- ¼ pound unsalted butter, at room temperature
- 1 shallot, thinly sliced, approximately ⅓ cup
- ½ garlic clove, mashed, approximately ½ teaspoon
- 2 ounces good-quality Gorgonzola cheese, crumbled, a generous ½ cup
- ½ teaspoon fresh thyme leaves, chopped
- 1 teaspoon red wine vinegar
- Salt and freshly ground black pepper

Melt 1 tablespoon of the butter in a small skillet over medium heat. Add the shallots and cook until soft, stirring and watching carefully so they don't brown, about 5 minutes. Add the garlic and cook for 1 to 2 minutes, stirring and not letting the garlic brown. Remove from the heat and set aside to cool.

Meanwhile, using a mixer or a wooden spoon, beat the remaining butter until it is soft and creamy. Add the cooled shallots and garlic and the cheese, thyme, and vinegar to the butter and cream together. Season with salt and pepper to taste. Adjust the seasonings if necessary.

Refrigerate until needed, placing a generous tablespoon on top of each portion of warm meat and allowing the butter to soften or melt slightly before serving.

MAKES 8 TO 10 SERVINGS

barbeque SAUCE

This is the sauce we use for pork spareribs, barbequed chicken, and meatloaf.

1½ cups ketchup
1 cup apple cider vinegar
¼ cup Worcestershire sauce
¼ cup soy sauce
1 cup packed brown sugar
1 tablespoon dry mustard
3 to 4 tablespoons chili powder, depending on how spicy you want the sauce
1 tablespoon fresh ginger, peeled and minced
2 garlic cloves, minced
2 tablespoons vegetable oil

Combine all of the ingredients in a saucepan over medium heat. Bring to a simmer and cook, stirring occasionally, until the mixture thickens, about 10 to 15 minutes. Cool and refrigerate. This sauce will keep up to a month in the refrigerator.

MAKES 3 CUPS

tomato SAUCE

This simple tomato sauce is easy to make and great for pizzas, polenta, and pastas. The sauce is only as good as your ingredients, so use only ripe tomatoes and a good olive oil. In the winter, we use high-quality canned Roma tomatoes instead of fresh. You can quickly chop the canned tomatoes in a food processor. Just pulse until they are in small chunks, not a purée. Cook the sauce a little longer to thicken if you will be using it for pizza sauce.

- 3 pounds ripe tomatoes, coarsely chopped, approximately 6 cups or two 28-ounce cans whole tomatoes and juice, chopped
- 3 tablespoons olive oil
- 1 medium yellow onion, finely diced
- 4 garlic cloves, finely chopped yielding 4 teaspoons
- ½ teaspoon sea salt
- ¼ teaspoon red pepper flakes
- 1 teaspoon dried oregano
- 2 tablespoons fresh basil, chopped
- Pinch of sugar (optional)

If using fresh tomatoes, skin them by immersing in simmering water for about 3 minutes or until the skins crack. Remove, cool, peel off the skin, and chop. Set the tomatoes aside.

Heat the oil in a heavy-bottomed saucepan over medium heat. Add the onions and sauté until softened and golden, stirring occasionally, about 5 minutes. Add the garlic and cook for 1 minute, being careful not to burn. Add the tomatoes, salt, pepper flakes, oregano, and basil and simmer, uncovered, for about 30 minutes, until thickened. Taste and adjust the seasoning if necessary. A pinch of sugar can be added if your sauce doesn't reflect the sweetness of fully ripe tomatoes.

MAKES APPROXIMATELY 4½ CUPS

chipotle RED CHILE CREAM

We drizzle this cream over quesadillas, shrimp and corn fritters, roasted potatoes, or pinto beans. Chipotle sauce can be found in the Mexican section of your local supermarket. It is made from dried and smoked jalapeño peppers. If this bottled sauce is not available, look for canned chipotles and purée them by forcing through a sieve or purée in a blender. We use Búfalo brand chipotle sauce but other brands are fine.

2 cups sour cream or crème fraîche
1 tablespoon Búfalo chipotle sauce
1 lime, juiced
1 tablespoon brown sugar
Pinch of salt

In a medium-sized bowl, whisk together ingredients until incorporated. Adjust seasonings to taste. Keep stored in an airtight container in the refrigerator for 1 week.

MAKES APPROXIMATELY 2 CUPS

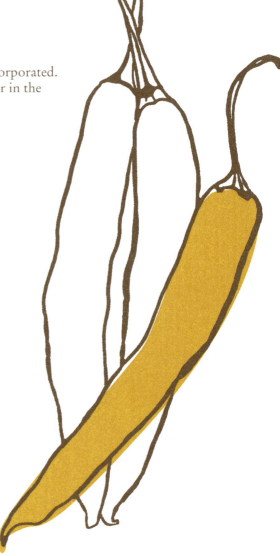

SALSA *verde*

This Italian green sauce is very good mixed with aioli for sandwiches or served with grilled fish, chicken, pork tenderloin, and roasted potatoes. This recipe can be prepared, up to the point of adding the vinegar and the lemon juice, hours ahead of time. Wait to add the vinegar and lemon juice until just before serving, or they will discolor the herbs. Of course, this can be made without a food processor by simply chopping the herbs with a chef's knife and blending them in a bowl.

1 bunch Italian parsley, leaves only, approximately 3 cups loosely packed
1 bunch basil, leaves only, approximately 2 cups loosely packed
2 tablespoons chives or scallions
2 sprigs fresh mint, leaves only (optional)
2 garlic cloves, coarsely chopped
¼ cup capers, rinsed
3 salted anchovies, rinsed and chopped
1 teaspoon lemon zest
2 teaspoons whole-grain Dijon mustard (optional)
½ cup olive oil
Sea salt and freshly ground black pepper
1 tablespoon red wine vinegar
A squeeze of lemon juice

Using a food processor fitted with a metal blade, pulse the parsley, basil, chives, mint, garlic, and capers until roughly chopped. Transfer to a bowl and stir in the anchovies, lemon zest, and mustard. Slowly whisk in the oil. Season with salt and pepper. If using immediately, add the vinegar and the lemon juice. Check for seasoning and serve.

MAKES 1½ CUPS

salmoriglio

This fresh sauce can be brushed on meat or chicken as it comes off the grill. It is also good on grilled vegetables. You can make it using a mortar and pestle or simply by hand with a chef's knife. It can also be made using a blender or food processor. Feel free to use a small amount of marjoram or thyme leaves in combination with the oregano.

> **1 cup fresh oregano, leaves only**
> **2 teaspoons salt, approximately**
> **Generous pinch red pepper flakes**
> **Juice of ½ lemon, approximately 1½ to 2 tablespoons**
> **½ cup olive oil**

Work in the bowl of a mortar and pestle or pulse in a blender or food processor until the mixture is slurpy and loose. The leaves of the herbs should be chopped fine in this process. Taste and adjust the seasonings. Store, covered, in the refrigerator, but use at room temperature.

MAKES 1 CUP

hummus

Hummus is a Middle Eastern garbanzo bean spread that is flavored with garlic, lemon juice, olive oil, and tahini (ground sesame seeds). You can find hummus in the deli section of most grocery stores, but it is also easy to make at home. If your garlic is strong or too sharp, you can mellow it by sautéing the peeled cloves in a bit of olive oil, on the stovetop for a few minutes, until they start to turn golden and brown on the tips.

> **2½ cups cooked garbanzo beans or one 16-ounce can garbanzo beans**
> **¼ cup lemon juice**
> **¼ cup olive oil**
> **2 to 3 garlic cloves, sautéed in oil**
> **⅓ cup tahini**
> **Sea salt**

Drain the beans, saving the liquid to use later if you want to thin the hummus. Put the lemon juice, oil, and garlic in a blender or food processor. Turn it on and slowly pour in the beans. Stop, scrape the sides, and continue puréeing. If the mixture seems too thick or dry, add some of the liquid from the beans. Taste, add salt and the tahini, and mix one more time. Remove to a bowl, cover, and refrigerate until ready to use.

MAKES APPROXIMATELY 3 CUPS

SALSA *fresca*

This is a basic recipe for fresh salsa, good with scrambled eggs and potatoes or any Mexican dish. A lot of substitutions are possible here. You could use lemon juice or rice vinegar in place of the lime juice or add some bottled chipotle sauce. This is definitely a recipe that requires you to sample and then make adjustments according to personal taste.

> 1 pound ripe Roma tomatoes, seeded and finely chopped, approximately 2 cups
> ¼ cup red onion, minced
> 1 small garlic clove, minced, approximately ½ teaspoon (optional)
> 1 tablespoon fresh lime juice
> 2 tablespoons cilantro, finely chopped
> ¼ jalapeño pepper, seeded and minced, approximately 2 teaspoons
>   or ¼ chipotle chile, canned, seeded and minced
> Salt and pepper

Combine all the ingredients in a bowl and let stand at room temperature for at least 30 minutes. Taste for seasonings and adjust if desired.

MAKES APPROXIMATELY 2½ CUPS

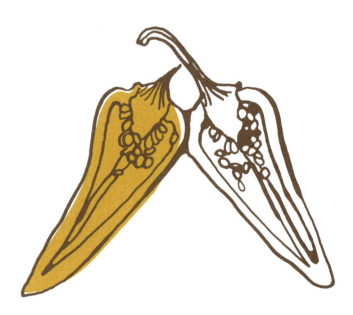

tropical FRUIT SALSA

This summery salsa is good on chicken, pork, and fish. It is fine to use jars of mango and papaya, if they seem better quality than what is available fresh.

1 medium shallot, minced
1 small garlic clove, minced
½ jalapeño pepper, seeded and minced
½ cup red or yellow bell pepper, very finely diced
1 mango, peeled, seeded, finely diced, approximately 1 cup
¼ cantaloupe, finely diced, approximately 1 cup
¼ medium papaya, peeled, seeded, finely diced, approximately 1 cup
¼ cup cilantro, chopped
Salt and freshly ground black pepper
Juice of 1 lime
Splash of seasoned rice vinegar

Combine the first 8 ingredients in a small bowl. Season to taste with salt and pepper, lime juice, and rice vinegar. Cover and refrigerate until ready to serve.

MAKES APPROXIMATELY 3 CUPS

crème fraîche

Unlike sour cream, which breaks or curdles when added to acidic ingredients, crème fraîche remains silky and intact. It also may be heated without separating. Try drizzling it over soups or stews, roasted potatoes, or any spicy Mexican dish. It is also delicious served with rich fruit desserts or pancakes and applesauce. Allow at least 24 hours for the cream to thicken and develop its nutty flavor.

> **2 cups heavy cream (not ultra-pasteurized)**
> **1 tablespoon cultured buttermilk**

Pour the heavy cream into a glass bowl or non-reactive container, add the buttermilk, and whisk the mixture together. Cover loosely, place in a warm spot, such as a top shelf in the kitchen, and let it sit for 24 hours. The crème fraîche should be thickened and usable after 24 hours, but, if desired, you could leave it out an additional 12 hours to develop the flavor more fully. Cover and refrigerate. This will keep for at least 2 weeks.

MAKES 2 CUPS

desserts

desserts

With dessert, our goal is to celebrate the end of a lovely meal. The dessert course is perfect for lingering over conversation and finishing with a refreshing or dramatic touch. Perhaps the most gratifying aspect of dessert is how beautiful and creative it can be. A few basic sauces can add pizzazz and elegance to your presentation and, with dessert, presentation is where you want to shine.

It is important to consider how the dessert will complete and complement the meal. Rich or heavy foods will be enhanced by a plate of fruit and biscotti or a scoop of sorbet. A lighter, simple meal might do well with a cheesecake or fruit crisp and ice cream.

Like other foods, desserts are tied to the seasons. Ripe strawberries become available in the spring, peaches throughout the summer, figs and pumpkin in the fall. All offer endless possibilities. Chocolate, fortunately, seems to have no season! So have fun and, by the way, did you notice that this section has the most recipes?

blueberry SAUCE

We serve this over pancakes, French toast, and lemon pound cake. It's delicious with cheesecake or vanilla ice cream too. We make this recipe in the winter from frozen berries and it is still good.

4 cups fresh or frozen blueberries
⅓ cup sugar
1 cinnamon stick (optional)
2 teaspoons cornstarch, mixed with 3 tablespoons cold water
1 tablespoon fresh lemon juice

In a non-reactive pan, combine the blueberries, sugar, and the cinnamon stick if you are including it. Cook the mixture, stirring occasionally, until the sugar dissolves, 5 to 10 minutes. Add the cornstarch mixture and stir to combine. Cook until the sauce is thicker and has lost the opaque appearance of the cornstarch, stirring occasionally, for about 5 additional minutes. Remove from the heat and add the lemon juice. Remove the cinnamon stick before serving. The blueberry sauce will keep for several weeks in the refrigerator.

MAKES 2¼ CUPS

raspberry SAUCE

Raspberry sauce is very simple to make and is a tangy addition to rich ice creams, chocolate desserts, angel food cake, or pound cake. It can be used in a squeeze bottle with a small tip to decorate the dessert plate.

- ½ cup water
- ½ cup sugar
- 4 cups fresh or frozen raspberries
- 2 teaspoons cornstarch mixed with ¼ cup cold water
- 2 to 3 teaspoons lemon juice

In a non-reactive saucepan, heat the water and sugar until the sugar is dissolved. Add the raspberries and bring to a boil, then simmer about 5 minutes. Add the cornstarch mixture and cook about 3 minutes longer. Remove from the heat and add lemon juice to taste. Put the sauce through a fine-meshed sieve to strain out all the seeds. This sauce will keep for several weeks in the refrigerator.

MAKES APPROXIMATELY 1½ CUPS

caramel SAUCE

We use this caramel sauce over ice cream, bread puddings, persimmon pudding, and apple or pear cake. Tightly covered, it will keep for up to one month in the refrigerator. It will become solid, so you will need to reheat, in either a double boiler or in a heavy saucepan over very low heat, adding a bit of water if it is too thick.

> 1 cup sugar
> ⅓ cup water
> 1 cup heavy cream

In a heavy-bottomed saucepan, combine the sugar and water and bring to a simmer until the sugar is dissolved and the liquid is completely clear. Swirl the pan if necessary to distribute the sugar, but do not stir with a spoon. Brush the sides of the pan down with water on a pastry brush if sugar crystals form. Cover the pan tightly with a lid and boil hard for a minute or so, until the bubbles are thick and large. Uncover the pan, swirl and cook the sugar until light amber or golden brown. Do not let it burn or smoke. Remove from the heat immediately and cautiously add the cream, stirring slowly with a long-handled spoon. The mixture will bubble up dramatically, causing a shot of hot steam so be very careful not to have your hands or face too close.

MAKES 1½ CUPS

crème anglaise

This is a fabulous sauce to drizzle over fruit crisps or to pool on a plate under a piece of chocolate torte or orange sponge cake. We use it with vanilla or mint flavorings.

Vanilla Crème Anglaise:
1 vanilla bean*
2 cups half-and-half
¼ cup sugar
4 egg yolks

Slice the vanilla bean in half lengthwise and, using a knife, scrape out the seeds into a non-reactive saucepan. Add the pod halves, half-and-half, and sugar and heat until just barely simmering, making sure all the sugar dissolves. Remove from the heat, cover, and let sit to infuse the vanilla flavor, about 20 to 30 minutes.

In a medium bowl, whisk the egg yolks and then slowly whisk in one-quarter of the warm half-and-half mixture. Add this mixture back into the rest of the half-and-half mixture and cook over medium heat, stirring constantly with a wooden spoon, until it thickens to coat the back of the spoon, about 6 to 8 minutes. Be very careful not to overcook as the eggs can scramble quite easily. Pour through a fine sieve and cool.

MAKES APPROXIMATELY 2½ CUPS

*Vanilla extract may be used in place of the vanilla bean. To substitute the extract, follow the directions for mixing and warming the half-and-half and sugar. Add the egg yolks and proceed with the directions for additional cooking. Strain, cool, and then stir in 2 teaspoons of vanilla extract.

Mint Crème Anglaise:

Substitute 1 cup chopped mint leaves for the vanilla bean and follow the same instructions for steeping. Strain out the leaves before cooking with the egg yolks.

MAKES APPROXIMATELY 2½ CUPS

pastry cream

We use this pastry cream as a filling for cakes, the base for fruit tarts, and for filling éclairs. The flavor can be changed by varying with vanilla, rum, almond, or other extracts and liqueurs. Also, you can lighten it by folding in a bit of whipped cream.

> 2 cups milk
> ⅓ cup flour
> 6 tablespoons sugar
> 6 egg yolks
> 2 tablespoons unsalted butter
> Vanilla extract or other flavoring

Scald the milk, that is, heat it to just under boiling. Remove from the heat and set aside. In a heavy and non-reactive saucepan, whisk together the flour and the sugar. In a large bowl, whisking by hand or with a mixer, beat the egg yolks until thick and lightened in color.

Stir the hot milk into the saucepan with the flour and sugar and cook over medium heat, whisking constantly, until the mixture has boiled for a minute or two. Whisk a small amount of the hot milk mixture into the egg yolks to warm them, then stir all the egg yolk mixture into the milk mixture in the saucepan. Mix well and cook over medium heat, stirring constantly, until the pastry cream thickens and begins to hold a slight shape as you move the whisk or spoon through it. It should cook to 170°F so that enzymes in the egg yolks don't cause it to break down later. Do not let it boil.

Remove from the heat and stir in the butter, then put the pastry cream through a medium-fine sieve. Stir in the vanilla or other flavorings to taste. Whisk occasionally to keep a crust from forming as it is cooling, but do not overbeat. This would cause it to thin. You can also simply cover it with plastic wrap, refrigerate it until cool, and then whisk before using. This will keep in the refrigerator up to 5 days if chilled right after it is cooked.

MAKES 2½ CUPS

caramel FROSTING

This delicious frosting is adapted from The New Joy of Cooking. *It is a handy recipe to have in your file because it can be made when you are out of confectioners' sugar. We have been using it with our banana cake ever since the day we found ourselves in that predicament! This recipe is easy to make, but please note that you need to allow enough time for the frosting to cool.*

- 2 cups packed brown sugar
- 1 cup heavy cream
  (if cream is unavailable, you can substitute ½ cup milk and ½ cup butter)
- 3 tablespoons unsalted butter
- 1 teaspoon vanilla extract
- 1 to 2 tablespoons rum (optional)

Have a candy thermometer and pastry brush ready to use. Combine the brown sugar and cream in a medium-sized, heavy saucepan and cook, stirring, over medium heat just until the mixture begins to simmer. Stop stirring, cover, and simmer for 2 minutes to dissolve the sugar. Uncover the pan and wash any sugar crystals from the sides of the pan with a wet pastry brush. Cook, uncovered, until the syrup reaches 238°F (softball stage) on a candy thermometer. Remove from the heat and add the butter. Do not stir.

Set aside without stirring, uncovered, until the butter is melted and the mixture cools to 110°F. This will take 45 minutes to one hour. When the mixture has cooled, add the vanilla and rum. Beat with a spoon until the frosting cools more and is thickened to a spreading consistency. It should become thick and creamy. If the frosting is reluctant to thicken, place the bowl in a larger bowl of ice water and continue beating. If it becomes too thick, it can be thinned with a little additional cream.

Use immediately or cover with plastic wrap. This will keep for up to 1 week at room temperature or 3 weeks refrigerated. It may be frozen also. Take out ahead of time to thaw and soften before using.

MAKES 3 CUPS

QUICK *orange icing*

It is important to watch this mixture carefully as it cooks. Have everything measured before you begin.

> **5 tablespoons heavy cream**
>   **(6 tablespoons unsalted butter may be substituted, but cream is preferred)**
> **3 cups sifted confectioners' sugar**
> **Zest of one orange**
> **3 tablespoons orange juice**
> **Pinch of salt**
> **1½ teaspoons vanilla extract**

Warm the cream (or melt the butter) in the top of a double boiler over low heat. When warm, remove from the heat and stir in the confectioners' sugar, zest, orange juice, and salt. Put the double boiler back on the heat and cook, stirring occasionally, over barely simmering water for 5 minutes. Remove from the heat and add the vanilla. Beat or whisk until cool and the desired consistency. You can place the pan in a larger pan of ice water to quicken the process. Pour over a cooled cake and smooth with a spatula if using immediately. To store, cover the surface of the icing with a sheet of plastic wrap. This keeps for up to 3 weeks refrigerated. Soften and beat until smooth before using.

MAKES 1¼ CUPS; ENOUGH FOR A 10 BY 4-INCH TUBE CAKE

CHOCOLATE *ganache*

This frosting is easy to make and has never failed to please.

- 2 tablespoons unsalted butter
- ¾ cup semisweet chocolate chips
- 6 tablespoons heavy cream or half-and-half
- 1¼ cup confectioners' sugar, sifted
- 1 teaspoon vanilla extract

Place all of the ingredients in a heavy saucepan over low heat and stir occasionally, just until melted. Remove from the heat and whisk until smooth. Cool slightly and pour over cake, brownies, or cupcakes. Smooth with a spreading knife and let cool until set. Any extra frosting can be stored in the refrigerator for a couple of weeks and then reheated gently over low heat or in a microwave.

MAKES APPROXIMATELY 1 CUP

CANDIED *citrus peel*

Candied citrus peel is easy to make, although you do need a little time. It can be added to ordinary gingerbread or cookies and is great to have on hand. Stored in an airtight container, it will keep in the refrigerator or freezer for up to 4 months. This recipe can be doubled.

Peel of 3 large oranges, 2 grapefruit, or 6 lemons, removed in large strips
2 cups sugar, divided
3 tablespoons light corn syrup
¼ cup water

Put the peel in a saucepan, add water to cover, and simmer for 30 minutes. Drain, cover with fresh cold water, and simmer until tender, about 15 minutes. Drain and rinse under cold water. Remove any remaining pulp or pith by scraping it away with a spoon. Cut the peel into ¼-inch-wide strips. Set aside.

Put 1 cup of the sugar, the corn syrup, and the water into a large, heavy saucepan and stir over low heat until the sugar is dissolved. Brush down the sides of the pan with cold water if sugar crystals begin to form. Add the peel and cook very gently over low heat until most of the syrup is absorbed. Remove from the stove, cover the pan, and let stand overnight. Bring to a simmer again, remove from the heat, and let cool slightly before draining. Spread 2 layers of paper towels on the counter and sprinkle with the remaining 1 cup of sugar. Roll the peel in the sugar until it is well coated. Transfer the candied peel to wax paper or parchment paper and let it dry for at least one hour. Store in an airtight container.

MAKES 2 CUPS

fruity OATMEAL COOKIES

Our present kitchen manager, Robin Miller, developed this recipe one day in a creative burst and it's been a favorite ever since. Be careful not to overbake these cookies as they are best when soft.

- 1½ cups unsalted butter, softened
- 1 cup firmly packed brown sugar
- 1 cup sugar
- 2 eggs, room temperature, lightly beaten
- 2 teaspoons vanilla extract
- ½ cup water
- 2 cups unbleached flour
- 2 teaspoons salt
- 1 teaspoon baking soda
- 1 cup unsweetened coconut, shredded
- 5 cups quick-cooking rolled oats
- 4 ounces pitted dates, coarsely chopped, approximately ¾ cup
- 1 cup dried cranberries
- 1 cup chopped dried apricot
- 1 cup dried currants

Preheat the oven to 350°F. In a large mixing bowl, cream the butter with the sugars until light and fluffy. Add the eggs, vanilla, and water and beat until well-blended.

In another bowl, sift together the flour, salt, and soda. Add this to the egg mixture and mix until well-blended. Stir in the rest of the ingredients and mix until evenly incorporated.

Wet your hands and roll pieces of the dough into balls the size of a walnut. Place the balls on a cookie sheet that is lightly greased or lined with parchment paper. Allow a few inches between each cookie because they will spread. Flatten each cookie just a little with a fork that has been dipped in cold water to prevent sticking. Bake for about 12 to 15 minutes, or until just lightly brown around the edges but still soft. Let them cool on racks before storing in an airtight container.

MAKES 48 COOKIES

persimmon COOKIES

How wonderful that our persimmon tree is filled with its beautiful orange fruit just as the Meyer lemons are ripening. They are the perfect combination for these tasty cookies that we make every late fall. Use soft Hachiya persimmons and make sure the fruit is transparent and thoroughly ripe. These cookies are soft and a bit sticky and best eaten within a day or so of being baked. No problem!

- 1 cup persimmon pulp, approximately 3 ripe persimmons
- ½ cup unsalted butter, softened
- 1 cup sugar
- 1 egg
- 1 teaspoon baking soda
- 2 cups unbleached flour
- 1 teaspoon baking powder
- 1 teaspoon ground cinnamon
- ½ teaspoon ground nutmeg
- ½ teaspoon ground cloves
- ½ teaspoon salt
- 1 teaspoon vanilla extract
- 2 teaspoons chopped lemon zest, up to 1 tablespoon if Meyer lemons are used
- 1 cup coarsely chopped walnuts
- 1 cup raisins

Preheat the oven to 350°F. Prepare the persimmon pulp by pulling the stems off the fruit, removing any bruised or black spots, and then either puréeing in a blender or smashing through a sieve.

Cream the butter and sugar in a large mixing bowl. Add the egg and beat well. Mix the persimmon pulp with the soda and then add to the butter mixture. Stir well. Sift the dry ingredients together and add to the butter mixture. Stir well. Add the vanilla and lemon zest and stir, then fold in the walnuts and raisins and mix all together.

Line a baking sheet with parchment paper or grease well. Using a large cookie scoop or tablespoon, spoon out 1 heaping tablespoon of dough for each cookie. Press on each to flatten a little. These cookies do not spread much so you can place them close together. Bake for 20 minutes or until nicely browned and done. Remove to a rack to cool and store in an airtight container.

MAKES 2 DOZEN COOKIES

cowboy COOKIES

This is one of our most popular cookies. If you make them without nuts and add a little spice, say one-half teaspoon of ground cinnamon, then you have Cowgirl Cookies!

1 cup whole almonds
1 cup unsalted butter
1 cup sugar
1 cup firmly packed brown sugar
2 eggs, beaten
1 teaspoon vanilla extract
1½ cups unbleached flour
½ cup whole wheat flour
½ teaspoon baking powder
½ teaspoon salt
1 teaspoon baking soda
2 cups regular rolled oats
1 cup semisweet chocolate chips

Heat the oven to 375°F. Toast the whole almonds until slightly brown. Cool and coarsely chop. Set aside. In a large bowl, cream the butter and sugars together, add the eggs and vanilla, and mix well.

Sift together the flours, baking powder, salt, and soda. Add to the wet ingredients and mix well. Stir in the rolled oats, chocolate chips, and the almonds and mix well.

Scoop the cookies and place onto baking sheets that are greased or lined with parchment paper.* Bake for about 15 minutes, or until the cookies are nicely browned.

MAKES 3 DOZEN LARGE COOKIES

*For a large cookie, we use a scoop that holds 2 tablespoons of dough. You can make them smaller if you prefer.

ORANGE *crispies*

If you like orange and oatmeal, this is the cookie for you. This is a refrigerator cookie, so you can make the rolls ahead, store them in the freezer, and bake as needed.

1 cup unsalted butter, softened
1 cup firmly packed brown sugar
1 cup sugar
2 eggs
1 teaspoon freshly squeezed orange juice
1¾ cups unbleached flour
1 teaspoon salt
1 teaspoon baking soda
Zest of 2 oranges
3 cups quick-cooking rolled oats
½ cup walnuts, chopped

In a large bowl, cream the butter and sugars until light and fluffy. Add the eggs and orange juice and beat until well-blended.

In another bowl, sift together the flour, salt, and soda. Add the flour mixture to the egg mixture and stir until incorporated. Add the orange zest, oats, and walnuts and stir until combined.

Lay down an 18-inch piece of plastic wrap. Divide the dough into 3 portions and spoon 1 of those portions onto the wrap. Roll it with your palms to form a 2-inch-wide by 12-inch-long log. You can make your logs square or round. Form all the portions of dough into logs and place them on a baking sheet. Put in the freezer for at least 2 hours or overnight.

Preheat the oven to 350°F. Remove the dough from the freezer, and cut the logs into ¼-inch-thick slices, and place on a baking sheet lined with parchment paper. Bake for 10 to 15 minutes, rotating cookies halfway through, until they are an even, golden brown. They will be crispy when cooled if baked until dark brown. For a softer cookie, do not bake as long. Cool on racks and store in an airtight container.

MAKES 40 TO 50 COOKIES

gingersnaps

This is the first cookie Liz learned to bake and it is still a family favorite. Studded with chunks of candied ginger, these gingersnaps feature the classic crackled top, shimmering with turbinado sugar. Granulated white sugar may be substituted for the turbinado, but the appearance of the cookie will be less striking.

- ¾ cup unsalted butter
- 2 cups sugar
- ½ cup molasses
- 2 medium eggs, beaten
- 4 cups unbleached flour
- ½ teaspoon salt
- 4 teaspoons baking soda
- 2 heaping teaspoons ground cinnamon
- 2 heaping teaspoons ground ginger
- 2 teaspoons ground cloves
- ¼ cup candied ginger, chopped
- 1 cup turbinado sugar, to dip cookies in

In a small saucepan, melt the butter over low heat. Let cool slightly. Put the butter into a large bowl, add the sugar and beat until light and creamy. Add the molasses and eggs and beat until well blended.

Sift together the flour, salt, soda, cinnamon, ginger, and cloves. Add the dry mixture to the egg mixture. Add the candied ginger and stir until thoroughly incorporated. The cookies can be formed and baked now or, for easier handling, you can let the dough chill in the refrigerator for 1 hour before forming.

Remove the dough from the refrigerator. Line baking sheets with parchment paper or lightly grease them. Preheat the oven to 350°F. Place the turbinado sugar in a shallow bowl next to the dough. Scoop about 2 tablespoons of the dough with a spoon or a 1-ounce cookie scoop and roll into a ball. Dip one side of the ball into the sugar and place on the baking sheet, sugar side up. Flatten the cookie slightly with your fingertips. Space the cookies 2 inches apart, as they will spread out while baking.

Bake for 15 to 20 minutes, or until the cookies have risen and fallen, are dark golden brown, and have a cracked appearance on top. You can control whether they are crispy or chewy by varying the baking time. A shorter baking time will yield a chewier cookie. Let the cookies cool a few minutes on the baking sheets before removing to racks for further cooling.

MAKES 4 DOZEN COOKIES

BLACK-FOOTED *macaroons*

These cookies are rich, moist, and especially delicious served with mango or pineapple sorbet.

> 1 cup egg whites (from 7 large eggs)
> 2¼ cups sugar
> 2 tablespoons honey
> 2 teaspoons vanilla extract
> 1 pound unsweetened coconut, finely shredded, approximately 5½ cups
> 1¼ cups unbleached flour, sifted
> 8 ounces semisweet chocolate (1 cup chocolate chips)

In the top of a double boiler, combine the egg whites, honey, and sugar. Whisk lightly and keep over heat until the mixture is warm to the touch, around 110°F.

Remove from the heat and fold in the vanilla, coconut, and flour. It will be easier to mix if you add the coconut in two portions rather than all at once. Refrigerate until the mixture is firm and chilled, about 1 hour.

Preheat the oven to 325°F. With a 1-ounce cookie scoop or a tablespoon, scoop the mixture into balls (a heaping tablespoon worth) and place on a baking sheet lined with parchment paper. With the scoop, you can scrape across the edge of the bowl to create a flat side for the bottom of the macaroon. Bake until the tops of cookies are lightly toasted, about 20 minutes. Let cool briefly on the baking sheets before moving to racks for further cooling.

Meanwhile, melt the chocolate in the top of a double boiler. Dip the bottoms of the macaroons in the chocolate and place back on the parchment to cool, flat-chocolate-side down. They will pull right off when cooled. That's the beauty of parchment! For rapid chocolate setting, place the macaroons in the freezer after dipping.

Store the macaroons in an airtight container. In extremely warm weather, you might want to keep them in the refrigerator to prevent the chocolate from melting. These cookies freeze well, but if you are freezing them for more than 1 week, it is best to freeze them without the chocolate and dip just before serving.

MAKES 75 MACAROONS

CHOCOLATE *mint* COOKIES

A thank you to Caroline Swift for this great recipe. Almond extract can be substituted for mint to give a different flavor. These cookies should be on the soft side so be very careful not to overbake them. They can be baked right after mixing but we usually make the dough into rolls, freeze, and bake when needed.

- 1¾ cups unsalted butter
- 2½ cups sugar
- 2 large eggs
- 2½ teaspoons vanilla extract
- 1 teaspoon mint extract
- 3¾ cups unbleached flour
- 1¼ cups unsweetened cocoa powder
- 1¼ teaspoons baking soda
- 1 teaspoon salt
- 1 cup chocolate chips

Preheat the oven to 350°F if not freezing the dough. Cream together the butter and sugar. Add the eggs and beat until fluffy. Add the vanilla and mint extracts and mix to combine. In another bowl, sift the dry ingredients together and then add to the egg mixture. Mix until all ingredients are well incorporated. Fold in the chocolate chips.

With a cookie scoop or spoon, scoop about 1 tablespoon of the dough and quickly roll it into a ball with your hands. Place on a cookie sheet lined with parchment paper and bake until just set, approximately 12 to 15 minutes. Let the cookies sit for a few minutes before removing with a spatula to the cooling rack.

If you want to bake later, divide the dough into 2 or 3 pieces and roll them into logs, approximately 2 inches in diameter. Wrap and freeze. To bake, remove the rolls from the freezer and let them sit at room temperature for 15 minutes to make slicing easier. Slice them about ¼-inch thick and bake following the directions above.

MAKES 8 DOZEN COOKIES

corn-lime COOKIES

The recipe for these tangy cookies came to us from a wonderful restaurant, Los Bagels, in Arcata, California. They are glazed after being baked and keep well. They also freeze well. You will need around 6 large limes to make this recipe.

- 2 cups unsalted butter
- 3 cups sugar
- 2 eggs
- 5 cups unbleached flour
- 1½ cups cornmeal
- 2 tablespoons zest of lime
- 1 teaspoon salt
- ½ teaspoon baking soda
- 2 tablespoons lime juice

Preheat the oven to 350°F. In a large bowl, cream the butter and sugar. Add the eggs and mix well. Combine the flour, cornmeal, lime zest, salt, and soda and add to the butter mixture. Add the lime juice and mix until all ingredients are thoroughly incorporated.

Using a small cookie scoop or a large spoon (to give about two tablespoons of dough), scoop the dough and roll into balls. Using a glass or a measuring cup, flatten each ball of dough to 2½ inches in diameter. A small piece of plastic wrap in between the dough and the implement will keep them from sticking.

Bake at 350°F until the cookies are just beginning to brown around the edges, about 15 minutes. Remove from the oven and cool. When cooled, make the glaze and spread on the cookies.

Lime Glaze:
- 3 cups sifted or sieved confectioners' sugar
- ¼ cup lime juice
- 1 teaspoon zest of lime

Mix all of the ingredients in the top of a double boiler and heat, stirring occasionally, just until liquid. You need to keep the double boiler warm, but be careful not to overheat it or the glaze will turn to syrup. Remove from the heat and brush the glaze on top of the cookies. Let the glaze cool and set before storing.

MAKES 6½ DOZEN COOKIES

ALMOND *biscotti*

We tried many biscotti recipes before we found this one, which is adapted from Fine Cooking *magazine. Hands down, it is our favorite biscotti.*

1⅓ cups whole almonds
1⅔ cups sugar
2¾ cups unbleached flour
1 teaspoon baking powder
½ teaspoon salt
Zest of 1 orange, minced
Zest of 1 lime, minced
Zest of 1 lemon, minced
½ teaspoon anise seed
3 egg yolks
3 whole eggs
1 teaspoon vanilla extract
½ teaspoon almond extract

Preheat the oven to 350°F. Toast the almonds on a baking sheet for 10 to 15 minutes or until they are golden brown inside and fragrant. Cool. Sift the sugar, flour, baking powder, and salt together in a large bowl. Add the citrus zests and anise seed and stir to combine.

In a separate bowl, whisk together the egg yolks, whole eggs, and the vanilla and almond extracts. Pour this mixture into the flour mixture and stir until the ingredients are almost incorporated. Add the whole almonds and mix until the dough barely comes together. Do not overmix.

Dump the dough out onto a lightly floured work surface and gently knead any dry remaining bits into the dough. If your eggs are especially large, you might need to add a little more flour to make the dough easy to handle. If the dough is extremely dry and won't hold together, add a drop or two of water and gently work it in. Divide the dough into 3 equal portions. With floured hands, roll and pat each portion of dough into a log, about 10 inches long and 2 inches wide. Place the logs 4 inches apart on a cookie sheet that is greased or lined with parchment paper.

Bake the logs for about 40 to 45 minutes at 350°F, until light brown on top but still soft. Remove from the oven and let cool for 10 minutes. Reduce the oven heat to 300°F. When the logs are cool enough to handle, slice them on the diagonal into ¾-inch-thick pieces. Place flat-side down onto the baking sheet and bake for 10 to 15 minutes. Remove the cookies from the oven, turn them over, and bake for an additional 10 minutes until the biscotti are just beginning to brown. Remove from the oven and cool on racks. When thoroughly cooled, store the biscotti in an airtight container.

MAKES APPROXIMATELY 36 COOKIES

CHOCOLATE & CANDIED ORANGE PEEL *biscotti*

This is one of our favorite biscotti recipes. You can make your own candied orange peel (page 205) or purchase it.

- 2½ cups whole hazelnuts
- 12 ounces bittersweet or semisweet chocolate (2 cups chocolate chips)
- 1 cup unsalted butter, at room temperature
- 4 large eggs
- 1 cup packed brown sugar
- 1 cup sugar plus ⅓ cup, for sprinkling
- 2 teaspoons vanilla extract
- ½ teaspoon almond extract
- 2 tablespoons instant espresso powder or finely ground coffee beans
- ¾ cup Dutch-processed cocoa powder, sifted
- 4 cups unbleached flour
- 1 teaspoon baking powder
- 1 teaspoon kosher salt
- 1 cup candied orange peel, chopped
- 2 egg whites
- ½ teaspoon orange extract (optional)

Preheat the oven to 350°F. Toast the hazelnuts on a baking sheet about 10 minutes or until browned. For this recipe you can leave the hazelnuts whole and with the skins on. Set aside. If not using chocolate chips, chop the chocolate into small slivers.

In an electric mixer, beat the butter until light and creamy. Add the eggs one at a time. Add the sugars and the vanilla and almond extracts. Mix together well. Add the espresso powder and the cocoa powder and mix. Scrape down the sides of the bowl as needed. Whisk together the flour, baking powder, and salt and add to the egg mixture along with the orange peel. Beat until thoroughly mixed. Add the hazelnuts and chocolate, mixing just to combine. The dough will be stiff and slightly sticky. Let the dough rest for 15 minutes before shaping.

Line baking sheets with parchment paper. Divide the dough into 6 equal pieces and, using as little flour as possible, form each piece into logs that are 12 to 14 inches long and about 1¼ inches wide. Transfer the logs to the baking sheets, keeping them about 3 inches apart.

In a small bowl, beat the egg whites with the orange extract until foamy. Brush the tops of the logs with this mixture and then sprinkle them with the sugar. Bake until firm in the center, about 35 minutes, rotating the sheets to ensure even baking. Remove from the oven and set the sheets on racks to cool for about 30 minutes.

Reduce the oven heat to 300°F. With a serrated knife, cut the logs, crosswise and on a diagonal, into ½-inch slices. Brush the tops again with the egg white mixture and sprinkle with sugar and then lay the slices flat on the baking sheets. Bake about 15 minutes. Then turn the biscotti over and bake an additional 10 minutes, until the cookies have dried out but the centers still feel a little soft. They will dry out more and harden as the cookies cool. Set the sheets to cool on racks and, when fully cool, store the biscotti in airtight containers.

MAKES APPROXIMATELY 10 DOZEN BISCOTTI

ITALIAN *sesame cookies*

These are wonderful little treats, not too sweet, and are delicious with tea, coffee, or a nice Zinfandel. They are easy to make and keep well.

- 3 cups unbleached flour
- 1 cup sugar
- 1½ teaspoons baking powder
- ½ teaspoon salt
- ¾ cup cold unsalted butter
- 2 teaspoons vanilla extract
- 3 eggs, beaten
- ½ cup sesame seeds

Preheat the oven to 350°F. Sift the flour, sugar, baking powder, and salt into a mixing bowl or into the work bowl of a food processor. Cut the butter into ½-inch cubes and work it into the dry ingredients until crumbly. Combine the vanilla and eggs and add to the flour mixture. Process, pulsing, or beat by hand until the dough is just moistened and uniformly mixed.

Put the sesame seeds in a shallow container, such as a pie tin. On a lightly floured surface, divide the dough into 4 equal pieces and shape each into a log, approximately 18 inches long and ½ inch in diameter. Brush the top of each log with water and cut it crosswise into 10 pieces, each about 1½ inches long. Dip the water-brushed tops in the sesame seeds and place the cookies 1 inch apart on baking sheets lined with parchment paper. Bake until golden and firm, about 25 to 30 minutes. Cool.

MAKES 40 COOKIES

vanilla nut WAFERS

This cookie is crispy and not too sweet. They are great alone or with tea or coffee. Make the dough into logs, freeze them, and then bake the cookies when needed.

1 cup unsalted butter, softened
½ cup firmly packed brown sugar
1½ cups sugar
2 eggs, beaten
1 tablespoon vanilla extract
4 cups unbleached flour
3 teaspoons baking powder
¼ teaspoon salt
1 cup walnuts, coarsely chopped

In a large bowl, with an electric mixer or by hand, cream the butter and sugars until light and fluffy. Add the eggs and vanilla and beat until well blended. In another bowl, sift together the flour, baking powder, and salt. Add the flour mixture to the egg mixture and stir until well blended. Add the nuts and mix until combined.

Divide the dough into 3 pieces. On a rectangular piece of plastic wrap or waxed paper, plop dough by the spoonful into the shape of a log, about 1½ inches wide by 10 to 12 inches long. Cover the dough with the wrap and roll back and forth to form a uniform cylinder. Place the rolls on a baking sheet and place them in the freezer for a few hours or overnight, until hard and set.

Preheat the oven to 400°F. Take the rolls out of the freezer and slice them into ¼-inch, or just a little thinner, slices. Lay them on a cookie sheet lined with parchment paper 2 inches apart. Bake until golden brown, about 15 minutes. Let them cool on racks before storing.

MAKES 5 DOZEN

butter tart BARS

This is a good dessert for a winter evening. The raisins or currants can be steeped in warm orange liqueur for 10 to 15 minutes before being added to the filling if desired.

Crust:
½ cup unsalted butter, softened
⅓ cup firmly packed brown sugar
1¼ cups unbleached flour

Filling:
2 eggs
1 cup firmly packed brown sugar
1 teaspoon unbleached flour
½ teaspoon baking powder
¼ teaspoon salt
¼ cup unsalted butter, melted
1 teaspoon vanilla extract
1½ cups raisins or currants
½ cup walnuts, coarsely chopped

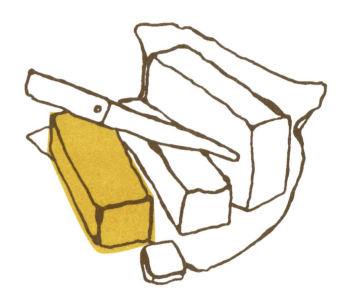

Preheat the oven to 350°F. For the crust, mix together the butter, brown sugar, and flour in a food processor or by hand, until all ingredients are equally incorporated and a ball is formed. Do not overmix. Press the dough into an ungreased, 8 by 8-inch pan and bake for 15 minutes, until golden brown. Cool.

To make the filling, lightly whisk the eggs in a mixing bowl. Add the remaining ingredients and stir to combine. Spread the filling over the cooled crust. Bake for about 20 minutes or until puffed and brown on top. Depending on your oven, this could take as long as 50 minutes. The filling should be starting to set when you take it from the oven. Cool on racks before cutting into bars.

MAKES 16 SMALL BARS

meyer lemon BARS

Meyer lemons are exceptionally juicy, with a low-acid, sweet fruit that works well in baking. If you are unable to find this variety, regular lemons can be used in this recipe with fine results.

Shortbread Crust:
1¼ cups unbleached flour
⅓ cup confectioners' sugar
10 tablespoons cold unsalted butter, cut into small cubes
2 teaspoons cold water

Filling:
1½ cups sugar
¼ cup unbleached flour
4 large eggs
Zest of 2 large Meyer lemons, finely chopped
⅓ cup Meyer lemon juice
3 tablespoons confectioners' sugar

Preheat the oven to 350°F. Grease a shallow 7½ by 11¾-inch baking pan. Combine the flour and confectioners' sugar in a food processor fitted with a steel blade. Pulse for about 5 seconds to mix. Add the butter and pulse for about 1 minute, until the butter is cut evenly into the dry ingredients and the mixture resembles coarse meal. Add the cold water and process until the dough just begins to hold together and form a ball. If necessary, add a few more drops of water, but do not overmix. This can be done by hand too, cutting the butter into the dry ingredients and then adding the water and mixing until the dough comes together.

Turn the dough into the baking pan and, using your fingertips, press it in evenly. Place in the preheated oven and bake for about 15 to 20 minutes, or until just starting to brown around the edge. Remove from the oven and allow to cool slightly.

Meanwhile, start preparing the filling by combining the sugar and flour in a medium bowl. Add the eggs and whisk until thick and creamy. Add the lemon zest and juice and mix until blended and smooth. Pour the lemon mixture over the crust and return to the oven to bake for about 20 to 25 minutes, or until the filling is set and the edges begin to color. Do not overbake. Remove the dish from the oven and allow it to rest until completely cooled. Cut into bars and sift confectioners' sugar over the top before serving.

MAKES 24 TO 28 SMALL BARS

FUDGE *brownies*

This is the chewiest and most delectable brownie ever! A chocolate ganache would top it off nicely or you could dust the top with confectioners' sugar.

- 12 ounces semisweet chocolate (2 cups chocolate chips)
- 1 cup plus 2 tablespoons unsalted butter
- 4½ cups confectioners' sugar
- 2¼ cups unbleached flour
- 6 tablespoons unsweetened cocoa powder plus a small amount, for dusting the pan
- 2¼ teaspoons baking powder
- ⅓ teaspoon salt
- 6 eggs
- 4½ teaspoons vanilla extract
- ½ teaspoon almond extract
- 4½ teaspoons corn syrup, light or dark style
- 1½ cups toasted walnuts or pecans (optional)

Preheat the oven to 350°F. Grease a 10 by 15-inch Pyrex baking dish and dust it lightly with cocoa powder. In the top of a double boiler, melt together the chocolate and the butter. Let this mixture cool to room temperature.

Meanwhile, sift the sugar, flour, cocoa powder, baking powder, and salt into a mixing bowl. In another large mixing bowl, whisk together the eggs, vanilla and almond extracts, and corn syrup until well blended. When the chocolate-butter mixture has cooled, add it to the egg mixture and stir until combined. With a spoon or using an electric mixer, slowly add the flour mixture to the chocolate mixture and stir until all ingredients have been incorporated and blended. Spread the brownie batter evenly into the greased and dusted pan and bake for about 25 to 30 minutes, or until the brownies have pulled away from the sides of the pan slightly and the batter has risen and set with a glazed and shiny appearance on top. Remove from the oven and place on a rack for 10 to 15 minutes to cool before cutting.

MAKES 24 LARGE BROWNIES

dream BARS

This is an old-fashioned favorite. These bars are very sweet, so make sure you cut them quite small.

Crust:
½ cup unsalted butter, room temperature
1 cup unbleached flour
1 tablespoon brown sugar

Filling:
2 eggs, beaten
1 cup firmly packed brown sugar
1½ tablespoons unbleached flour
¾ teaspoon baking powder
Pinch of salt
¾ cup unsweetened shredded coconut
½ cup walnuts, coarsely chopped
1 teaspoon vanilla extract

Vanilla Icing Glaze:
3 tablespoons unsalted butter, softened
1½ cups confectioners' sugar, sifted
½ teaspoon vanilla extract
1 tablespoon milk or water, enough to make the icing spreadable

Preheat the oven to 350°F. For the crust, combine the butter, flour, and brown sugar in a food processor fitted with a metal blade and pulse until mixture comes together in a ball. Press the dough into the bottom of an 8 by 8-inch Pyrex pan. Bake the crust for 15 minutes, or until lightly browned. Let cool on a rack.

Turn down the oven to 275°F. While the crust is baking, mix together all of the ingredients for the filling. Evenly spread the filling over the cooled crust and bake for about 1 hour, or until golden brown and the filling has set. Remove from the oven and let cool slightly. Combine all of the ingredients for the glaze and mix until smooth. While the bars are still slightly warm, glaze them with a thin layer of the vanilla icing. Let cool completely before cutting into small squares.

MAKES 16 BARS

citrus-olive oil CAKE

This cake came to us from Oliveto's Restaurant in Berkeley, California. We like to think of it as a somewhat "healthy" dessert because it uses olive oil instead of butter. Certainly it is a favorite for aroma and taste. Serve with softly whipped, slightly sweetened cream.

- 2 small navel oranges
- 1 lemon
- 6 ounces almonds, approximately 1½ cups
- 4 eggs
- ½ teaspoon salt
- ½ cup sugar
- 1 cup unbleached flour
- 3 teaspoons baking powder
- ⅔ cup olive oil

In a small saucepan, cover the oranges and lemon with water and simmer for 30 minutes. Drain. When cool enough to handle, cut off the stem ends and cut the fruit in half. Scoop the pulp and seeds out of the lemon and discard. Cut the oranges into lengthwise sections and examine for seeds if you used Valencia instead of navel oranges. Either by hand or pulsing in a food processor, chop the oranges and the lemon rind very fine. Put into a sieve and let sit to drain out any excess liquid.

Preheat the oven to 350°F. Chop the almonds in a food processor or by hand until they are almost as fine as crumbs. Set aside.

Beat the eggs and salt together until they are foamy and light. Then gradually add the sugar, while beating, until the mixture is light-colored and thick. Sift together the flour and baking powder and add to the egg mixture until blended. Mix in the chopped citrus, the ground almonds, and the oil. Do not overmix.

Grease a 9- or 10-inch springform pan. Line the bottom with parchment paper. Turn the batter into the pan and bake for 1 hour, or until a toothpick inserted into the middle comes out clean. Let cool before cutting. This cake keeps exceptionally well.

MAKES 12 TO 16 SERVINGS

lemon pudding CAKE

For many, this will be a familiar taste from childhood. This old-fashioned dessert has become popular again. You can make it with either lemon or orange;* both are equally good. Meyer lemons would be your best option and, if you use them, you can increase the amount of zest you use.

- **4 egg whites, beaten stiff**
- **4 egg yolks**
- **¾ cup sugar**
- **4 tablespoons flour**
- **½ cup lemon juice**
- **1 tablespoon grated lemon zest**
- **2 cups light cream or milk**

Place a rack in the middle of the oven. Preheat the oven to 350°F. Butter either a 1-quart ceramic soufflé dish or a 9 by 13-inch glass pan. You will also need a larger, ungreased 10 by 15-inch pan to use during the baking process. You will need boiling water for the water bath.

Separate the eggs and beat the egg whites until stiff but not dry. Set aside. Cream the butter until light, and then add the sugar and flour and beat until light and fluffy. Add the egg yolks, one at a time, beating well after each addition. Add the lemon juice, zest, and light cream. Mix together. Fold in ¼ of the beaten egg whites and mix to lighten, then slowly fold in the remaining egg whites, being careful not to overmix. Transfer the mixture to the prepared baking dish, pour boiling water into the larger pan to a depth of at least 1 inch. Set the baking dish with the cake inside the large pan and place all in the oven.

Bake for about 1 hour or until the top is golden brown, the center is just set, and the top springs back when pushed lightly with your hand. Let the cake cool on a rack for 10 minutes. Serve warm, scooping up some of the pudding from the bottom with each serving.

*If you wish to make the orange version, simply increase the flour to ⅓ cup, the orange juice to 1 cup, and use 2 tablespoons of orange zest. All other ingredients remain the same.

MAKES 6 TO 8 SERVINGS

black magic CAKE

Caroline Swift donated the recipe for this easy-to-make chocolate cake. It is a delicious, classic, birthday-style-cake, excellent with a simple chocolate frosting or served with a mint crème anglaise sauce. It can also be made into cupcakes.

- 2½ cups sugar
- 2¼ cups flour
- 2½ teaspoons baking soda
- 1¼ teaspoons baking powder
- 1¼ teaspoons salt
- ¾ cup plus 3 tablespoons unsweetened cocoa powder
- 1¼ cups freshly brewed, strong coffee, cooled
- 1¼ cups buttermilk
- ½ cup plus 2 tablespoons vegetable oil
- 1¼ teaspoons vanilla extract
- 3 eggs

Preheat the oven to 350°F. Butter and flour a 10 by 15-inch Pyrex pan or two 9-inch round cake pans. Measure the sugar into a large mixing bowl. Sift the remaining dry ingredients into the bowl of sugar and whisk together. In another bowl, whisk together all of the wet ingredients until well blended. Add the wet ingredients to the dry and whisk until evenly incorporated and blended.

Pour this batter into the prepared pan and bake for approximately 40 to 45 minutes, or until the cake is pulling away from the sides of the pan and the top of the cake springs back when it is lightly pressed with your hand. A toothpick inserted into the cake should come out clean. Let cool on racks for 10 minutes before removing from the pan for further cooling.

MAKES 16 TO 24 SERVINGS OR APPROXIMATELY 3 DOZEN CUPCAKES

CHOCOLATE *torte*

We serve this creamy chocolate torte year-round with raspberry sauce or mint crème anglaise. You can make it with bittersweet or semisweet chocolate. It keeps and freezes well.

> 8 ounces bittersweet or semisweet chocolate, chopped
> ¾ cup unsalted butter
> 6 large eggs, separated
> 1 cup sugar
> ¼ cup flour
> ¼ teaspoon salt
> Confectioners' sugar, for dusting

Preheat the oven to 325°F. Butter a 9-inch round cake pan and line the bottom with parchment paper. Melt the chocolate and butter together over low heat. When melted, set aside and let cool.

In a medium bowl, whip the yolks with ½ cup of the sugar until they are pale yellow and thick. Mix in the flour and then the chocolate mixture. In a separate bowl, whip the egg whites with the remaining ½ cup of sugar and the salt until soft peaks are formed. Do not overwhip. Fold the egg whites into the chocolate batter.

Spread the batter into the prepared pan and bake until the center is firm, about 45 minutes. It should be moist, but not runny, when tested with a toothpick. The cake will have risen dramatically and will have a crust on the top. As it cools, the cake will fall and the crust will shatter a little. After the cake has cooled, run a knife around the edges and turn the pan over to release the cake. Dust with confectioners' sugar and cut into 12 or 16 pieces.

MAKES 12 TO 16 SERVINGS

almond TART

This is a classic almond tart, a wonderful way to end a meal.

Tart Dough:
1⅓ cups unbleached flour
¼ teaspoon salt
4 teaspoons sugar
⅔ cup unsalted butter, chilled and cut into small pieces
1 teaspoon vanilla extract
1 tablespoon cold water

Put the flour, salt, sugar, and butter into a food processor fitted with a metal blade and pulse until the dough begins to come together. Add the vanilla and as little of the water as possible and continue to process until the dough forms into a ball. Using your hands, press the dough into a 9-inch tart pan. Place in the freezer to chill for about 30 minutes before baking. This will help reduce shrinkage.

Preheat the oven to 425°F. Bake the chilled crust about 15 minutes, checking at least once to prick and deflate any big air bubbles that might form. Bake until the shell appears dry and is just barely starting to change color but is not brown. Remove from the oven to a rack and let the shell cool completely.

Filling:
¾ cup heavy cream
¾ cup sugar
⅛ teaspoon almond extract
1 tablespoon orange liqueur (Cointreau, Triple Sec, or Grand Marnier)
1 cup coarsely chopped almonds

Preheat the oven to 425°F. Place the cream and sugar in a small saucepan and cook over medium-low heat until the sugar is dissolved and the mixture is beginning to appear translucent. Add the almond extract and the orange liqueur and stir to blend. Stir in the almonds and pour the filling into the tart shell, spreading evenly. The filling will be fairly shallow in the shell.

Line a baking sheet with foil and place the tart on it. Place it in the oven and bake for about 25 minutes, rotating the tart halfway through to get even browning. The top should be a deep golden brown. Remove the tart, and as soon as it is cool enough to handle, ease it gently from the rim, loosening the sides with a knife or small spatula if needed.

MAKES ONE 9-INCH TART

banana cake
FILLED WITH RUM PASTRY CREAM

Occasionally we like to make this cake into The Banana Rum Extravaganza. That includes both pastry cream and the rum-glazed bananas, which are explained below. However, the cake itself is delicious served simply with a dusting of confectioners' sugar and a dollop of whipped cream. It can also be frosted with the Caramel Frosting on page 202.

Cake:
2 cups flour
1 teaspoon baking soda
1 teaspoon baking powder
1 teaspoon salt
½ cup vegetable oil
½ cup buttermilk
1¼ cups mashed ripe banana
2 eggs
1½ cups sugar
½ cup chopped, lightly toasted walnuts or pecans (optional)

½ recipe of pastry cream, mixed with 1 tablespoon rum (page 201)

Rum-Glazed Bananas:
2 bananas, sliced
⅓ cup sugar
¼ cup unsalted butter
⅓ cup dark rum

Confectioners' sugar to dust the top of the cake

Preheat the oven to 350°F. Grease two 10-inch spring form pans and line with wax paper or parchment paper.

Into a large mixing bowl, sift the flour, baking soda, baking powder, and salt. Add the oil, buttermilk, and bananas. Beat with a whisk or electric mixer for about 30 seconds to form a smooth batter.

In a separate bowl, beat the eggs until thick and foamy. Gradually add the sugar, and continue beating for three minutes. If using walnuts, toast for about 10 minutes in the 350°F oven and then rub them in a towel to remove some of the bitter skin. Add the walnuts or pecans to the egg-sugar mixture.

Fold this egg-sugar-nut mixture into the batter. Pour the batter evenly into the prepared pans. Bake for 35 to 45 minutes, or until a knife comes out clean when inserted in the center and the cake is pulling away from the sides of the pan. Remove the cakes from the oven and let sit on the rack to cool for ten minutes, run a knife around the cakes, and turn them out. Let the cakes cool.

Make the pastry cream.

Slice the bananas and sauté them briefly in the sugar, butter, and rum. When the bananas have softened a bit, remove from heat. Spread the rum pastry cream on one of the cakes, arrange the sliced bananas on top. Place the remaining cake on top. Dust with confectioners' sugar and serve.

MAKES 12 SERVINGS

orange *chiffon* CAKE

This is a light cake that goes well with vanilla ice cream. The cake should not be baked in a convection oven because the fan will disturb the fluffy batter.

Dry:
2 cups sifted flour
1 cup sugar
1 tablespoon baking powder
1 teaspoon salt

Wet:
7 egg yolks
½ cup vegetable oil
Zest of 2 oranges
¾ cup orange juice

Egg Whites:
7 egg whites
½ teaspoon cream of tartar
½ cup sugar

Preheat the oven to 325°F. Sift the flour, 1 cup of sugar, baking powder, and salt into a large bowl. Set aside. Beat the egg yolks until light and fluffy. Add the vegetable oil, zest, and orange juice and stir to blend.

In a dry bowl, whip the egg whites with the cream of tartar. Gradually add the ½ cup of sugar, while beating, until the egg whites are stiff but not dry. Fold about one-quarter of the egg whites into the egg yolk mixture. Then fold half of the egg yolk mixture into the dry ingredients, then half of the remaining egg whites, then the remaining egg yolk mixture, and finally, the last of the egg whites.

Scoop the batter into a 10 by 4-inch angel food cake pan (tube pan) with a removable bottom. It should not be a nonstick pan; do not grease the pan. Bake until the top springs back when lightly pressed with your hand and a toothpick inserted in the middle comes out clean, approximately 1 hour. Let cool upside down for at least 1½ hours. To unmold, turn right-side-up and run a knife around the edge. Turn out.

We frost this cake with Quick Orange Icing (page 203), drizzling it over the top and letting the extra drip down the sides of the cake.

MAKES 16 SERVINGS

pumpkin-ginger
CAKE WITH PRALINE PECANS

This is a cake that always receives many favorable comments. Sami Koelker shared this with Liz when they worked together in Alaska.

Cake:
- 4 eggs
- 2 cups sugar
- 1 cup vegetable oil
- 2 cups canned pumpkin
- 2 cups unbleached flour
- 2 teaspoons ground cinnamon
- ½ teaspoon salt
- 1 teaspoon baking soda
- 2 teaspoons baking powder
- ½ teaspoon ground ginger
- ½ teaspoon cloves
- ½ teaspoon nutmeg
- 4 tablespoons minced, candied ginger

Praline Pecans:
- 1½ cups pecan halves
- ⅓ cup sugar

Whipped Cream:
- 1 pint whipping cream
- ¼ cup sugar
- ½ teaspoon vanilla extract

Preheat the oven to 350°F. In a large bowl, combine the eggs, 2 cups sugar, oil, and pumpkin and mix well. In a separate bowl, sift together all the dry ingredients. Add the dry ingredients to the wet, mix just until blended, and then stir in the candied ginger.

Pour the batter into two 9-inch cake pans, greased and lined with parchment paper.

Bake for 40 minutes or until done. Let rest a few minutes, then turn out on racks to cool.

For the final assembly, the nuts may be done ahead, but the cream should be whipped and the cake assembled within a few hours of service.

To make the praline pecans, lightly toast the pecans in a 350°F oven for about 10 minutes. Melt the ⅓ cup sugar in a skillet over low heat. When it is dissolved and a light brown color (310°F on a candy thermometer), add the pecans and stir until coated with the sugar. Remove immediately from the heat and pour onto a piece of parchment paper or a sheet pan. Stir to separate the nuts. Reserve 12 pecans to put around the top edge of the cake and coarsely chop the remaining nuts.

To assemble the cake, whip the cream with the ¼ cup sugar and vanilla until stiff enough that it will hold its shape. Spread about one-third of the whipped cream over the bottom cake layer and sprinkle the chopped pecans over it. Place the top layer over the bottom layer and then spread the remaining whipped cream over the sides and top of the cake. Decorate with the reserved pecan halves.

MAKES 12 TO 16 SERVINGS

fresh pear CAKE

This simple, homey dessert can be dressed up with a sprinkling of confectioners' sugar and served with vanilla ice cream or whipped cream on the side. It is a moist cake that keeps for days in the refrigerator. It can also be made with apples.

- 1 cup coarsely chopped walnuts
- 2 cups unbleached flour
- 2 teaspoons baking soda
- ¾ teaspoon salt
- 2 teaspoons ground cinnamon
- 2 eggs
- ¼ cup sugar
- 2 cups packed brown sugar
- ¼ cup water
- 1 teaspoon vanilla extract
- ½ cup vegetable oil
- 4 cups pears, peeled and cut into ½-inch cubes

Preheat the oven to 325°F. Toast the walnuts at 325°F for 10 to 15 minutes, until they have a slightly roasted flavor. Rub them with a towel to remove some of the bitter skins.

Sift together the flour, baking soda, salt, and cinnamon and set aside. In a bowl large enough to hold all of the batter, beat the eggs, sugars, water, vanilla, and oil. Add the flour mixture and nuts. When thoroughly mixed, add the pears and stir just to blend.

Pour into a greased 9 by 13 by 2-inch pan and bake at 325°F for 65 to 75 minutes. The cake should have pulled away from the edge of the pan. It should appear moist but not wet. Serve with softly whipped cream, slightly sweetened.

MAKES 12 TO 18 SERVINGS

summer fruit TART

This dessert is easy to make and really shows off the luscious fruits of summer. A simple shell is baked, covered with flavored cream cheese, topped with ripe fruit, and then glazed. The shell can be made early in the day, but we prefer to add the filling, fruit, and glaze just a few hours before serving, so the crust remains crisp and the fruit colors stay unmixed. For example, cut strawberries will stain pineapple red.

Crust:
½ cup unsalted butter, softened
¼ cup confectioners' sugar
1 cup unbleached flour

Filling:
One 8-ounce package cream cheese
½ cup sugar
1 teaspoon vanilla extract
Ripe fruit such as peaches, nectarines, strawberries, pineapple, blueberries, or cherries

Glaze:
2 tablespoons cornstarch
1 cup pineapple juice
½ cup sugar
1 teaspoon lemon juice

Preheat the oven to 350°F. Mix the butter, confectioners' sugar, and flour together and press into the bottom of a 10-inch springform or tart pan. Bake until the crust is just starting to brown, about 12 minutes. Remove from the oven and cool.

Cream together the cream cheese, sugar, and vanilla and spread onto the cooled crust. Refrigerate if not serving immediately.

Prepare your choice of fruit and arrange attractively over the topping.

In a small, non-reactive saucepan, whisk together the cornstarch, pineapple juice, sugar, and lemon juice. Bring to a simmer over medium heat, stirring occasionally, and cook until the cornstarch is clear and the mixture is slightly thickened. Pour the glaze over the fruit and refrigerate the tart to chill the glaze. To serve, remove the outer rim of the springform and cut.

MAKES 12 TO 16 SERVINGS

BUTTERMILK-LEMON *pound cake*

This is a wonderful dessert for the winter, when lemons are in season. Equally good with an afternoon cup of tea or as a dessert garnished with blueberry sauce and softly whipped cream, this cake is simple and easy to make and it freezes well.

- 3 cups unbleached flour
- ½ teaspoon baking powder
- ½ teaspoon baking soda
- 1 teaspoon salt
- 1 cup unsalted butter, softened
- 2 cups sugar
- 4 eggs, room temperature
- 2 tablespoons fresh lemon juice
- 1 teaspoon lemon extract
- 1 tablespoon lemon zest, minced
- 1 cup buttermilk
- Blueberry sauce (page 197)
- Whipped cream

Preheat the oven to 350°F. Grease and flour two 8 ½ by 4 ½ by 2 ½-inch loaf pans. Sift together the flour, baking powder, soda, and salt. Set aside. In a large mixing bowl, beat the butter until smooth and creamy. Slowly add the sugar, beating constantly, until the mixture is smooth and a light lemon color. Add the eggs and beat until the mixture is light and fluffy.

Stir the lemon juice, lemon extract, and lemon zest into the buttermilk. Sprinkle about half of the flour mixture over the butter mixture and beat until blended. Beat half of the buttermilk mixture into the batter. Add the remaining flour and buttermilk mixtures and beat until the batter is smooth and well blended.

Pour the batter into the prepared pans and bake for 40 to 45 minutes, or until a toothpick comes out clean when inserted into the center of the cake. The cake will have pulled away from the sides of the pan a bit and will bounce back slightly when pressed with your hand. The tops of the loaves will be cracked. Remove from the oven and let the loaves cool for 5 minutes before turning them out onto a rack to finish cooling. Slice 1-inch thick. To serve as a dessert, place 2 slices on the plate. Spoon over the blueberry sauce and add a dollop of whipped cream.

MAKES 2 LOAVES

ginger-peach UPSIDE-DOWN CAKE

This is an excellent variation on the gingerbread theme. We love the moistness of the cake and the caramelized top with the fruit peeking through. Sometimes we add minced candied ginger to the batter for an extra kick. Although we usually recommend using fruit in season, we have made this successfully with canned pears and peaches. This cake keeps well, and it looks beautiful with a dollop of lightly whipped cream or crème fraîche.

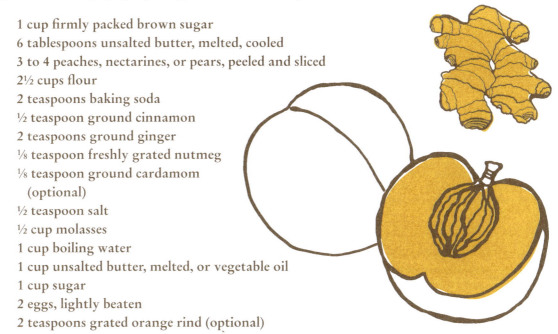

- 1 cup firmly packed brown sugar
- 6 tablespoons unsalted butter, melted, cooled
- 3 to 4 peaches, nectarines, or pears, peeled and sliced
- 2½ cups flour
- 2 teaspoons baking soda
- ½ teaspoon ground cinnamon
- 2 teaspoons ground ginger
- ⅛ teaspoon freshly grated nutmeg
- ⅛ teaspoon ground cardamom (optional)
- ½ teaspoon salt
- ½ cup molasses
- 1 cup boiling water
- 1 cup unsalted butter, melted, or vegetable oil
- 1 cup sugar
- 2 eggs, lightly beaten
- 2 teaspoons grated orange rind (optional)

Preheat the oven to 350°F. Butter the sides of a 10 by 3-inch springform pan and line the bottom with a circle of parchment paper. Combine the brown sugar with the melted butter and spread evenly on the bottom of the pan. Place the sliced fruit decoratively and in a tight concentric circle atop the butter and brown sugar.

Sift together the flour, baking soda, cinnamon, ginger, nutmeg, cardamom, and salt. Set aside. In a bowl, combine the molasses and water and set aside.

In a large mixing bowl, combine the butter or oil and sugar and beat until smooth and light. Beat in the eggs and orange rind until well blended. Add the molasses and water and blend. Stir in the dry ingredients until well incorporated.

Pour the batter over the fruit in the springform pan. Place the pan on a baking sheet. (This will protect your oven from drops of sugar and butter that might leak from the pan while baking.) Place the cake in the oven and bake for approximately 1 hour, or until a knife or toothpick comes out clean. If the top of the gingerbread looks like it's burning halfway through baking, place a piece of foil loosely on top. Let the cake cool for 30 minutes on a rack before pulling off the sides of the springform and inverting the cake onto a plate. Be careful, when pulling off the bottom, to keep the fruit intact. Serve warm or at room temperature.

MAKES 12 TO 16 SERVINGS

APPLE-CRANBERRY *crisp*

Fruit crisps add a homey touch to meals throughout the year. Vary your choice of fruit to take advantage of what is in season. We give a recipe for Apple-Cranberry Crisp here, but other flavorful combinations include apple with rhubarb or strawberries, peach and blueberry, or rhubarb and raspberries. The crisp topping is easy to make and keeps well in the freezer or refrigerator, ready for an impromptu dessert, so make extra. If using frozen cranberries, strawberries, or blueberries, it is not necessary to thaw them first. We usually do add a squeeze of lemon and some lemon zest to the fruit.

Topping:
½ cup unsalted butter, room temperature
¼ to ½ cup brown sugar
¾ cup unbleached flour
½ cup regular rolled oats
1 teaspoon ground cinnamon
½ teaspoon ground ginger
¼ teaspoon grated nutmeg
Toasted almonds, walnuts, or pecans, coarsely chopped, approximately ½ cup (optional)

Put all of the ingredients, except the nuts, into the bowl of an electric mixer fitted with a paddle attachment. Mix until everything begins to hold together but is still crumbly. If mixing by hand, work in the butter with your fingers until the topping is crumbly and begins to hold together. If adding toasted nuts, add them at the end and stir in just to blend. Do not overmix. This makes enough for a 9 by 13-inch pan.

Apple-Cranberry Crisp:
6 cups peeled and sliced apples, approximately 5 to 6 apples
1 cup fresh or frozen cranberries
¼ to ½ cup firmly packed brown sugar
4 tablespoons flour
1 teaspoon ground cinnamon
Zest of 1 lemon
1 teaspoon lemon juice

Preheat the oven to 350°F. Cut up the apples, mix with the cranberries, and measure. You will need 6 to 7 cups for a 9 by 13-inch pan. Mix the sugar, flour, and cinnamon and stir into the fruit. Add the lemon zest and juice. Put the fruit mixture into the baking pan and crumble the topping over it. Bake for 1 hour or until the top is browned and crisp, the fruit is soft when pierced with a fork, and the liquid is bubbling up. Serve the crisp with a scoop of vanilla ice cream or a dollop of crème fraîche.

MAKES 12 TO 15 SERVINGS

ALL-BUTTER *pie crust*

This is a flaky crust that rolls out easily. We give you quantities to make either a single or a double crust. Remember to keep all of the ingredients cold and work the dough as little as possible. This will ensure a light and flaky crust.

Single 9-inch Pie:
1½ cups unbleached flour
¼ teaspoon salt
9 tablespoons unsalted butter (1 stick plus 1 tablespoon), cut into small pieces
3 tablespoons ice water

Double 9-inch Pie:
2¼ cups unbleached flour
½ teaspoon salt
14 tablespoons unsalted butter (1 stick plus 6 tablespoons), cut in small pieces
4½ tablespoons ice water

Whisk the flour and salt together in a bowl or a food processor. Add the butter and cut it in with a pastry cutter or pulse in the food processor, until the mixture resembles coarse meal and the butter is in ¼-inch pieces. Sprinkle on the water and combine just until the dough comes together.

Dump the dough onto a work surface and press into a ball, then flatten into a disk. Wrap in plastic wrap and let rest for at least one hour in the refrigerator. When ready to use, lightly flour a work surface and roll the dough into a circle that is ⅛-inch thick and about 12 inches in diameter. Gently fold the dough in half and lift into a 9-inch pie pan. Unfold and settle into the pan, then fold and crimp the edges.

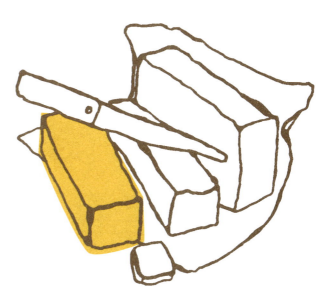

desserts . PAGE 235

MOM'S BEST EVER *pumpkin pie*

This is a legendary family recipe, much beloved for its light and creamy texture. It is, of course, best made with fresh homemade pumpkin, but if you don't have time for steaming or baking a pie pumpkin or butternut squash, then canned pumpkin works fine. We always make two pies so there will be some leftover for breakfast the next day.

- **1 single recipe All-Butter Pie Crust (page 235), unbaked**
- **½ cup sugar**
- **1 cup cooked pumpkin**
- **2 eggs**
- **½ teaspoon salt**
- **½ teaspoon ground cinnamon**
- **½ teaspoon ground or grated nutmeg**
- **½ teaspoon ground ginger**
- **1½ cups whole milk**

Preheat the oven to 450°F. Whisk together the sugar, pumpkin, eggs, salt, cinnamon, nutmeg, and ginger in a large bowl, whisking until the eggs are beaten in. Add the milk and stir. Do not get this mixture frothy. Roll out the pie crust and place in the pie pan. Pour the filling into the unbaked pie shell. Bake at 450°F for 10 minutes. Turn the oven down to 350°F and bake until the filling has puffed up and most likely has a crack around the edge. A knife inserted about 2 inches from the edge should come out clean. This will take 45 minutes to 1 hour. When the pie is done, remove from the oven and cool. The filling will settle as it cools. Serve with softly whipped cream if desired.

MAKES ONE 9-INCH PIE

cherry-peach PIE

This combination makes a beautiful pie, with yellow peaches nestled in pink juice and dark cherries scattered throughout. Frozen cherries work fine, but do use fully ripe yellow peaches. Fruit pies are best if they have at least two hours to cool before cutting.

- 1 double recipe All-Butter Pie Crust (page 235) with ½ tablespoon lemon zest added
- ¾ cup sugar plus more for sprinkling
- ¼ cup minute tapioca
- Pinch of salt
- 1 tablespoon lemon juice
- 4 cups yellow peaches, skinned and sliced into large, ¾-inch chunks
- 1 cup pitted red pie or Bing cherries, fresh or frozen
- 1 tablespoon unsalted butter

Preheat the oven to 450°F. Mix together the sugar, tapioca, salt, and lemon juice in a medium bowl. Prepare the fruit and stir into the sugar mixture. Set aside and let rest for at least 15 minutes.

Roll out one circle of dough and place onto a pie pan, settling the dough into the bottom without stretching it. Spoon the fruit mixture onto the crust. Break the butter into tiny pieces and scatter them over the fruit. Roll out the top crust, place it over the fruit, and crimp and flute the two crusts together. Cut steam vents decoratively in the top crust. Brush the top of the crust with water and sprinkle sugar over the top.

Place the pie in the lower half of the oven and bake for 15 minutes. Lower the temperature to 400°F and continue baking for 30 minutes. If the pie seems to be browning on top too much, you can turn the oven down to 350°F. If the top needs more browning, move the pie to a higher rack. Continue baking for an additional 15 to 20 minutes, or until the juices are translucent, thick, and bubbling up through the vents. Let cool and serve.

MAKES ONE 9-INCH PIE

suggested reading

Aidells, Bruce and Denis Kelly. *The Complete Meat Cookbook.* New York. Boston. Houghton Mifflin. 1998.

Child, Julia. *The Way to Cook.* New York. Alfred A. Knopf. 1989.

Corriher, Shirley O. *Cookwise.* New York. William Morrow and Company, Inc. 1997.

Clayton, Bernard Jr. *The Complete Book of Breads.* New York. Simon and Schuster. 1973.

Cunningham, Marion. *The Breakfast Book.* New York. Alfred A. Knopf. 1988.

Cunningham, Marion. *The Fannie Farmer Cookbook.* New York. Alfred A. Knopf. 1993.

Greenspan, Dorie. *Baking with Julia.* New York. William Morrow and Company. 1996.

Katzen, Mollie. *Sunlight Café.* New York. Hyperion. 2002.

Madison, Deborah. *The Greens Cookbook.* New York. Bantam Books. 1987.

Ortiz, Joe. *The Village Baker.* Berkeley. Ten Speed Press. 1993.

Pence, Caprial. *Caprial's Café.* Berkeley. 1994.

Reinhart, Peter. *Brother Juniper's Bread Book.* Menlo Park. Addison-Wesley Publishing Company. 1991.

Rodgers, Judy. *The Zuni Café Cookbook.* New York-London. W.W. Norton and Company. 2002.

Rombauer, Irma S. with Marion Rombauer and Ethan Becker. *The All New Joy of Cooking.* New York. Scribner. 1997.

The San Francisco Chronicle Cookbook, edited by Michael Bauer and Fran Irwin. San Francisco. Chronicle Books. 1997.

Somerville, Annie. *Fields of Greens.* New York. Bantam Books. 1993.

Magazines:

Fine Cooking. Taunton Press. Newtown, CT.

Saveur. World Publications. New York, NY.

index

a

Aioli, basil, recipe, 180; 112
Apple
    Apple-Cranberry Crisp, 234
    Apple Strudel, 34

b

Balsamic Vinaigrette, 84
Bananas
    Banana Cake with Rum Pastry Cream, 227
    Banana Coconut Muffins, 39
Barbeque Sauce
    Braised Beef Short Ribs, in, 123
    Sauce recipe, 186
Bars, dessert
    Butter Tart Bars, 218
    Dream Bars, 221
    Fudge Brownies, 220
    Meyer Lemon Bars, 219
Basil Aioli, recipe, 180; 112
Beans
    Black Bean Chili, 77
    Black Bean Salad, 92
    Corn, Bean and Squash Stew, 70
    Green, Roasted with Shallots and Hazelnuts, 165
    Hummus, recipe, 191; 100, 120
    Lentil soup, 78
    Pinto Beans, Homemade, 174
    White Bean Soup, 74
Beef
    Beef Stew with Cabernet and Hoisin Sauce, 124
    Grilled Hanger Steak, 122
    Short Ribs Braised in Barbeque Sauce, 123
Biscotti
    Almond, 214
    Chocolate and Candied Orange Peel, 215
Biscuits, herbed, 44
Blueberries
    Blueberry Buckle, 35
    Blueberry Muffins, 41
    Blueberry Sauce, recipe, 197; 29, 232
Braised Chicken with Thyme and Apple Cider, 110
Braised Sweet and Sour Red Cabbage, 169
Breads, discussion of, 46–48
    Breadsticks, 61
    Cheese Onion Poppy Seed, 57
    Cornbread with Chiles and Cheese, 62
    Focaccia, 58
    Fruit Bread, 60

Italian Herb Bread, 54
　　Onion Rye Caraway, 56
　　Seeded Dinner Rolls, 51
　　Sourdough , 52
　　Struan, 55
　　Walnut Rosemary Beer, 50
　　Whole Wheat, 49
Broccoli
　　Chinese-Style Broccoli with Oyster Sauce, 164
　　Winter Curry, 138
Brussels Sprouts, Roasted
with Sage and Squash, 159
Buckle, blueberry, 35
Butternut Squash
　　Butternut Squash Galette, 154
　　Corn, Bean and Squash Stew, 70
　　Cornish Game Hens with
　　Butternut Squash and Sage, 114
　　Curried Butternut Squash Soup, 69
　　Roasted Brussels Sprouts
　　with Sage and Squash, 159

C

Cabbage, Braised Sweet and Sour Red, 169
Cakes
　　Banana, 227
　　Black Magic, 224
　　Buttermilk-Lemon Pound, 232
　　Chocolate Torte, 225
　　Citrus-Olive Oil, 222
　　Fresh Pear, 230
　　Ginger-Peach Upside Down, 233
　　Lemon Pudding, 223
　　Orange Chiffon, 228
　　Pumpkin-Ginger, 229
Candied Citrus Peel, 205

Carrots
　　Maple-Glazed Carrots, 162
　　Roasted Winter Vegetables, 170
　　Spicy Carrot Soup, 80
　　Winter Curry, 138
Champagne Vinaigrette, 89
Cheese
　　Cheese and Nut Loaf, 137
　　Cheese and Tomato Galette, 155
　　Cheese Onion Poppy Seed Bread, 57
　　Chilaquile Casserole, 141
　　Cornbread with Chiles and Cheese, 62
　　Creamed Swiss Chard, 168
　　Feta, in Middle Eastern platter, 100
　　Feta, in pizza, 145
　　Feta, in spanakopita, 140
　　Fiesta Rice, in, 176
　　Fontina with baked polenta, 148
　　Fontina with pesto and tomato lasagna, 150
　　Fontina with pizza, 144
　　Gorgonzola with baked polenta, 148
　　Gorgonzola with pizza, 146
Chicken
　　Braised with Thyme and Apple Cider, 110
　　Chicken Breast with Lemon-Caper Sauce, 107
　　Enchilada Mole, 111
　　Focaccia Sandwich with Chicken, 112
　　Grilled with Adobo Sauce, Citrus Butter
　　and Fruit Salsa, 109
　　Korean-Style, 106
　　Lemon-Chicken Pasta Salad, 96
　　Orange with Olives and Thyme, 105
　　Pizza with Smoked Chicken, 146
　　Roasted with Rosemary and Garlic, 108
Chilaquile Casserole, 141
Chinese Noodle Salad, 97
Chipotle Red Chile Cream, recipe, 188; 127, 134

Chocolate
    Black Magic Cake, 224
    Black-Footed Macaroons, 211
    Chocolate and Candied
    Orange Peel Biscotti, 215
    Chocolate Mint Cookies, 212
    Chocolate Torte, 225
    Fudge Brownies, 220
    Ganache, 204
Chutney, Red Tomato, recipe, 182; 138
Citrus, see also under orange,
grapefruit, lemon or lime
    Citrus butter, with grilled chicken breast, 109
    Citrus Marinade, with Fish Kabobs, 134
    Citrus peel, candied, 205
    Citrus Vinaigrette, 87
    Citrus-Olive Oil Cake, 222
Cilantro Pesto, 179
Coconut
    Black-Footed Macaroons, 211
    Dream Bars, 221
    Winter Curry, 138
Condiments and other accompaniments
    Candied Citrus Peel, recipe, 205; 215
    Caramelized Nuts, 184
    Cilantro Pesto, 179
    Citrus Butter, 109
    Garlic Rouille, 132
    Gorgonzola Butter, recipe, 185; 122
    Hummus, recipe, 191; 100, 120
    Pickled Red Onions, recipe, 181; 93
    Red Tomato Chutney, recipe, 182; 138
    Salmoriglio, recipe, 190; 122
    Tamari Sunflower Seeds, 183
    Yogurt-Mint Sauce, 121
Cookies
    Almond Biscotti, 214
    Black-Footed Macaroons, 211
    Chocolate and Candied
    Orange Peel Biscotti, 215
    Chocolate Mint, 212
    Corn-Lime, 213
    Cowboy, 208
    Fruity Oatmeal, 206
    Gingersnaps, 210
    Italian Sesame Cookies, 216
    Orange Crispies, 209
    Persimmon, 207
    Vanilla Nut Wafers, 217
Corn
    Corn, Bean, and Squash Stew, 70
    Cornbread, in, 62
    Fritters, Sweet Corn with Rock Shrimp, 127
    Hillary's Salad, in, 101
    Potato Corn Chowder, 71
    Stock, Fresh Corn, 67
Cornmeal, see also polenta
    Corn-Lime Cookies, 213
    Cornbread, 62
Cornish Game Hens with Butternut Squash
and Sage, 114
Cranberry Muffins, 40
Curry
    Curried Butternut Squash Soup, 69
    Winter, with vegetables, 138
Crust, pie, 235

d

Dessert sauces, see Sauces
Dressings, see also vinaigrettes
    Buttermilk-Herb, 86
    Fresh Tomato, 88
    Ginger-Soy with Chinese Noodle Salad, 97
    Gorgonzola, 85
    Lime-Honey with Roasted Vegetable Salad, 98

Dried Fruit
- Fruit Bread, 60
- Granola, 27
- Scones, 42

e

Egg Foo Yong, Vegetable, 149
Eggplant
- Roasted in Chinese Noodle Salad, 97
- Roasted in focaccia sandwich, 112
- Roasted in pizza, 144
- Roasted in Summer-Vegetable Ragoût, 160
- Roasted Vegetable Salad, 98

f

Fish
- Baked Cod with Basil and Parmesan, 130
- Fish Kabobs with Citrus Marinade, 134
- Fish Stew with Garlic Rouille, 132
- Grilled Salmon with Italian Salsa Verde, 131
- Pescado con Jugo de Naranja, 129

Focaccia
- Focaccia, recipe, 58
- Focaccia Sandwich with Chicken, 112

Fritatta
- Spring Vegetable Fritatta, 33
- Zucchini Fritatta, 32

Frosting, Caramel, 202
Fruit, see also under individual listing
- Bread, 60,
- Dried Fruit Scones, 42
- Tart, 231
- Tropical Fruit Salsa, 193

g

Galettes
- Galette Dough, 152
- Butternut Squash, 154
- Cheese and Tomato, 155

Garlic rouille, with fish stew, 132
Gazpacho, watermelon, 79
Ginger, fresh
- Ginger-Soy Dressing with Chinese Noodle Salad, 97
- Sesame-Ginger Vinaigrette, 83
- Winter Curry, 138

Ginger, ground and candied
- Ginger-Peach Upside-Down Cake, 233
- Gingersnaps, 210
- Pumpkin-Gingercake, 229

Gorgonzola
- Baked Polenta Layered with Spinach, Mushrooms, Fontina, and Gorgonzola, 148
- Gorgonzola Butter, 185
- Gorgonzola Dressing, 85
- Pizza with Caramelized Onion, Smoked Chicken, and Gorgonzola, 146

Granola, 27
Grapefruit, Ruby with Romaine, Jicama and Avocado, 93

h

Hoisin sauce, in beef stew, 124
Honey Butter, with pancakes, 29
Hot and Sour Soup, 75
Hummus, recipe, 191; 100, 120

i

Icing
- Caramel Frosting, 202
- Quick Orange, 203
- Chocolate Ganache, 204

j

Jicama
- Jicama with Lime and Chili, 102
- Romaine with Ruby Grapefruit, Jicama and Avocado, 93

k

Kale, in wilted greens, 167

l

Lamb Moroccan Kabobs, 120
Lasagna, Summer Pesto and Tomato, 150
Lemon
- Almond Biscotti, 214
- Buttermilk-Lemon Pound Cake, 232
- Caesar, in salad dressing, 94
- Citrus-Olive Oil Cake, 222
- Lemon Pudding Cake, 223
- Lemon-Caper Sauce, 107
- Lemon-Chicken Pasta Salad, 96
- Lemon Vinaigrette with Middle Eastern Platter, 100
- Meyer Lemon Bars, 219
- Sesame-Ginger Vinaigrette, 83

Lime
- Almond Biscotti, 214
- Citrus Vinaigrette, 87
- Corn-Lime Cookies, 213
- Jicama Salad, 102
- Lime-Honey Dressing with Roasted Vegetable Salad, 98

m

Meatloaf, turkey, 115
Middle Eastern Platter with Pita Triangles, 100
Mole
- Enchilada chicken mole, 111
- Turkey mole, 116

Muffins
- Banana Coconut, 39
- Blueberry, 41
- Coffee-Spiked Poppy Seed, 37
- Cranberry, 40
- Oatmeal, 38
- Pumpkin Date, 36

Mushrooms
- Baked Polenta Layered with Spinach, Mushrooms, 148
- Cheese and Nut Loaf, 137
- Curried Butternut Squash Soup, 69
- Shiitake Mushroom Ragoût, 147
- Spanakopita, 140
- Turkey Meat Loaf, 115

n

Noodle, Chinese Salad, 97
Nuts
- Almond Biscotti, 214
- Almond Tart, 226
- Almonds in Citrus-Olive Oil Cake, 222
- Almonds in granola, 27
- Caramelized Nuts, 184
- Cheese and Nut Loaf, 137

Hazelnuts in chocolate biscotti, 215
Hazelnuts with roasted green beans, 165
Pecans, Praline with
Pumpkin-Ginger Cake, 229
Pecans, Spicy with Roasted Potato Salad, 99
Vanilla Nut Wafers, 217
Walnuts in Butter Tart Bars, 218
Walnuts in Dream Bars, 221
Walnuts in Rosemary Beer Bread, 50

O

Oatmeal
    Cookies, 206
    Granola, in, 27
    Pancakes, Oatmeal with Buttermilk, 30
    Struan Bread, 55
Onions
    Cheese Onion Poppy Seed Bread, 57
    French Onion Soup, 73
    Red, pickled, 181
Orange
    Almond Biscotti, 214
    Candied Citrus Peel, 205
    Chocolate and Candied Orange
    Peel Biscotti, 215
    Citrus Vinaigrette, 87
    Citrus-Olive Oil Cake, 222
    Cranberry Muffins, in, 40
    Orange Chicken, 105
    Orange Chiffon Cake, 228
    Orange Crispies, 209
    Orange Currant Scones, 43
    Orange Icing, 203
    Pescado con Jugo de Naranja, 129
    Soft Polenta, in, 173
Oyster sauce, with broccoli, 164

P

Pancakes
    Bishop's Ranch Pancakes with
    Honey Butter, 29
    Buttermilk Oatmeal Pancakes, 30
    Potato Pancakes, 171
Pasta
    Fettuccine with Rock Shrimp, 128
    Lemon-Chicken Pasta Salad, 96
    Summer Pesto and Tomato Lasagna, 150
Peach
    Cherry-Peach Pie, 237
    Ginger-Peach Upside-Down Cake, 233
Pears, in cake, 230
Pesto
    Cilantro, 179
    Summer Pesto and Tomato Lasagna, 150
Pickled Red Onions, 181
Pie
    Cherry-Peach, 237
    Crust, 235
    Pumpkin, 236
Pita Triangles, with Middle Eastern Platter, 100
Pizza
    Caramelized Onion and Smoked Chicken, 146
    Greek-Style with Spinach,
    Feta and Oregano, 145
    Pizza Dough, 142
    Roasted Eggplant, Red Bell Pepper,
    Fontina, 144
Polenta
    Baked Polenta Layered with
    Spinach and Mushrooms, 148
    Shiitake Mushroom Ragoût, 147
    Soft Polenta, 172
    Soft Polenta with Red Pepper and Orange, 173

Struan Bread, 55
Poppy seed, in muffins, 37
Potatoes
    Marinated Vegetables with Fresh Herbs, 166
    Oven-Baked Home Fries, 28
    Pancakes, 171
    Potato Corn Chowder, 71
    Potato Leek Soup, 72
    Roasted Potato Salad, 99
    Roasted Winter Vegetables, 170
    Winter Curry, 138
Poultry, see under chicken,
Cornish game hens, or turkey
Pork
    Grilled Tenderloin. 118
    Slow-Roasted with Sage and Garlic, 119
Pumpkin
    Pumpkin Date Muffins, 36
    Pie, 236
    Pumpkin-Ginger Cake, 229

r

Rice
    Fiesta Rice, 176
    Fragrant Rice, 175
Rolls, Seeded Dinner, 51

s

Salads
    Black Bean Salad, 92
    Caesar, 94
    Chinese Noodle with Roasted Eggplant, 97
    Hillary's, 101
    Jicama with Lime and Chili, 102
    Lemon-Chicken Pasta with Greens, 96
    Middle Eastern, 100
    Roasted Potato with Bacon
    and Spicy Pecans, 99
    Romaine with Ruby Grapefruit,
    Jicama and Avocado, 93
Salmon, Grilled with Italian Salsa Verde, 131
Salsas
    Salsa Fresca, 192
    Salsa Verde, recipe, 189; 122, 131
    Tropical Fruit, 193
Sauces, dessert, savoury and others,
see also under condiments
    Basil Aioli, recipe, 180; 112
    Barbeque, 186
    Blueberry, 197
    Caramel, 199
    Chipotle Red Chile Cream,
    recipe, 188; 127, 134
    Crème Anglaise, recipe, 200; 224, 225
    Crème Fraiche, 194
    Egg Foo Yong Sauce, 149
    Hoisin with Beef Stew, 124
    Honey Butter, 29
    Lemon Caper Sauce, 107
    Pastry Cream, 201
    Raspberry, 198
    Tomato, 187
    Yogurt-Mint, 121
Scones
    Dried Fruit Scones, 42
    Orange Currant Scones, 43
Shrimp
    Fettucine with Rock Shrimp. 128
    Rock Shrimp with Sweet Corn Fritters, 127
Soup
    Black Bean Chili, 77
    Corn, Bean and Squash, 70
    Curried Butternut Squash, 69
    Fish Stew with Garlic Rouille, 132
    French Onion, 73

    Hot and Sour, 75
    Lentil, Moroccan-style, 78
    Potato Corn Chowder, 71
    Potato Leek, 72
    Spicy Carrot, 80
    Tomato, 76
    Watermelon Gazpacho, 79
    White Bean, 74
Spinach
    Baked Polenta, Layered with Spinach, 148
    Greek-Style Pizza, 145
    Spanakopita, 140
    Wilted Greens, 167
Spreads, see condiments
Squash, see butternut squash
Stock
    Chicken, 66
    Corn, 67
    Fish, 68
    Vegetable, 65
Strudel, apple, 34
Swiss Chard
    Chard Tart, 156
    Creamed Swiss Chard, 168
    Wilted Greens, 167

t

Tamari Sunflower Seeds, 183
Tarts, dessert
    Almond Tart, 226
    Summer Fruit Tart, 231
Tarts, savoury
    Chard Tart, 156
    Tart dough, 152
Tofu
    Hillary's Salad, 101
    Hot and Sour Soup, 75
    Scrambled Tofu with Vegetables, 31
Tomatoes
    Baked Polenta Layered with Spinach, 148
    Braised Chicken with Thyme and Apple Cider, 110
    Cheese and Tomato Galette, 155
    Fettucine with Rock Shrimp, Sun-Dried Tomatoes, 128
    Fish Stew with Garlic Rouille, 132
    Fresh Tomato Dressing, 88
    Herb-Baked Tomatoes Provençal, 163
    Red Tomato Chutney, 182
    Roasted Summer-Vegetable Ragoût, 160
    Salsa Fresca, 192
    Summer Pesto and Tomato Lasagna, 150
    Tomato Sauce, 187
    Tomato Soup, 76
Tropical Fruit Salsa, 193
Turkey
    Bishop's Ranch Turkey Meatloaf, 115
    Turkey Mole, 116

v

Vegetable Egg Foo Yong, 149
Vegetables, mixed
    Frittata with spring vegetables, 33
    Marinated, 166
    Roasted Summer, 160
    Roasted Vegetable Salad, 98
    Roasted Winter, 170
    Scrambled Tofu with Vegetables, 31
    Stock, 65
    Vegetable Egg Foo Yong, 149
    Winter Curry, 138
Vinaigrettes, see also dressings
    Ariel's, 90
    Balsamic, 84

Bishop's Ranch, 91
Champagne, 89
Citrus, 87
Cumin Vinaigrette with Black Bean Salad, 92
Sesame-Ginger, 83

W

Watermelon Gazpacho, 79

Z

Zucchini
- Chilaquile Casserole, 141
- Fritatta, 32
- Roasted Summer-Vegetable Ragoût, 160